AF323644

Soul of the Israelites

A "Solomonic" Cherub, five-inch ivory plaque from Syria, ninth to eighth century BCE. Descriptions, similar to those of this plaque, of the "Cherubim" that decorated the foot of the throne of YHWH in the Tabernacle of Solomon's Temple in Jerusalem, are mentioned many times in the Hebrew Bible to reflect the syncretic Yahvism that characterized the religion of Judah and Israel at this point in their history.

Seymour W. Itzkoff
Smith College

WHO ARE THE JEWS?—I

Soul of the Israelites

PAIDEIA PUBLISHERS
Ashfield, Massachusetts

Library of Congress Cataloging-in-Publication Data

Itzkoff, Seymour W.
  Who are the Jews? / Seymour W. Itzkoff
        v. cm.
Includes bibliographical references and index.
Contents: 1. Soul of the Israelites -- 2. A nation of philosophers.
    ISBN 0-913993-17-4 (v. 1) -- ISBN 0-913993-18-2 (v. 2)
    1.   Jews--History--To 1500. 2.   Judaism--History--To 1500.
O.T.--History of Biblical events.   I. Title
    DS117.I89 2004
    909'.04924--dc22

                                                    2003066433

Paideia Publishers
P.O. Box 343
Ashfield, Massachusetts 01330

Printed in the United States of America

Dedicated to Our Magical Seven

BOOKS BY SEYMOUR W. ITZKOFF

Cultural Pluralism and American Education	1969
Ernst Cassirer: Scientific Knowledge and the Concept of Man	1971, 1997 (2nd edition)
A New Public Education	1976
Ernst Cassirer, Philosopher of Culture	1977
Emanuel Feuermann, Virtuoso	1979, 1995 (2nd edition)
The Evolution of Human Intelligence, a theory in four parts:	
The Form of Man, The Evolutionary Origins of Human Intelligence	1983
Triumph of the Intelligent, The Creation of Homo sapiens sapiens	1985
Why Humans Vary in Intelligence	1987
The Making of the Civilized Mind	1990
How We Learn to Read	1986
Human Intelligence and National Power	1991
The Road to Equality, Evolution and Social Reality	1992
The Decline of Intelligence in America, A Strategy for National Renewal	1994
Children Learning to Read, A Guide for Parents and Teachers	1996
The Inevitable Domination by Man, An Evolutionary Detective Story	2000
2050: The Collapse of the Global Techno-Economy	2003
Intellectual Capital in Twenty-First-Century Politics	2003
Who Are the Jews? I: *Soul of the Israelites*	2004
Who Are the Jews? II: *A Nation of Philosophers*	2004

"The Song of Moses"

"YAH is my strength and song, and he has become my salvation: he *is* my God, and I will prepare him an habitation; my father's God, and I will exalt him."

"The LORD *is* a man of war: the LORD *is* his name."

"Who is like unto thee, O LORD, among the gods? Who is like thee, glorious in holiness, fearful *in* praises, doing wonders"?

"Thou in thy mercy hast led forth the people *which* thou hast redeemed: thou hast guided *them* in thy strength unto thy holy habitation."

"Thou shalt bring them in, and plant them in the mountain of thine inheritance, in the place, O LORD, *which* thou hast made for thee to dwell in, *in* the Sanctuary, O LORD, *which* thy hands have established."

"The LORD shall reign for ever and ever."

{Exodus 15: 2, 3, 11, 13, 17, 18—"J"-source—King James Translation}

The "Song of Moses," written in high archaic Hebrew verse, may be the oldest original document in the Hebrew Bible. Some authorities see a more recent monarchical era (King Solomon) authorship, since some references could be interpreted as alluding to the Temple in Jerusalem. Other parts of the poem refer to some of the then-tribal enemies of the Israelites. However, the sense of power and presence of YHWH reflects a most ancient stratum of reverence to wherever the LORD may dwell, upon mountaintop, in pasture, or sanctuary. Everywhere, forever.

Contents

Maps and Illustrations

Preface

It is a good thing that exposure to the Hebrew Bible can still occur late in the development of a scholar's experience and study. It seems to be a discovery of innocence to realize that, by comparison with all other literary traditions, here exists a human and civilizational achievement, unparalleled in the moral, historical, and philosophical development of any people. Much of the Hebrew Bible, the Old Testament, was being chronicled before the time of Homer in the north Aegean. Indeed, the events that spurred this chronicle of devotion to a higher law were occurring in the era about which Homer wrote. But his work was put to the pen three or four centuries later, as the sagas of the *Iliad* and the *Odyssey*.

The comparison of the two literary traditions is instructive, because it refracts the character and destiny of two extraordinary, if different peoples. In one it will lead to an extroverted, secular, curious, and confident people, physically and intellectually destined to conquer the world—the Greeks. In the other it will lead to a brooding, introspective, uncensored examination of the depths of human nature, the strengths and the weakness of the inner man—the Israelites.

This interpretation of man and God was to enfilade the moral and affective dimension of human perception. It transformed our sense of identity and purpose in the outside world. The psychological richness to be found in the Hebrew Bible, the willingness to confront the limitations of human nature, the need to aspire to a higher order of moral behavior, the suzerainty of a supreme God that is more than an honorific place name, all these are explanation enough for its historically regarded holiness. It is a guide for the human soul amidst the degradation that constitutes the ordinary life of humans throughout history. The Hebrew Bible shows us the path given to us by an abstract, yet personal deity, YHWH, his messenger Moses, and those prophets who followed in his steps. Chronicled here are untold examples of humans striving against their own bio/social nature to live in disciplined accordance with a higher set of rules. It is a tough and often tragic struggle. YHWH gives no quarter to the weak.

What I have attempted in this book is to trace the origins of the Israelites as part of the ancient southerly migration of peoples. That which is hinted at in Genesis. It concludes with the great collapse of a dream, the shredded hopes of this covenanted people. We see their expulsion from the land that YHWH promised them, if only they would uphold His laws. And they experience the destruction of their "city" and their Temple.

Who were they to begin with? What allowed them to rise in obligation, as the "chosen," a nation of priests? Moses is the key to this transformation. After Moses' death, and on their native soil, they did become a true nation, only to fall away from the Law. How could they again hope to regain the covenant between YHWH and the descendants of David in Jerusalem? These are some of the themes that intrigue. The Bible itself must be testament in this deeply philosophical, religious, but human tale. History and scholarship help to give it context and a degree of factual verisimilitude for our modern understanding. But herein is human experience that rises beyond the mundane bricks and mortar revealed by the archaeologist's pick.

In helping me find my way through a vast literature, including the Hebrew Bible, I must acknowledge with pleasure, the stimulus of fruitful conversations with my colleagues in the Smith College Department of Religion, and the Chapel.

Northampton, Massachusetts, January 2004

1

Testimony and History

Heritage

No matter one's faith or creed, the existence of the traditions, beliefs, and community of the Hebrews, Israelites, Jews, the *people of the book*, must give notice to an epochal experience in the history of the human race. In understanding the origins of this community of faith and experience, we understand a bit more of ourselves today. That Judaism gave birth to two other great and dominating religions of our time is but one of its important contributions to our heritage. More important is the total civilizational contribution of the religion and the experience of the Hebrews. The events of their interaction with history, their response to the evolving awareness of humans of their own nature, have catapulted humankind forward both in intellectual perspective and moral discipline. They and we, too, face the reality, always fraught with tension and conflict, of the significance of ethnicity and community.

It is correct to view human history as a unilinear path forward, *time's arrow*. We cannot go back and re-learn nor can we re-do the errors along the path. We have to take the knowledge that humans have gleaned from their experience with the forces of biological evolution as they have been spelled out in our spontaneous creation of culture, our dawning awareness of frailty. We tend to be imperious today as we look back at the scratchings at the earth of our ancient predecessors, their struggle to ward off starvation, the seemingly spontaneous predation of humans against each other. But, in reality, have these ancient weaknesses been solved by sequentially more powerful understandings and controls over material nature? We have the Internet, supersonic transportation, but also, the atomic bomb, all-too-terrible genocidal and terrorist pogroms against our fellow humans.

This book is a small attempt to understand the contributions as well as the tragic dilemmas of a people on its way, from first formation to first frustration, disillusion, and recurring hope. By tracing the very beginnings of a people along with their confreres, as they emerge from the northern Eur-Asian mists of pre-history, I hope to set the moral, historical, and political origins of a people in the context of this earliest stage of self-consciousness.

Levantine Setting

The Israelites were originally part of that great migratory descent down into the Middle East that occurred toward the end of the Pleistocene Ice Age, after c.12,000 BCE. They came in trickles, in small tribal clans that could exist off the land, hunting and gathering, as they wandered south from an environment that in the north had radically changed. At one time, even just south of the ice caps, the ecology was a rich and benign hunting environment. In the new modern era of sharp climatic contrasts, very warm summers and bitterly cold winters, where the forests now sufficed to give easier cover to the animals of the hunt, the south loomed ever more welcoming. This land was diversely covered with forests and plains, not nearly the modern desertified product of extensive overgrazing by goat and sheep, the erosions of over-cut forests, even the silt clogged lands adjoining the intensely irrigated rivers. Yes, hard to believe, but it was then a luxuriant enticement, a land of "milk and honey."

I trace the civilizational beginnings in Sumer and Egypt noting the historical connection to those as yet undefined populations, soon to become Israelites. Into the land that was to be Judah and Israel, deeply etched into the memories of Pharaonic Egypt, the presence of these people became tangible. They were for the most part Indo-European invaders, given their clear tribal and ethnic marks, as Hurrians, Hittites, Sea Peoples. Yet, as the Sumerians noted in their own traditions, deeper layer of migrants existed before the late-coming Indo-Europeans trickled into the south. The ancient pre- and post-Ice Age settlers, and then the Semites and Hamites, had left an indelible linguistic mark, even a religious tradition that the newcomers could not merely displace. Thus at all points in this history, the power of place, of geography and history, served to absorb the newcomers into the old. But, with that one exception, ancient Sumeria. Perhaps the Semites were too few at the conjunction of the two great rivers, when these northerners arrived. They remained a burr of ethnic indigestibility.

Eventually the Sumerians were enveloped by surrounding Semite Akkadians, Amorites, and Arameans north along the two great rivers. The authors of the Hebrew Bible were, as with others throughout western Asia, deeply in debt to the technological, esthetic, religio-mythological and legal achievements of the Sumerians. But, of course, it was the invention of writing that brought all of the peoples of this area into their circle of thought and culture. Even as the Sumerians were overlain by the surrounding peoples and new national ideals of expansion and mastery, their intellectual, religious, and literary heritage remained deeply imbedded in the minds of the new learners of civilization. In consequence Sumeria and its tradition became a classical heritage.

The permanence and renewability of Egypt's Nilotic ecology did not allow Egypt the cultural dynamic that gave to the empires of the two rivers and the coasts of the Mediterranean the stimuli toward a vigorous intellectual heritage. Egypt's wealth and stability became an inviting magnet to the plundering outsider, an under-populated reservoir for the salvation of the dispossessed. Whether they came as Indo-European Hyksos conquerors, perhaps symbolized as Joseph, during their century or so of domination, or as Shasu herders, as with Abraham or Jacob, the outsiders viewed Egypt as eternal and receptive in its immobile fecundity. So, too, as the Hebrew Bible testifies with regard to Jeroboam 1 and Jeremiah, Egypt was an ever-available political refuge.

The Light of History

As we will later show, the Israelites appear in history in a victory stele of an Egyptian Pharaoh, of the late thirteenth century BCE. This was a tumultuous period in the Mediterranean littoral, coinciding with the wanderings and raiding of various displaced and marauder peoples, later chronicled from the bardic traditions by Homer in the north Aegean. It is now posited that the Israelite tribes, described in much detail in Joshua and Judges, on their supposed entrance into Canaan, were already existent prior to the coming of the Exodus escapees from Egypt, led by Moses and Aaron. Genesis is a synthesis of both local Canaanite tradition as well as more ancient but powerful memories, north Mesopotamian experiences, then stretching back some 2000 years, to Sumer. Still there seems to be a core of facticity to the existence of most of the twelve tribes that constitute the later Israelite confederation.

The breakup of the United Monarchy in the tenth century BCE and its division into Israel in the north and Judah in the south is echoed in the historic and archaeological record. Both the northern and southern tribes are roughly etched in the Biblical presentation. And it appears that the northerners, with their sanctuaries in Shechem, Shiloh, Bethel, reflected an ancient worship of the traditional Levantine gods, El (Lord), Elohenu, or the Elohim. Some would be named after Baa-el, from whom so many heroic Israelite figures, "Eli," "Samu-el," for instance, including the very name of the land from whom the people was derived.

It is to the people of the south, the hills of Judah, the lands of northern Arabia, the Sinai, the Negeb, east of the Jordan River on the plains of Syria and the Trans-Jordan, that we will find ancient mention of the fierce warrior god, YHWH. Indeed, the references throughout the Hebrew Bible to these southern peoples, the Midianites, Edomites, Kennizites, Calebites, Rechabites, reflect a differing religious tradition from that in the north. There is more than a hint of the nomadic life, the Shasu. YHWH does not seem to emanate from that traditional Mid-eastern heritage, richly developed along the two rivers, the Tigris and Euphrates, and passed on both south and west (to Europe).

The above two tribal constellations probably comprised the setting for the great moral and theological drama provided by the Exodus. As to whether Moses was an historical figure, or whether the Exodus actually occurred, or whether it was a fictive creation of much later Biblical redactors during the exile and after cannot now be proved one way or another. There was much ferment in Egypt and along the coasts of Canaan in what was later called Phoenicia during this period, c.1250-1150 BCE. Transitional dynasties surfaced, then dissolved during a series of invasions by the Sea Peoples from the north, Asia Minor, the Aegean, and also from the west, Libya, Sardinia, Sicily.

My own tentative conclusion is that the Exodus of Moses was beyond mere invention, especially since it was known, written down, and hallowed in the time of Solomon and before. There is renewed archaeological and historical evidence for a memory of monotheism to have spilled over to the Nile Delta from the days of Akhenaton and Amarna, c.1350 BCE. And it is not inconceivable that a holdover tradition in belief from this era could have inspired a gifted "seer," Moses, to lead a group of "stiff-necked" Semitic riff-raff out of a tough situation in Egypt. They were, no doubt, resident Asiatics filled with the hope of getting back to the open spaces and tribal freedoms of Canaan. But these remainder peoples from the east, serving in the Egyptian construction gangs, could not have expected to deal with a Moses, who had a vision of his own.

The acknowledgment by the Biblical writers of Moses' marriage in the wilderness to the daughter of Jethro, a Midianite priest of YHWH, and the two sons that she bore him, tells us something about intermarriage in the earliest period of Israelite history. This was very different from the line-in-the-sand drawn by post-exilic priests toward intermarriage, even with YHWH-worshipping "non-Jews," but of cousinly ethnicities. Moses' own tribal relationships are almost extraneous issues to his compelling struggle to bring his diverse and susceptible flock under the tutelage of the law of YHWH, to agree to a covenant that constituted their only hope for survival in a bleak and hostile world. Peoplehood would be the key to their achievement of the Promised Land.

Today, skepticism about the historicity of the Book of Joshua is universal. The evidence increases against the reality of Joshua's apocalyptic military sweep, the emptying of the land and opponents by the invading children of Israel. It is the argument here that, indeed, the incoming followers of Joshua found a world of discord and chaos among the indigenous warring tribes. All the while, the now dominant and sharply different Sea Peoples (blatantly Greek at first) were increasingly encroaching along the southern Canaanite coast. Probably in response to these new invaders, well-organized, iron-using Philistines, the old time 'Apiru Israelites in the highlands absorbed the newcomers from Egypt, and especially the new tutelage being given by the God known to the wilderness peoples, YHWH. This YHWH was different from the increasingly hated Canaanite Baaels now being adopted by the Philistines. YHWH might now provide the supernatural and moral force for their mutual survival.

Ultimately the simple tribespeople, agriculturists as well as herders, would have to transform their military judges—fighters, tribal elders, seers, and prophets—into a king who could unify and weld them into a nation capable of resisting the Philistines and Canaanites on the western shores, the Ammonites on the east. But also the great and dangerous empires far to the north along the rivers that were ever moving south. Yes, opportunistic, even slow-moving Egypt, could once more transform them into vassals, then slaves.

Moses' message was sophisticated, certainly influenced by ancient Egyptian traditions of law as well as the now-internalized Hammurabic system of law (c.1800 BCE) in the various cities and nations of the north. But, as we shall explain below, there was much more, a deeper understanding of the nature of the mind, theodicy, the yearning of human beings for a moral structure to life that would defend any community from the weaknesses in human nature. There was a clearer recognition of the dangers inherent in those beliefs and behaviors that could dissolve the social fabric and send a people down a path to oblivion. The power of Moses' message was understood by the intellectual leadership of these peoples who were now entering the light of civilizational experience. Call them priests, seers, and prophets. They were the teachers, philosophers, scientists of that era. That their knowledge was visionary, that it was derived from a sense of higher force, a God of man, does not denigrate their capacity for understanding those deep human murmurings and relationships that they could not yet clearly articulate.

Nationhood

Was nationhood a success? As with all political hegemony, it had to practice accommodation to the highest as well as the lowest in human nature. Three generations of a United Monarchy encompassing the numerous northern tribes as well as a new force in the south, Judah, was all that could be sustained. Jerusalem, an ancient fortress on high, of a mysterious Indo-European people, the Jebusites, became the powerful capital of David, leader of Judah. David's grandson, Rehoboam, half-Ammonite son of Solomon, lost half the realm. The northern tribes withdrew to their richer kingdom, taking on the ancient name of the land, Israel.

Thence, the Deuteronomic Historians tell us of the universal corruptions of the north, the happenstance corruptions of the south, Judah, with the exception of two kings, Hezekiah and Josiah. These two attempted to rally their people politically around a more purified, centralized Yahwism. On either side of their reigns were fathers and sons who reverted to the lowest common denominator of moral and religious beliefs. The irony was that these "evil-doers" were as likely as not to achieve greater political and economic success. Biblical history is testimony to the weakness in mind and soul of any people regardless of whether they were filled with urban wealth and power, or labored in the orchard, vineyard, or in the field with the herd.

The prophets, now a dislocated and wandering repository of memory of the Mosaic law, attempted to turn these nations from their weakness of moral resolve. They could only warn, as Moses had done, that the pervasive corruption in social and ritual behavior would bring down the wrath of YHWH. No nation committed to such apostasy could escape its day of retribution and destruction. The material cause might bear the name Ashur or Chaldea, but in reality it was the guiding hand of YHWH that shaped the events at all moments in history.

The Meaning of Exile

Abraham entered Canaan as a stranger from the north. Near Hebron, he purchased from the resident Hittites a burial place for his wife, Sarah, and himself. Jacob did the same with the Shechemites further north in the highlands. Joseph, now empowered by a Pharaoh, led his family to Egypt where they remained at the Pharaoh's pleasure. Moses took his disparate flock from that land, through the strangeness of the wilderness for forty years, to attempt to teach his people God's laws, hoping for success bringing them to this alluring land. Moses himself failed, as did the generation that he had led to Kadesh Barnea. He was thence privileged only to gaze upon the "Promised Land."

The Covenant with YHWH might be thought of from a historical point of view as a product of the Israelites' wandering in the wilderness and overcoming its dangers. These were hostile byways, constantly challenged by resident tribal peoples who saw these exilic searchers as threats. The laws and regulations, and the punishments, if one studies both the early Books of Exodus and Numbers, and later, Leviticus, were harsh, often pitiless. Later, ensconced in their lands, now as homeland, they forgot the principles and the conditions for leanness, discipline, reverence, and purity.

Fortunately, after again being forced from their homeland so many hundreds of years after arriving, they now had a written record of their hegira. They could now study and contemplate the meaning of Moses' message, the Temple on Zion, the prophets who ineffectually goaded them to take the higher path. One long stage in the history of this people had been completed.

They entered our consciousness as Israelites searching for a home in a land that truly brimmed with "milk and honey." But they lost this land as they themselves had lost their way as a people. They turned their backs on a God that demanded much of them, though not in material achievements and offerings.

Fate, a gift of YHWH, gave them another chance, this time as Jews, people of Persian Yehud. What had they learned as the chosen bearers of the faith: the ark, the tabernacle, the law, the scrolls? That then became the question underlying this next act of the great historic drama.

Reinterpreting the Bible

In tune with the spirit of our own day, many writers on Biblical themes have attempted to read back into the Pentateuch, and the Deuteronomistic History especially, a political/theological ex-post-facto interpretation. Gosta Ahlstrom's admirable 1986

work, *Who Were the Israelites*? is an example.[1] While developing a worthwhile historical perspective on the central Canaanite tribes as the original Israelites, Ahlstrom shunts
the writing of the relevant historical portions of The Hebrew Bible to the post-exilic period, after 539 BCE. In Ahlstrom's view, this writing of history anew, this rationaliza-
tion of the past by the priests in the Yehud of Persia, was an act essential for the rebuilding of the Temple.

Richard E. Friedman's excellent and popular 1987/1997 work, *Who Wrote the Bible*?[2] placed the "P" (priestly—see Chapter 3) writer in the first five books of Moses to
the period of King Hezekiah of Judah, c.715 BCE. Most scholars still view this "P"
author's redacting and interweaving of earlier materials to the post-exilic period. "P" is
the sole authorship of the Book of Leviticus, in the Pentateuch. Friedman sees these
authors as being Aaronite priests intent on downgrading the Mushite (Moses) school,
and legitimizing the priestly tradition of Solomon's priest, Zadok. Friedman also sees
the Deuteronomist writer(s) as originating in King Josiah's reign, c.630 BCE, when the
discovery of these "ancient scrolls" in the precincts of the First Temple was announced.
Here the authors are Shilonite priests associated with the prophet Jeremiah. Friedman's
placing of the work of the Deuteronomists is not radical. Ahlstrom's tendency to place
all these fundamental writings, parts of the Pentateuch and the Deuteronomist Histories,
as a more recent and creative endeavor, after 539 BCE, is subtly radical.

The most sensational factual challenge of our historical understanding of The Hebrew Bible is the 2001 work of Israel Finkelstein and Neil Silberman, *The Bible Unearthed.*[3] Using the recent dating techniques of archaeological science, Finkelstein and
Silberman presume to downgrade the material achievements of Solomon, (c.950 BCE).
Instead, they place the building technologies and the imputed wealth that these denote
into the northern regions of the Divided Monarchy, in Israel, a product of the dynasty of
Omri, from c.875 BCE. This syncretic Yahwist dynasty was much hated and feared by
the Judeans, the Deuteronomistic Historian, and the prophets Elijah and Elisha. As such,
to authors Finkelstein and Silberman, the history of the Israelites, both in Judah and Israel, as laid out from Joshua to 2 Kings, as written by priests and scribes from Judah,
constitutes political propaganda against the Northern Kingdom. They view the Biblical
historians as illegitimately elevating Solomon's achievements in Jerusalem, c.970-931
BCE.

Insofar as the archaeological approach to Biblical history, simpler responses are
possible than with the Biblical scholars. If one can show that the basic dating processes

used by the authors, Finkelstein and Silberman, might err by a hundred or so years, especially from a perspective of almost 3,000 years in the past, the argument would be over, the Hebrew Bible vindicated. Nicolae Roddy, to name just one evaluator, has rejected the above authors' debunking:. "Contrary to the claims of *The Bible Unearthed*, the Bible's witness to the presence of kingdoms in and around tenth-century Israel [Solomon's reign], is based on the reality of institutional-type structures. One cannot easily dismiss this as simply the projection of a golden age superimposed upon history from some later date."[4]

Who Wrote What?

The work of Friedman and Ahlstrom involves complex textual issues. Most scholars accept Deuteronomy 1 as being, in the main, pre-exilic. Deuteronomy 2, which introduces several of the books, and writes the epitaph to the independent political entity, Judah, clearly is post-exilic. As with most of the other Biblical writings, there is later redacting and editing. Early in the history of the Deuteronomic writings, the Book of Deuteronomy itself was probably attached to Joshua and the following books of the history, as an introduction. Later it was separated, and then included as the fifth book of the Torah, the Pentateuch.

If we go forward in time to the period after the exile, perhaps even to the time of Ezra and Nehemiah, a century after the first returnees from Babylon, some interesting facts become evident. Ezra, who, it is said, assembled the *golah* (the initiated) in Jerusalem for a reading of the full Torah, c.458 BCE, may have indeed had an important part in its final editing. At the same time, in the province of Samarina (Samaria) there was now a history of separation, c.722-539 BCE. This produced a growing a sense of alienation and rejection by the returnees of the resident Samarian/Israelite syncretic Yahwism. This different ethnic Yahwism had rooted itself in the above lands since the Assyrian deportations and population exchanges. Inevitably, the original stock of the ten tribes of Israel had been diluted. As worship on Mt. Gerizim, outside Shechem, developed in opposition to Mt. Zion in Jerusalem, a separate Samaritan schismatic version of Judaism evolved. This schismatic trajectory rejected all the writings of the prophets subsequent to the five books of Moses, the Pentateuch. It is interesting to compare these Samaritan books with those that seemingly were in existence in Yehud at that time.

In examining the fragments of the Dead Sea scrolls, c.250-100 BCE, as well as the translation of the Pentateuch for the Greek-speaking Alexandrian Jews, c.280 BCE, the

Septuagint, scholars have found few differences with these early versions as compared with the much later Masoretic text of the Rabbis of the early Middle Ages. Even more surprising is that there are even fewer differences with the ancient Samaritan Pentateuch. What this seems to tell us is that a version of the Pentateuch existed shortly after the exile, which was then complete and acceptable to all the Yahwist communities of the ancient homeland.

Insofar as Richard Friedman's claims, it is clear that sections of "P" must precede the writing of Deuteronomy and were not written after the exile. On the other hand, most scholars adhere to the opinion that the major redaction of "P" into the Pentateuch took place at a time when priestly dominance was most highly valued. And this could have existed among the exilic communities, and those returnees, at the behest of the Persian emperors, involved in the construction of the Second Temple. Clearly, to have persuaded the Samaritans, the Pentateuch had to have been completed either during or shortly after the return from Babylon, because soon after this period, c.450 BCE, the breach between Samaria and Jerusalem became irreconcilable.

The critical issue in the historical status of the Hebrew Bible is the facticity of the writings identified as "J" (Jahwist source in Judah) and "E" (Elohist source in Israel). "J" dates to the end of Solomon's reign, or early in that of Solomon's son, Rehoboam, c.950-900 BCE. "E" dates to the reign of Jeroboam and his immediate successors in Israel, c.900-850 BCE. Both these documents were based on a number of earlier writings mentioned in the Hebrew Bible and were used as a resource by the two groups of priests/scholars who shared this conjoint heritage. If the historicity of both "J" and "E" holds up, the reality of the Mosaic experience will be strengthened historically, and we will be able transcend the present-minded politicization of these extraordinary writings that comprise the Hebrew Bible. Certainly it will be seen as true that in the period of the Babylonian exile, or shortly after, these early documents were collated with "P". This had probably been an ongoing process since it is generally believed that "J" and "E" might have been joined before "P".

The Hebrew Bible Not a Political Tract

One cannot read the Hebrew Bible, even given the serious limitations of translation, without wonder and awe. There is here so much humanity, strength, weakness, ferocity, tenderness. Above all, one encounters a majestic sense of the limitations in our human nature, the need for a powerful organizing force or principle, a moral God that will guide us. Several examples follow to argue against the above simplistic political view.

In {1 Samuel 2:22*f*}, an oracle condemns the house of the prophet Eli, because of the corruptions of his sons and affiliates, implying also that the descendants of this heir of Moses shall be cut down at an early age and become beggars. Presumably, these verses serve to prepare the way for the ascendancy of Solomon's Zadokites, who are priestly followers of Aaron. In the very next chapter {1 Samuel 3}, we witness a young Samuel who does not believe that the LORD has anointed and then spoken to him. He runs back and forth to the room of an aged and dying Eli, thinking that it was Eli who was calling him. Both aged prophet and young anointed are here joined together, Eli, finally saying in acceptance, "It is the LORD; let him do what seems good to him."

There may be a political semantic involved in these passages, but the humanity, tenderness, and poetry of the writing overcomes and transforms what could be a crass rationale for a change in priestly governance. The politics of power fades in the presence of the authenticity of conception.

In {1 Samuel 9*ff.*}, the tribes of Israel demand that Samuel find them a king to unite and then lead them in war. Against his better wishes, but with the approval of YHWH, Samuel identifies Saul of the tribe of Benjamin, who is first pictured as wandering in confusion in search of his father's lost donkeys. The word painting that here describes Saul is rich and complex. Saul, a man of prophetic frenzy, is reluctantly, if formally crowned at Mizpah, c.1030 BCE, in the same town where the last regent of Judah Gedaliah, will be assassinated, c.582 BCE. Saul returns to his home in Gibeah, (a place where his tribe had earlier sinned and had been almost destroyed by the other Israelite tribes for an act of terrible depravity, oddly similar to the primeval behavior of the men of Sodom and Gomorrah). {Judges 19; Genesis 19:4-11-J-source}. A call to liberate the tribes of Jabesh-Gilead across the Jordan River is received by the western tribes. The Ammonites have besieged them. This newly-crowned King of Israel is informed of the danger while plowing his family's fields with oxen. He answers the call and liberates Jabesh-Gilead.

Later, he sacrifices unlawfully while preparing for battle with the Philistines, grants life to the defeated king of the Amalekites, consults the witch at Endor, acts further in-curring Samuel's wrath, and that of YHWH. He is thus condemned. In his life actions he is painted as jealous and treacherous toward David, a Judean, his true equal in military skill. But in his last battle against the Philistines, on Mt. Gilboah, near the valley of

Jezreel, Saul and his three sons perish, with great valor. And he is honored in death by the men of Jabesh-Gilead who come and steal his body from the Philistines.

Certainly the authors of {1 Samuel} have a bias toward Judah and the house of David who will soon capture Jerusalem and claim Mt. Zion, as against a Benjaminite from the hamlet of Gibeah, such as Saul. Neither Shakespeare nor even Euripides, the latter writing in Athens two hundred years after the time of the Deuteronomists, could have painted such a vivid portrait of a man of power, humility, frenzy, tortured jealousy, and ultimate heroism. These chapters in that ancient manuscript are not tracts; they are poetry containing deep psychological insight and sobering historical testimony.

In {2 Kings 6:24-7:21}, written about events that probably took place during the reign of the Yahwist-named King of Israel, Jehoahaz c.815-802 BCE, a scene is described of a siege of Samaria by an Aramean king. Great starvation ensued, a donkey's head sold for eighty shekels of silver (a huge amount of money). Women negotiated with each other about which of their sons should be eaten first. One woman complains that in such a bargain with another woman, she and this neighbor have killed, cooked, and eaten her own son, but the neighbor did not fulfill her side of the bargain, and hid her son. The king of Israel walks along the ramparts, listens, as the woman cries out for justice:

"When the king heard the words of the woman he tore his clothes—now since he was walking on the city wall, the people could see that he had sackcloth on his body underneath—and he said, 'So may God do to me…'" with a threat to Elisha whom he believed to have cursed the kingdom, and brought on this tragedy. Elisha saves himself with an omen of good fortune from YHWH. The story concludes in mystery, but for the good, as two hungry lepers sitting outside the gates decide to defect to the Arameans. At the camp, they find that the Arameans have disappeared leaving behind untold booty. "For the LORD had caused the Aramean army to hear the sound of chariots, the sound of a great army, so that they said to one another, 'The king of Israel has hired the kings of the Hittites and the kings of the Egyptians to fight against us'….the man of God [Elisha] had said to the king, [in Samaria] 'two measures of barley shall be sold for a shekel, and a measure of choice meal for a shekel…'" And the people of Samaria were saved.

This was written in Judah about the corrupt leadership of Samaria and Israel. Yet, this tale is here inserted in {2 Kings} as a vignette about human life under extreme duress, a moral lesson about divine punishment. Indeed, it is a tale populated with ordinary people, even kings, with whom Israelites, Judeans, all humans, could identify.

With these Deuteronomist writers there is no mere subservience to a king, even such opportunistic, yet committed Yahwist rulers as Hezekiah and Josiah. The writers of the Deuteronomistic History, and the Prophets who explicitly discoursed on human weakness and need, allowed to flow into their writings a truth that was explicitly stated to the Israelite elders by an aging Samuel {1 Samuel 8} at his home in Ramah, in Benjamin, just north of Jebuz (Jerusalem).

Again, at an earlier chronological point in Israelite history, it is entered as a hymn, sung by Jotham, surviving son of the tribal Judge, Gideon {Judges 9:8-15}, on Mt. Gerizim, near Shechem.

Simply, there are higher principles in the universe than the powers of kings. These are the laws of YHWH, which apply to all things in the universe, and endure for an eternity.

Endnotes, Chapter 1

[1] Ahlstrom, Gosta. 1986. *Who Were the Israelites?* Winona Lake, IN: Eisenbrauns.

[2] Friedman, R. E. 1987/1997. *Who Wrote The Bible?* San Francisco: Summit/Harper.

[3] Finkelstein, I., and Silberman, N. A. 2001. *The Bible Unearthed*, N.Y.: The Free Press.

[4] Roddy, Nicolae. 2001. "Archaeology's 'New Vision' or Myopia?" review critique of Finkelstein and Silberman, *The Bible Unearthed, op. cit.,* in *Journal of Religion* and *Society*, Vol.3, p. 9 of 9 pp.

2

Northern Genesis

Birth of Modernity

Modern humans, the creators of literate civilizations, including the ancestors of the Jews, and far distant beyond the ken of history, originated in the north, somewhere west of Siberia, east of the Danube, north of the Mediterranean and Black Sea, and south of the ice flows. We are not sure when this process began or ended. We only see both its direct and indirect results. The direct outcomes were the modern humans we have discovered both in fossil bone and in their material cultural artifacts. They were the Cro-Magnon Caucasoids of Europe and West Asia, with their modern bone and body structure and their unprecedented sophistication of tool making and art, so different from any group of humans that then existed on our planet.[1]

The indirect results of this mysterious genesis shows itself in the relatively sudden modernization of humans around the world, from about 150,000 years ago, well before we see the bones and culture of Cro-Magnon.[2] As with the unknown force that moved the planet Uranus in surprising ways, observed well before we discovered the culprit, Neptune, these as yet undiscovered progenitors unstuck the human race from a well-grooved primitive form of life.[3] These other humans, whatever taxonomy we give them, as *Homo* erectines, or borderline *sapiens*, were heavy of bone, with thick skulls, small brain, brow ridges, similar to the Caucasoid Neanderthals of Eur-Asia. All earlier forms of *Homo*, who eventually shared the same neighborhoods as the Cro-Magnons, and for

many thousands of years, succumbed to the inevitable scythe of Darwinian natural selection.[4]

This is not to imply that these other peoples of the world, including the Neanderthals were butchered into oblivion. Rather, through interbreeding, as well as being
pushed into the isolation of reproductive lethargy, they gradually disappeared from the
world scene.[5] This process is still continuing. Natural selection does not disappear because the results happen to be politically unpalatable to the momentary powers-that-be.
Nature has perfected its strategies for life on this Earth for over 4 billion years. A few
thousand years here or there are insignificant in the inertia of Darwinian inevitability.[6]

The creation of modern humans who would fabricate the first great civilizations of
the southern river valleys was a biological long shot, but wholly consonant with evolutionary theory and history. Ancient *Homo*, born in Africa, was endowed, as were all
primates, with wandering, venturesome, exploratory genes. Between two and one million years ago, some of these human primates left their Ur-homeland for the Eur-Asian
land masses. Eur-Asia had by then been connected to Africa through Arabia and the
Middle East for at least 10-15 million years. Many other primate lines, apes and mon-
keys had taken the plunge before them.[7]

Clearly, to the north was a new plenitude. Perhaps the word got back to those left
behind. Recently, in the Republic of Georgia, an early human, 1.7-million-years old, was
uncovered.[8] Similar-looking cousins, *Homo ergaster*, have been found at the same time
level in East Africa. This is not controversial material, as we have found thousands of
fossil remnants from the East Indies, China, the Middle East, and Europe, at time levels
similar to the above fossil. As time passes this ancient human cast of characters seems to
grow brainier in terms of skull size and the tools that they are now fabricating. But the
primeval, heavy bone, thick brow ridges, prognathous human model remains basically
the same. Indeed, there begin to be discerned racial differences in these geographically
separated human lines, differences, which in spite of much recent out-breeding and mis-
cegenation still identify the ancient eras of separation.

As with all times of plenty, the scene clearly changed. We call this period of evolutionary history the Pleistocene period, the Ice Ages. The ebb and flow of the glaciers,
and the changes from benign to horrific climatic environments, maintained a two mil-
lion-year pulsation. No doubt many groups, unprepared for life in the frost zone, succumbed. Others including the Neanderthals survived, gradually developing a suite of
cold climate adaptations—hairy bodies, wide nostrils to buffer the cold air, short squat

physical builds to retain body heat. We will always wonder about those groups, clans or tribes of inbreeding humans, caught in any one of the successive frigid periods, who disappeared. We have some of their fossils. Their descendants, if any, are absorbed into our genetic structure.[9]

Somewhere in Eur-Asia, certainly within the last 200-250 thousand years, one of these climatic crises of the Ice Ages in the north brought one group of humans to the brink. Likely, the majority of the group disappeared, one small remnant surviving, to reproduce another day.[10] How can we be sure about such an improbable set of events? Answer, by the radical results then and now impacting the nature and structure of the human species, and by comparison with those humans who stayed behind in the complacent south.

Conditions of Conception

Had this revolution in the form of *Homo* not occurred, the traditional small-brained, thick boned humans all over the "Old World" might have remained in place and probably become separate, intersterile species. As it was, the aggressive expansionism of this highly corticalized human sub-species from the north, spread its genes far and wide, especially in the last 100,000 years. In so doing it spun the entire human genus over the sapiens *Rubicon*.

How did those genes for a larger brain and skull settle on these people? First, it is important to emphasize that a larger brain was a characteristic of all placental mammals in comparison with other forms of life. The primates were especially specialized in the use of their brain to survive by looking out for danger and avoiding it. As alert and highly mobile creatures, able to live under a variety of external conditions, the brain that made this possible became a highly adaptive and positively selected physical attribute. In a word, a large information processing brain was smiled upon by "Mother Nature" for many millions of years.

Further, brain size has been critically adaptive, every small increment that happened to occur in a small group, even an individual, made that particular deviant more adaptable, even more powerful than others born with less. In general this principle holds to this day. In more ancient times such skills and the resultant energies usually led to "mating power," and thus more progeny. Over time, the mutations for ever larger brain size kept on appearing in these more able survivors, because it was positively adaptive. The challenges for the use of intelligence in a threatening world both external and internal to all human communities never wane. Natural selection either positively selects a characteristic or suppresses it, depending on its usefulness in bringing progeny to reproductive maturity. We call this process directional evolution. It can enhance or suppress antler size, tooth shape, beautiful feathers, ferocity, or brain/intelligence.[11]

Into that ancient and terrible climatic vale of crisis went a short, prognathous, heavy-boned, small-brained creature. Unknown thousands of years later, a small band of survivors emerged, thin-boned faces, skulls without brow ridges, bleached in body, tall and lean, with bulging cortical protuberances vaulting above their high brows. Here arose a baby faced and soft-boned animal whose body had become sexually mature while most of his body and brain remained infantile in structure. The body had grown in height, the skull soaring above, an exploding neurological mass within.[12] The grossness of bone and body, now an evolutionary memory. Instead, a brain searching to play, think, master—*Homo sapiens sapiens*.

A. R. Wallace, Darwin's contemporary, once wondered why had nature created a creature with a vaulting 1600cm^3 skull/brain when the average *Homo erectus* of 500,000 years ago, with a brain of 1000cm^3, skull/brain was doing fine?[13]

It certainly was not because humans needed a bigger brain to fend off lions, chimpanzees, snakes, and wild dogs. A bigger brain kept appearing genetically because in the environment in which the northerners lived, the dynamic challenges both natural and social that impacted on these humans, as we well know even today, never lessened.

To understand contemporary human life and behavior we should view the creation of this human brain not as a stereotyped selective response to specific survivalistic needs, whether they be the protection of the young, one's related kin, even gaining brute reproductive advantage. Rather the human brain surged upward and outward in response to inner structural relationships that nature alone could predict. It was a product of an ancient and inner directional trend in brain growth the end result of which was surprising for evolutionary history.[14] That is why we today are not merely thinking machines, rigidly fixated on survival schemes. Rather we are replete with religious, ascetic, emotional visions, fascinations, obsessions, all of which belie the purely practical adaptive sociobiological functions of the typical primate brain.

As the *Homo sapiens sapiens* brain exploded in size it not only expanded in the thinking dimensions of its structure. It also brought to the fore enormous emotional affect of the more ancient primate and mammal levels of behavior, but now permanently integrated with the power of logical thought. Its selective evolutionary value lay in the fact that despite the paradoxical suite of cultural behaviors and emotions, the irrational frenzies, myths and wars, its cognitive intellectual power overrode these many accompanying negatives in human nature. In the history of all peoples, including that long hegira of the Jews, this tension between a brain of reason and a brain of uncontrolled emotionality and the often violent behavior that these torrents of passion induced became the ruling theme of our species.

In the long run, however, this new brain could shine and create practical and scientific reasoning to allow us to perceive the causes of things, even when events were seemingly novel. In this way we could learn to exploit and control our environment. It is striking to consider that nature valued this brain so highly, as to give it survival priority over the needs of that ancient and basic structure, the still narrow primate pelvis of modern human females. An ancient recidivistic morphology of a sudden had to extrude a huge and tearing skull, the brain within, often at the cost of a mother's life.

Stages

There is an interval of approximately 60,000 years between the lives of two humans. One was found at Qafzeh in Israel, and now dates from approximately 95-90 Ka BP.[15] The other was uncovered in Mladek, Bohemia, and dates from c.35-30 Ka BP. The former skull was found in the context of Mousterian-Neanderthal tools. The latter was found in the context of Aurignacian, Cro-Magnon tools. Both skulls are extremely similar showing more ancient characteristics than traditional Cro-Magnon, *Homo sapiens sapiens,* yet certainly far beyond the Neanderthal stage. They probably connote a hybrid ancestry, yet lean more toward modernity. Why does one reflect the Neanderthal mentality, the other the Cro-Magnon, at least by evidence of the tools? The burial traditions seem modern. Mladec seems to have survived in a context of Cro-Magnon life that had existed in Central Europe for almost 10,000 years.[16] Why do we not find evidence for the existence of Qafzeh types in Western Asia, after this period, even while much Neanderthal skeletal material shows up in the Levant at time levels far more recent?

This is a mystery. Let us hypothesize that this as yet archaic skull, Qafzeh, and another hybrid cousin Skhul, found nearby, had the internal neurological potential for producing the beautiful and diverse tool kit of *Homo sapiens sapiens.* In the particular historical context in which they lived, one of probably several hybrid communities, they apparently had not yet been exposed to the fully evolved Cro-Magnon culture. This modern culture probably had not as yet been invented 90,000 years ago. If a Cro-

Magnon, Aurignacian culture was already in existence, then Qafzeh and Skhul had probably been absorbed into the existing and surrounding Neanderthal way of life.

Mladec, on the other hand, may have been part of a population that still retained these ancient phenotypic or surface physical characteristics even while its beneath-the-skull neurology was quite as modern as other contemporary Cro-Magnons then living throughout Eur-Asia. In Central Europe the old morphology gradually disappeared, apparently retained as a recessive trait thousands of years later, as evidenced in the burial grounds of Iron Age European populations.[17] It tells us that we should be wary of 'judging a book by its cover,' for we humans have buried within us a long and complex heritage leading back to our founding "Adams and Eves."

Civilization: Preconscious Discovery

We do not know when the Eur-Asian Cro-Magnons developed their advanced Aurignacian culture. Scientists have identified a number of post-Mousterian, (Neanderthal), cultural locations, the tool kits of peoples not yet identifiable, no skeletal remains. Some of these suggestive cultural types have names: the Szelettian, Ahamarian, Emiran, Illuzian, Chatelperronian.[18] The last, interestingly, is highly controversial because of its association with both Neanderthal and Cro-Magnon skeletal remains.[19] But it is the Aurignacian culture, when it first appears in West Asia, Bulgaria, Russia, at about 45,000 BP that draws a new line in the sand in terms of a leap forward, now associated with a distinctive people, along a relatively huge geographical swath, and over a timeline of development and expansion moving toward the present.[20]

These Caucasoid northerners seem to have advanced suddenly and overwhelmingly out of an unknown and mysterious "Garden of Eden." Perhaps this incubator lay in the Caucasus, Eastern Anatolia, even the Dnieper River basin in western Russia, certainly products of the northern latitudes. Yet, they show few signs of specialization for life in bitterly cold climates, such as the Neanderthals' sturdy bones, wide nasal openings to warm the cold air, short and stocky physiognomy, not too different from many contemporary paleo-arctic peoples. The Cro-Magnons, tall, c.5'10" on average, with slender bones, thin brain case, all hint at an origin in the moderate climate conditions that existed below the glacial ice during most of these eras over the past two million years in Eur-Asia.

The Aurignacian culture of the Eur-Asian Cro-Magnids, the prototype of all historical civilizations to come, lasted from about 45,000 to about 12,000 years ago. Then another interstadial climatic period took over, the glaciers receding rapidly to the north, and modern, extreme continental climatic conditions taking over. Before this transition, climates during this period had been benign.[21] In the winter months it was cool, autumnal. Summers were cool, spring-like, vegetation rich and variegated in terms of types, some plants today found only in more tropical climes. Clearly the Mastodons, Mammoths, Irish Elk, Great Wild Ox, others dependant on vast amounts of forage throughout the 12-month cycle, could not have long survived on minus-0 Celsius temperatures, or the heavy layerings of snow universally found in recent Eur-Asian winters.

Northeast of Moscow, at c.27,000 B.P, a gravesite was discovered that included fossils of a mature man and several children. They wore clothing of animal leather whereon were sewn dozens of bone, ivory, and horn decorative items; the skeletons also wore necklaces and wrist charms of similar materials. These were clearly persons of high social rank.[22] The importance of the find is not only in the illustrated stratifications within early Cro-Magnon communities meriting such ceremonial funerary decoration. What astounds is the implied specialization and time available from subsistence hunting that allowed for the development of craft skills and the time available to fabricate these decorative and clearly valued items. It reveals, in terms of the chronology of Cro-Magnon occupancy of this very northerly location, and the relatively early articulation of Aurignacian culture, how quickly the skills of these people came to fruition once they stabilized their economy. It reveals how the human mind thirsted for other delights, the leisure provided by efficient satisfaction of *Homo's* basic requirements of food and shelter. It also gives evidence for the many faceted skills available to *Homo sapiens sapiens* from that eruptive brain, a hint for a future that is still ours to explore.

The hunting was good, human populations sparse, tribes freed from the sharp land contentions of later ages. And the minds of our Cro-Magnon ancestors poured forth. We all know about the cave paintings, the sculptures of humans and animals in their outdoor amphitheaters, the bone, horn, ivory, and stone jewelry, often sewn onto their animal skins, wonderfully delicate, yet functional. Then there were the chronometric incisions on bone and rock that seemed to fathom the natural rhythms and meaning of the world outside.[23] The cave paintings are especially intriguing. Always, they are situated deep in the pitch-black interiors. Stone lamps, having saucer like depressions holding animal fat-wax, with a long-lasting vegetative wick, were the source of their light. The paintings often were situated—as with Lascaux in the French Dordogne—in caves high up on a hill overlooking the campsite in the valley, that, alongside the sustaining river.[24]

Think of the Sistine Chapel, in the Vatican in Rome, a product of sixteenth-century Renaissance genius. Here, too, in an interior room unlit by natural light, on all the walls and ceiling is an artistic panorama of the interaction of gods and humans amidst the mysteries of holy meanings. So, too, at Lascaux, some 17,000-20,000 years earlier, the same kind of human mind and intentionality gave expression to a dynamic vision of life, tempered by artistry and skill. Whether this dark cave was a religious shrine, a men's club for relaxation after the hunt, or a place to do art for one's inner soul, we can only speculate. The international flavor of Cro-Magnon's art and technology, across Western Europe to the portals of Siberia, mystifies. Instinct and repetition have here disappeared from the ancient mental template of both ape and man. Throughout this many thousand square mile range of these humans, the similarity of their external appearance as well as the products of their internal intellectual effusions impresses.

Power in Thinking

If one travels to the Dordogne in France, to the areas around rivers Lot, Vézère, Dordogne, to the village of Les Eyzies, where the original Cro-Magnon skull was discovered in the mid-nineteenth century, one will find in every farm house, hotel, shop, municipal building, glass case after glass case exhibiting Upper Paleolithic, Cro-Magnon tools, decorative jewelry made of stone, bone, and ivory, reflective of these many thousands of years of residence, and the long symbiotic infatuation of these humans for the animal life from which they lived and prospered. As with all civilizations they needed time and stability, the luxury of leisure and economic plenty to create their civilization, to mine the inner potentiality of this brain that nature had thrown up seemingly adventitiously, onto the surfaces of practical evolutionary life. We are still making new discoveries from our long distance timeframe. Recently, the dating of the sensational art work in the Chauvet Cave along the Ardèche River in the Massif Central in the south of France has been revised back in time to c.35,000 BP.[25]

What this indicates, since these people are thought to have arrived in France and the West from Eastern Europe and Western Asia, within several thousand years of this date, is how quickly their economic stability allowed them the time and mental freedom to create so unselfconsciously this very advanced artistic sensibility in both technique and esthetics. These new uncoverings of the past further reveal the richness of mind in these northern Eur-Asians. No one taught them to value the esthetic, the intellectually intriguing nature of human experience. Philosophers they probably were not, as yet. Their making of evolutionary history, as with all of life before them, was an act of inner spontaneity.

What they were telling us was that, in the first place, perhaps even before the physical activity of hunting, a need existed for abstract thinking. Far beyond survival and physical surfeit, humans now demanded something that had never existed before, to paint, to carve, to figure out meaning and abstraction. Two outdoor friezes, one of animals at Cap Blanc on the Vézère River, and one, to the north, of animals and Venuses at Angles sur l'Angles on the Creuse River, both in France, are reminiscent of the Parthenon and the Erectheum, carved 20,000 years later in Athens. While dynamic and masterful art, both hint at a common philosophical awareness of the connectivity of life. The modern mind demands order, structure, relationships, at the very least to bind up this florescence of emotive energy, the sensual tides that well up from our reconstructed mammal brain. In the Upper Paleolithic of France, from 35,000 years ago, it was symbolized in the pulsations of animal life. In Athens we observe it carved into the friezes of the Parthenon, the processions of gods pictured as humans.

We cannot know about the inner community life of these Cro-Magnon peoples, their social relations, their sexual discipline, their religious rituals and worship. Their brain was given to them from "Mother Nature," a product of an ancient inertial movement in placental animal life, with which we are still grappling. Given as-yet unclear conditions within human culture and the world outside, awesome civilizations would henceforth be created, else humans could voluntarily dam up the power of mind, now expressed in random doodlings, pornographic exploitation, electronic noise.

What is interesting is that one does on occasion find in the caves of Cro-Magnon and in their outdoor amphitheaters such doodlings and carvings. One must assume accompanying lascivious dances and noisy celebrations, Ice Age "rock." Thus, *Homo sapiens sapiens* could go down the evolutionary hierarchy of symbolic expression for a lark. Could the "Neanderthals" go up? But for the most part, where the brain power and the cognitive urgings existed, the most intensive, explosive, and satisfying use of this sensual energy, pouring out through their cortex without surcease, would be fulfilled in the mind's intellectual concentration.

For example, at La Marche, Lussac-les-Chateaus, (now displayed in the Musée des Antiquités Nationales, Saint Germain en Laye) there must have been a communal area in front of the cave. Blocks of stone surrounding this area were found engraved with animals and Venuses, again emphasizing sharply-incised female torsos and triangled vulvas. All the above amphitheaters and their sculptings date from the culminating period of the Ice Ages, the Magdalenian period, c.16,000-12,000 BP.[26] We find the same graphic sexual incisions in the fertility statuettes of the goddesses in Canaan, 3,000 years ago.

The Cro-Magnons did not merely hibernate in their grottos and caves. In the final icy surge of the Magdalenian period they were already wandering east and south in numbers, searching for better climes and opportunities. Within this general time frame we encounter their tools and arrowheads in Siberia, on their way across Beringia and into the Americas.[27] Of course, in the process they encountered many human groups on the fringes of their original mental and cultural domain. Their genes were thus spread far and wide in concentric waves of influence. By the time these small trickles of people were coming on-shore in North and South America they had been transformed from the original ethnic template. They were now of mixed Caucasoid and Mongoloid heritage. And we find this to be true to the Cro-Magnon's immediate south, the borderlands of South Asia and Africa.[28]

The power of this mentality was not always benign. We find no direct evidence of violence against the Neanderthals as cause for their disappearance as a separate ethnicity, c.27,000 years ago. Knowing what humans were in historical times has to sober us with regard to the question of life style during the Ice Age "Garden of Eden," times of happy prosperity. With the new powers of mind, *Homo sapiens sapiens* was still an untutored aggressive, expansive, dominating creature, as he is today.

Inside the skull was a great and throbbing computer attempting to organize this information, to find meaning in the dark clouds, the lightning, and the stormy rain, to correlate events and to act with regard to an understanding of cause and consequence, before one was washed out of one's tent. These peoples needed to learn to take note of the angle of the sun at different times of the year, to relate it to the migration of animals and fish, so that they could plan and secure a steady supply of food. They had to learn that in the hunt what was necessary was only to sneak up on a grazing animal and with spear, spear thrower, or bow and arrow, deliver a wound that would bleed, then to follow the animal to its ultimate fate. No risk here of body and soul in a fatal physical encounter.

They would learn that the fruits of the hunt could be smoked and preserved for use in times of want, else traded to other tribes for their shells, ivory or amber.[29] Indeed, accidents of cooking might explain the origin of what is the first recorded instance of fire hardened pottery amalgam, in this case, the Venus of Dolni Vestonovice in what is now the Czech Republic, c.20,000 BP.[30] Consider the mentality of these humans contemplating traditional stone tools made by earlier humans. Then, imagine the Cro-Magnon hunter examining the bone, ivory, antler detritus remaining from the last hunt: "If it can be done with stone, wouldn't using bone, ivory or horn be easier, perhaps more beautiful, too?"

The world of Cro-Magnon, instead of being a life experience of events close to his body and those of his intimate kin and fellows, expanded in mental range of observation and planning both spatially and over time. In earlier epochs, new and seemingly frightening events were translated into the spirits and daemons of the primitive mind. To the Cro-Magnids, they were translated into questions, challenges to be figured out. This secular response to the potentially fearful could happen only if humans were able to control and discipline the enormous emotions that often flooded their beings. Without the requisite brain power, such passion could propel a people down a road of stupid and impetuous deeds. If only such fears, explosive aggressivity could be poured into a strategy of feint, retreat, encirclement, then organized attack, wouldn't these powerful feeling be culminated in a very different conclusion, an exuberant hymn of victory over the destroyed foe?

The heretofore unrevealed capacity of the animal brain to discipline behavior by a consideration of possible causes and effects, instead of through automatic instinctual responses, now became part of life lived in the new symbolic world of ideas. More and more, as the brain constructed this abstract system of relationships of the causes of things outside one's own body, or that of the immediate social group, life or death would depend on the ability to calculate the significance of events in a "secular," dispassionate manner.

Expulsion from Eden

Think of the Amero-Indians, the pleasure and freedom of the hunting/gathering life, so different from the grind of agricultural farming, the dawn-to-dusk routine/regime. The pleasant climate, the animal plenty, a steady and satisfying sexual life, the excitement of the hunt, the openness of the land to fill the wandering urge—migration—all deeply fulfilling of primeval human urges. More sinister in this elemental human nature were the easy explosions of nervous and physical energy, the excitement of war and combat for the men, the exhilaration of personal challenge, even perhaps, heroic death for the honor of the clan or tribe.

The northern Eur-Asian paradise still echoed a life with mundane perils. The discovery of many graves with the skeletons of young women with either their newborn dead or infants, or very young children buried alongside, testifies to the fragility of life under these relatively primitive conditions of survival. The birth of very large-headed babies ultimately would add to the power of the group in defense of its way of life. However, this extremely high hominid intelligence was clearly offset, if to a lesser extent by the fact that many women, especially adolescent women, died in the Paleolithic complexities of childbirth.[31] The struggle for existence kept populations to a minimum. Death as a result of warfare does not seem to have been a common event with the Cro-Magnons; the paucity of skeletal remains showing battle wounds is but one piece of evidence.[32]

The ice began to retreat between 12-10 Ka BP. The period that follows is called the Mesolithic. The forests began to encroach upon the tundra/plains ecology of northern Eur-Asia, as warm summers and extremely cold winters drove the great herds either into extinction or into the depths of the forests. There are occasional exemplars in the following Mesolithic period, c. 7000 BP, of beautiful art or architectural endeavors. One cave illustrated at the National Museum in St-Germain-en-Laye near Paris shows the walls incised with row after row of decorative grooving.[33] There are many encampments in which are found numerous painted stones, carvings of animals, extremely miniaturized. Yet these cannot compare in conception and richness of style or quantity with the Upper Paleolithic era before it. Many tribal groups remained. There was still good hunting in the forests, but it was more difficult now.

The hunting economy had not permitted either large-scale settlement, or often, not permanent settlement. These Cro-Magnids followed the herds of animals, the animals themselves sensitive to climatic or ecological changes. Thus, populations per square mile were thin as compared with later southern oases such as Jericho where a steady supply of water from the Judean hills allowed for irrigation and the growth and harvesting of crops year round as well as specialized crafts and a differentiated economy.

The environmental changes forced many groups to reconsider their life commitments. They began to trickle south, often in numbers, gradually fabricating a new economy, but with effort and travail. Humans will stay with the pleasurable, living off the land. They will try to preserve the status quo. Their ability to break out into a new economy, a complex civilization based on sedentary agricultural patterns clearly necessitated the capacity to attain to a wholly new mental perspective, truly revolutionary. It had to have taken time for them to work out new possibilities, often pushed to decision-making by the ever larger population densities now drawn into these magnetic river valley ecologies.

In the south it was more difficult to store large quantities of meat for food reservoirs. Grain reaped through agricultural techniques could be baked and preserved indefinitely. Without the surpluses accruing to the agricultural societies of the later river valley civilizations, the ability and the means to domesticate and feed herd animals could not have been stabilized. Herding had been practiced in the north with reindeer in the final and frigid Magdalenian period.[34] As knowledge gradually accumulated in the river valleys of the south, including the Danube in Europe, as well as around the entire Mediterranean littoral, new possibilities for a northern agriculture became possible. Animal domestication, mining, lumbering with steel axes, riverine trade with other communities, followed.

For the most part, the Cro-Magnon communities seem to have first taken the path of least resistance, as word came back that the warm river valleys to the south beckoned. As with Florida, for retirees, the new frigid continental climate of the Holocene interstadial, from c.12,000-10,000 BP, could no longer provide for a life of easy excitements and pleasures. It was now to be a time of grind, close to the precipice.

We have evidence of a settlement in Jericho, the land of Canaan, at about 9,000 BCE (11,000 BP). In what is now Asiatic Turkey, the settlements date to about the same time period. A thousand years later, along the southeastern course of the Danube, perhaps simultaneously with the first northern settlements along the Nile, began the gatherings of wild grain. In all cases herding begins with humans and animals sharing precious water. Horses and dogs had been domesticated by the Cro-Magnons, long before.[35]

In these lands water was precious, a source for life and possible prosperity, and thus a new economy had to be mastered, in this case systematic agricultural production. Demographic expansion along the rivers gradually excluded the hunting/gathering way of life of the northerners, long patterned to the time when they lived on the savannahs under the rim of the ice-flows. But then, there were still opportunities beyond the river valleys.

This openness beyond the intensive agricultural economies did not mean that the independent northern wanderers were then alone in the world. Inevitably they encountered earlier settled peoples. Soon, that world would see war-learned communities venturing forth besides their flocks, in a plains ecology that was still not wholly desertified. The forested hills of the Middle East were for a while, secure from the corvées of laborers with their iron axes.

Endnotes, Chapter 2

[1] Klein, R. G. 1989. *The Human Career,* Chicago: Univ. of Chicago Press, pp. 348-350.

[2] Dennel, R. 1997. "The World's Oldest Spears," *Nature*, Feb., 1997, 385:27:767-768; Wilford, J. N. 1997. "Ancient German Spears Tell of Mighty Hunters of Stone Age," *The New York Times,* 3/4/97.

[3] Simeons, A. T. S. 1962. *Man's Presumptuous Brain,* N.Y.: Dutton, p. 276.

[4] Schwarcz, H. P. 1994. "Chronology of Modern Humans in the Levant," in Bar Yosef, O., and Kra, R. S., eds., *Late Quaternary Chronology and Paleoclimates of the Eastern Mediterranean,* Tuscon, Ariz.: Univ. of Arizona, p. 27; Trinkaus, E., and Shipman, P. 1993. *The Neanderthals*, N.Y.: Knopf, *passim.*

[5] Wolpoff, M .H., and Caspari, R. 1997. *Race and Human Evolution*, N.Y.: Simon and Schuster, Ch. 11.

[6] Itzkoff, S. W. 2000. *The Inevitable Domination by Man, An Evolutionary Detective Story*, Ashfield MA.: Paideia Publishers.

[7] Andrews, P., and Stringer, C. 1993. "The Primates' Progress," in Gould, S., ed. 1993. *Life,* N.Y.: W. W. Norton, p. 233.

[8] Gabunia, L, *et. al.* 2000. "Earliest Pleistocene Hominid Cranial Remains from Dmanisi, Republic of Georgia: Taxonomy, Geological Setting, and Age," *Science*, 288:12, May:1019-1025.

[9] Tattersall, I. 1995. *The Last Neanderthal*, N.Y.: Macmillan/U.S.A., p. 117, Illus. 82, 83.

[10] von Koenigswald, G. H. R. 1962. *The Evolution of Man*, Ann Arbor, MI: Univ. of Michigan Press, p. 125.

[11] Wright, S. 1963. "Adaptation and Selection," in Jepson, G. L., Simpson, G. G., Mayr, E., eds., *Genetics, Paleontology and Evolution,* N.Y.: Atheneum, pp. 365-391; Simpson, G. G. 1953. *The Major Features of Evolution,* N.Y.: Columbia Univ. Press.

[12] deBeer, G. 1958. *Embryos and Ancestors,* 3rd ed., Oxford: Oxford Univ. Press; Bolk, L. 1926. *Das Problem der Menschenwerdung*, Jena: G. Fischer.

[13] Eisley, L.1957. *The Immense Journey*, N.Y.: Random House.

[14] Simpson, G. G. 1944. *Tempo and Mode in Evolution,* N.Y.: Columbia Univ. Press.

[15] Tattersall, I., *The Last Neanderthal, op. cit.,* Illus. 115; pp. 168-169.

[16] Klein, R. G., *The Human Career, op. cit.,* p. 277.

[17] Coon, C. S. 1962. *The Origin of Races,* N.Y.: Knopf, p. 584.

[18] Davidson, I., and Noble, W. 1993. "Tools and Language in Human Evolution," in Gibson, K. R., and Ingold, T., eds., *Tools, Language, and Cognition in Human Evolution*, Cambridge, Eng.: Cambridge Univ. Press, pp. 380-382.

[19] Harrold, Francis B. 1989. "Mousterian, Chatelperronian and Early Aurignacian in Western Europe: Continuity or Discontinuity, in Mellars, P. A, and Stringer, C. P.,

eds., *The Emergence of Modern Humans*, Edinburgh: Univ. of Edinburgh Press, pp. 696-697.

[20] Bar Yosef, O. 1994. "Introduction: Dating Eastern Mediterranean Sequences," in Bar Yosef and Kra, eds., *op cit.*, pp. 1-12.

[21] Guthrie, R. Dale. 1984. "Mosaics, Allelochemics and Nutrients," in Martin, P. S., and Klein, R. G., eds. 1984. *Quaternary Extinctions*: a *prehistoric revolution*, Tucson, Ariz.: Univ. of Arizona Press, pp. 259-298.

[22] Tattersall, I., *The Last Neanderthal, op. cit.,* Illus. 129, pp. 186-187.

[23] Marshack, A. 1972. *The Roots of Civilization,* London: Weidenfield and Nicolson; Marshack, A. 1974. "The Meander as a System, etc.," in Ucko, P., ed., *Biennial Conference of the Australian Institute of Aboriginal Studies*, May-June, 16, Canberra, Australia.

[24] Itzkoff, S. W., *The Inevitable Domination by Man, An Evolutionary Detective Story, op. cit.,* p. 279.

[25] Clottes, Jean. 2001. *La Grotte Chauvet: L'Art des Origines,* Paris: Editions du Seuil; Clottes, Jean. 2001. "Chauvet Cave," in *National Geographic*, August, 104-121.

[26] Campbell, B. 1985. *Human Evolution,* 3rd ed., N.Y.: Aldine De Gruyter, Fig. 10.3, p. 296.

[27] Wilford, J. N. 1996. "American Arrowhead Found in Siberia," *The New York Times* Aug.2; from article in *Science*, Aug. 2, 1996 by King, M., and Slobodin, S. B.

[28] Brues, A. 1977. *People and Races,* N.Y.: Macmillan; Asley-Montagu, M. F., and Brace, C. L. 1977. *Human Evolution,* N.Y.: Macmillan, pp. 399-401.

[29] White, R. 1989. "Production Complexity and Standardization in Early Aurignacian Bead and Pendant Manufacture: Evolutionary Implications," in Mellars, P.A., and Stringer, C., eds. 1989. *The Human Revolution—Behavioral and Biological Perspectives on the Origins of Modern Humans*, Princeton: Princeton Univ. Press, pp. 374-376; Mellars P. A. 1996. *The Neanderthal Legacy,* Princeton: Princeton Univ. Press, pp. 398-400.

[30] Klein, R. G. *The Human Career, op. cit,.* p. 303.

[31] In the Natural History Museum in Les Eyzies, Dordogne area of France, where the original Cro-Magnon skeleton was found in the mid-19th century, there are several skeletons of very young women, with their infants buried besides them.

[32] Bar-Yosef, O.1993 "The Role of Western Asia in Modern Human Origins," in Aitkin, M. J., *et al.,* eds. 1993. *The Origin of Modern Humans and the Impact of Chronometric Dating*, Princeton, N.J.: Princeton Univ. Press, pp. 132-147; Tattersall, I. 1995. *The Last Neanderthal, op. cit.*

[33] Musée des Antiquités Nationales, Saint-Germain-en-Laye, Paris.

[34] Leakey, R. 1981. *The Making of Mankind.* N.Y.: Dutton, pp. 193-196.

[35] Wills, C. 1998. *Children of Prometheus,* Reading, Mass.: Perseus Books, p. 41.

3

Wandering Patriarchs

Israel's Northern Origins

"So Abram went, as the Lord had told him; and Lot went with him. Abram was seventy-five years old when he departed from Haran…and they set forth to go to the land of Canaan." {Gen. 12:4-5-J-source.}

" and he drove away all his livestock…that he had acquired in Paddan-aram, to go to his father Isaac in the land of Canaan…and Jacob deceived Laban the Aramean, in that he did not tell him that he intended to flee. So he fled with all that he had; starting out he crossed the Euphrates [Hebrew—the river], and set his face toward the hill country of Gilead." {Gen. 31:17, 20-21—E-source.}

"Terah took his son Abram and his grandson Lot son of Haran, and his daughter-in - law Sarai, his son Abram's wife, and they went out together from Ur of the Chaldeans to go to the land of Canaan; but when they came to Haran, they settled there." {Gen. 11:31; also Gen. 12:5; 15:7; 25:20; 28:2-7—P-source.}

[In the Hebrew Bible scholars attribute "J" to the time of Solomon, tenth century, latest to his son, Rehoboam, early ninth century in Judah; "E" is considered to have been written in the Northern Kingdom, Israel, sometime during the ninth to the eighth century. Both "J" and "E" have much older material, written and oral, added to the texts. "P" is controversial, scholars divided as to whether its main components, in addi-

tion to the inclusion of more ancient materials, were written in the era of Hezekiah, King of Judah, toward the end of the eighth century. Else, it was written in exile in Chaldean-Babylonia, or shortly after, on the return to Judah (Yehud), now part of the Persian Empire, in the sixth century. (Possibly both views are reconcilable). Deuteronomy through 2 Kings, although consisting of much original and relatively old documentation and tradition, was probably written in Judah in the time of Josiah, latter seventh century, with numerous addenda; Deuteronomy 2, completed in the early sixth century, is exemplified in later descriptions of the destruction of Jerusalem and the First Temple.

Two sources are here used to identify the various strands of Biblical tradition, with regard to which group of writers wrote what: Norman Gottwald. 1985. *The Hebrew Bible, A Socio-Literary Introduction*, Philadelphia: Fortress Press; Friedman, R. E. 1987/1997. *Who Wrote the Bible?* San Francisco: Summit/Harper.]

In the Hebrew Bible there are three versions of the same tale of the patriarch Abram's journey south to Canaan at the command of God. The city of Ur of the Chaldees was originally a Sumerian city, c.3000 BCE, at the junction of the Tigris and Euphrates rivers as they entered the Persian Gulf. But at the time of the writing of the "P" source, Ur was in the domain of the neo-Babylonian or Chaldean Empire. Haran, mentioned in all three versions, is located in northern Mesopotamia, and during the historical period of the patriarchs as envisioned by the authors of these excerpts, was a Hurrian (Indo-European) city.[1]

Clearly this pathway down into Canaan was characteristic of the migration of people probably as far back as the closing millennia of the Pleistocene Ice Ages, c.13,000-9,000 years before the present (BP). The Ice-Age history of the southern river valley geographies reflects a quieter impact of new arrivals, Cro-Magnons, on older populations, less developed from an evolutionary standpoint than the newcomers. The older indigenous peoples were receptive genetically to the scattering migrants that entered their lands, else they moved out of the way as the Neanderthals had done in the north thousands of years earlier. There was still an emptiness of humans on our earth.

The northerners had to learn to deal with this new ecology. At first it was a bare eking out a livelihood of mixed hunting, gathering, even marginal cultivation of indigenous grains and fruits. The climate was relatively benign, and thus allowed for a time of slow genetic and cultural absorption of new into old. This is why the so-called indigenous peoples of the river valleys of southwest Asia and northern Africa are unclear ethnically in the early post-Ice Age period.

In the land of Canaan, the so-called Natuftians have been identified as the earliest core post-Ice-Age populations, 12,000-8,000 BP. Physically, as compared with the ancient Mousterian Neanderthals, the Natuftians evince reduced "head size, jaw size, and tooth size."[2] They were shorter than the classic Cro-Magnons or even the ancient hybrid Skhul populations, 90,000 BP, male Natuftians 168cm. *versus* Cro-Magnons 180cm. As compared to more modern successor Neolithic (pottery making) populations, after c.5500 BP, the only significant trend that continues is reduction in tooth size.[3] In general, the Natuftians can be described as short to medium in stature, with long, narrow skulls, broad faces, quite prognathous in facial appearance.[4]

Throughout the Fertile Crescent after 11,000 BCE, sickles of flint blades cemented into wooden or bone handles suddenly begin to appear in the fossil record. These would have been used for harvesting wild grains, probably would not have been too different from tools fabricated in the north to harvest wild vegetables and fruit. Also, we discover baskets woven of vegetative materials in which to carry the grains home from the hillsides where they grew, and mortars and pestles, or grinding slabs, to remove the husks. Evidence exists of the use of techniques for the roasting of grains so that they could be stored without sprouting; and underground storage pits, some of them plastered to make them waterproof.[5] Clear changes in technology were now occurring in the south.

The next interval, 8,000-4,000 BP, reveals a more significant morphologically identifiable change in the population. This period was characterized by more significant incursions of northern peoples, ever going south, as well as migrations within the general Near East geographical complex, between the Tigris-Euphrates and Nile River systems, including the Arabian peninsula. Pre-pottery Neolithic eras give way to the Neolithic and then the early Bronze Age cultural traditions, spurred to some extent by incoming influences, but now also reflecting the increasing demographic weight, maturation and sophistication of these populations in acclimatizing themselves to the new ecological context of life in the post-Ice-Age Holocene period.

The most ancient populations of historical peoples in North Africa, now found especially in the recesses of the Atlas Mountains, are the Berbers, who seem, in their blue eyes, pinkish skin, and round faces, to be descendants of the Cro-Magnons who during the Ice Ages had migrated across the Straits of Gibraltar. Clearly they preserved their ethnicity, either because of self-imposed geographical isolation in the mountains, else, and more probably, they came in force and pressed the indigenous peoples south into the desertifying savannahs. Later, easterners from the Semitic states along the Mediterranean, and northerners flowing south out of southern Europe, into the islands of this sea and then south into Africa, repeated a migratory tradition dating from the late-Pleistocene Ice Age.

In the Nile Valley, the Egyptian dynastic tradition overlaying fairly significant pre-existing populations had been developing from at least 3500 BCE. They represent an incoming group of invaders, again of larger stature and northern physiognomy.[6] The bronze statuette of the designer of the earliest surviving terraced building of stone, the "renaissance" architect, physician, wise man, Imhotep, c.3000 BCE; the diorite portrait of Khafre, the Pharaoh responsible for the building of the second pyramid at Gizeh, c.2900 BCE; the bronze portrait of Pepi 1, c.2600 BCE, here with rock-crystal inlaid eyes, all testify to the early if historically unheralded northern Eur-Asian presence among the ruling classes, at the least, here in the Nile Valley.[7]

This dominant tradition was the final phase of more ancient shepherd wanderers from around 5000 BCE who brought the Hamitic class of languages first into Egypt, thence across North Africa, finally deep into the south of the continent. The pharaonic classes, whether or not they came as invading warriors from the river valleys of Meso-potamia, or up the Red Sea, or indeed, as but another migrating people from the north, c.3500 BCE, were similar in heritage to those who settled in numbers in the Holy Land, somewhat later. The language differences between the Hamites and Semites are no doubt due to the barrier constituted by that sliver of sacral desert, the Sinai.

Civilizational Memories: Sumer

The steady rhythmic pulsations of the Nile as it flowed north to the Mediterranean Delta, the insulation of this ecological anomaly in the desiccated flatlands surrounding the river gave a certain placidity to the cultural advances that mark Egypt as a unique civilization. In the north it was different. The great rivers, Tigris and Euphrates, flowing down from the Iranian and Anatolian highlands were like a conduit guiding the flow of the populations southward. To the original Semitic inhabitants of these valleys a new presence suddenly appeared about 3500 BCE, lured by the rich marshy delta lands at the confluence of these rivers as they entered the Persian Gulf.

Their original homeland may have been near the Caspian Sea, from a city-state they called Aratta, with whom they had trade and political relationships throughout their rule in the south.[8] Clearly, this is a relatively late post-Ice Age date for the first northern civilizational occupation of such an important source for economic sustenance as were these rich river valleys. The predecessors have been called "Proto-Euphrateans," "Ubaidians," or later in time, "Subarians." Many of the root Sumerian words for cities, rivers, occupations, reveal a non-Sumerian character, now attributed to these earlier productive and acculturated people who were absorbed into the Sumerian city-states.[9] Also, there exist on some of the earliest Sumerian written inscriptions, writing, itself a truly Sumerian innovation, Semitic loan words, as with the names of a number of adopted deities of seemingly Semitic origin.[10]

The first dynasty of the Sumerians in the city of Kish, according to their own epic writings, began after the "Great Flood," with rulers having Semitic names, "Etana," for example, at the beginning of the third millennium BCE, c.2900. The immigration south into the fertile valleys was probably gradual. The exhilaration of the new geographical setting, which stimulated agricultural as well as mercantile and industrial innovation, brought about the necessity and innovation of written forms of record keeping, including the laws of the magistrates. Only then do we find the Sumerians attending to their literary talents, the poetry, mythology, and literature that became the glue of Mesopotamian education and civilization.

The prosperity produced by these advances brought them into contact with peoples far and wide. The paradisiacal country of Dilmun, either on the Persian Gulf, else the Indus River Valley, the land of the black people, Meluhha, probably Ethiopia, and, of course, Egypt, where they contributed their knowledge as traders, architects and engineers, possibly even as conquerors, c.3000 BCE.[11] Meluhha is also known from the later time of the Semite "Akkadian" King Sargon. Boats from Meluhha rode at anchor at the port of "Agade" on the Euphrates. The poem, "The Curse of Agade," refers to Naram-Sin, grandson of Sargon. "The meluhhaites, the men of the black land, Bring to him all kinds of exotic wares." A reference to the black people of Meluhha continues to the first millennium BCE.

S. N. Kramer describes the Sumerians as they first appear in the historic record as follows: "...the aggressive penchant for controversy and the ambitious drive for pre-eminence provided no little of the psychological motivation which sparked and sustained the material and cultural advances for which the Sumerians are not unjustly noted: irrigation expansion, technological invention, monumental building, the development of a system of writing and education....There is little doubt that the Sumerians considered themselves a kind of 'chosen people,' 'salt of the earth,'" as it were.[12] In the myth of "Enki and the World Order," which treats of the god Enki's creating and organizing the natural and cultural entities and processes essential to civilized society, we find Enki blessing Sumer in winged words which reveal that the Sumerians thought of themselves as a special, hallowed community more intimately related to the gods than to mankind in general, a community noteworthy not only for its material wealth and possessions, not only for its powerful kings, but also for its honored spiritual leaders, the *en's*, a community that all the fate-decreeing heaven-gods, the Anunnaki, had selected as their abode.[13]

The Sumerians called themselves the "black-headed" people in contradistinction to other ethnicities around them and at a distance. "After An, Enki, and Ninhirsag/ Had fashioned the black-headed people,/ Vegetation luxuriated from the earth,/ Animals, four-legged (creatures) of the plain were/ were brought artfully into existence."[14] {Genesis in the Hebrew Bible?.} In the epics of the Sumerians, Emmerker, lord of Erech goes on journey to Aratta, to make it a vassal state. He joins with seven heroes, especially the hero Lugalbanda; they arrive at Mt. Hurum.[15] Kramer argues that Mt. Hurum was the original home of the Hurrian people who figure so largely in the Hebrew Bible, "in the neighborhood of Lake Van," now in eastern Turkey.[16]

Where did they come from, with their greatly different spoken language, perhaps related to the Uralic/Altaic family, Hungarian Magyars, Turkic peoples, Kazahks? The awareness of their separate heritage perhaps was accentuated by the fact that they were dark-headed people in contrast to the light-haired Semites and early dominating Hamites. This may hint of a people in contact in their northern homelands with peoples of mixed Mongoloid heritage. The Sumerians, could have been a people who swerved south instead of wending their way east, as did so many of the advancing northerners— first, Amero-Indians, later, people of Pazaryk (Siberia), and the Tokharians (Shang Dynasty).

The Sumerian civilization of city-states flourished from 3500-1900 BCE. The impact of their civilization on the Semites around them was tangible. The growing sophistication of the neighboring Semitic Akkadians led by Sargon, c.2350 BCE, ended their political independence for several hundred years, but not their cultural domination in terms of the accoutrements of civilizational life—law, literacy, technology, myth, literature and history, morality, personal and civic discipline, technological innovation, the arts, the sense of beauty.

"Sargon, the mighty king, king of Agade, am I/ My mother was a *changeling*, my father I knew not./ The brother(s) of my father *loved* the hills./ My city is Azupiranu, which is situated on the banks of the Euphrates./ My *changeling* mother conceived me, in secret she bore me./ She set me in a basket of rushes {Exodus: Moses story?}, with bitumen she sealed my lid./ She cast me into the river which rose not (over) me./ The river bore me up and carried me to Akki, the drawer of water./ Akki, the drawer of water lifted me out as he dipped his e{w}er./ Akki, the drawer of water, {took me} as his son (and) reared me./ Akki, the drawer of water, appointed me as his gardener./ While I was a gardener, Ishtar granted me {her} love,/ And for four and {...} years I exercised kingship./ The black-headed {people} I ruled, I gov{erned};/...Whatever king may come up after me,/ {...},/ Let him r{ule, let him govern} the black-headed {peo}ple..."[17]

Writing and thus reading were invented in Sumer, c.3000 BCE. The Sumerians' first use of pictures to denote numbers and objects was necessitated by the need to organize increasingly complex legal and bureaucratic affairs in a society with an urban economy, highly differentiated and specialized occupations and professions. Their cuneiform symbols for concrete objects, such as for bread and head, were gradually combined to create the ideas, "eat," for example. Many such signs were soon found, as was true later in Egypt, to be confusing, often because of the homophonic overlap of spoken words that stood for the pictures—"son" and "sun." Thus the conceptual logographic system of ideograms was gradually streamlined intellectually with additional signs so that it reflected the syllabic structure of the spoken language. This was an important step toward a purely abstract code of conveying information, yet still sensuously related to the spoken and listened to language.

The conquering Akkadians were a minority military elite of light-haired people that ruled a large population base of black-headed Sumerians. Sargon envisioned a rule over these cultured yet politically subservient peoples well into the future. Inscriptions by his successors reveal ever more attempts to integrate the Semitic Akkadian cuneiform with the older classic Sumerian. About 2150 BCE, after 200 years of Semitic Akkadian rule, a revived Sumerian dynasty (Gudea) reasserts its power from the cities of Lagash, Nippur, and Ur. Internecine wars and gradual cultural/economic decline ultimately heralds the rise to power of Semitic, Amorite Babylon, and the rule of Hammurabi, c.1800 BCE, whose famous law code is based on established Sumerian written law and practice. But the mysterious Sumerian language, whose agglutinative structure is reminiscent of the Uralic/Altaic family of languages, as well as the extraordinarily talented Sumerian ethnicity, now goes underground, absorbed as a classic rivulet of memory into the Semitic ocean.

Certainly the emphasis in Genesis of the "P" writers (c.550 BCE), as to Abram and his family's ultimate origins in Ur of the Chaldeans, was not a bow toward this revived neo-Babylonian empire, (reasserted after the rule of Israel's nemesis, Assyria), whose capital was now far from Ur of the delta lands. It was a historical recognition of relatedness that had to be aligned to the then-contemporary reader's notice of the powerful empire that had brought down Judah. The archaeologist Leonard Wooley was one of the first to note the parallels between the story of the Flood and Noah and events related in the Gilgamesh legend far back in time at the Sumerian city of Ur. There is thus a tradition of peoples sharing a common heritage, coextensive with the written Sumerian, "...narratives of the Creation, the first human pair, the rise of sin, and the Flood."[18]

The Biblical parallels with Sumer derive from the many Sumerian influences on other peoples, Elamites, Akkadians, Assyrians, Hittites, Hurrians, neo-Babylonians, Canaanites. Tablets about Enki, the god of water, referring to King Ziusudra, were found in Shurrupak, in Sumer, that dated back to c.2900 BCE. In tablets at Kuyunjik (Palace of Sennacherib, 700 BCE, late Assyrian), at Sippar I Babylonia, (1646-1626 BCE, King Ammisaduqa), the Flood theme is reiterated. As Paul Johnson notes, these earlier tales, even the epic of Gilgamesh, lack moral and historical depth, whereas Noah's tale is replete with human strivings and weaknesses, moral ambiguities, also the question of providential design. "Whoso sheddeth man's blood, by man shall his blood be shed: for in the image of God made he man." {Genesis 9:—P-source.}[19] Of course, the tale of the Flood in Genesis is a conflation of the work of the "J" and "P" writers, completed much later in time, and more experienced in the travails of humankind.

The linguist Arno Poebel believed that the name Shem, oldest son of Noah, derived from the Sumerian way of saying Sumer. Also, Ur of the Chaldees, c.600 BCE, would relate back through a timeline to "Urim" in Sumerian, but pronounced in Sumerian "Ur." The Hebrews wrote it down as the Sumerians had pronounced it.[20]

In the "J" version of Genesis we find added an even older tale about Noah after the deluge. It is inserted after the Covenant between God and Noah, his son, their descendants. "And I will establish my covenant with you; neither shall all flesh be cut off any more by the waters of the flood; neither shall there be a flood to destroy the earth." {Gen. 9:11; also 1-17; 28-29—P-source.} Noah, "a man of the soil," quickly planted a vineyard, harvested the grapes, turned them into wine, and became drunk. Ham, the middle son, saw his father lying uncovered in the tent and committed a sin. The other two brothers, Shem and Japheth, discreetly cover Noah. Noah awakens, understands what has happened and issues this prophetic hymn to his sons who will become the progenitors of the modern peoples on the earth: "Cursed be Canaan; lowest of the slaves shall he be to his brothers...Blessed by the Lord my God be Shem; and let Canaan be his slave. May God make space for Japheth, and let him live in the tents of Shem; and let Canaan be his slave." {Gen. 9:18-27—J-source.}

The descendants of Ham: Cush (Arabia), Egypt, Put (Mesopotamia), Canaan. The descendants of Japheth: Gomer, Magog, Javan, Tubal, Mesheck, and Tiras..."From these the coastland peoples spread," *.i. e.,* peoples of the Aegean peninsula, Asia Minor, Medes, Cimmerians, Cretans, Scythians.

"To Shem also, the father of all the children of Eber [Ibrim—Hebrews="beyond"], Elam, Asshur, Arpachshad, Lud and Aram," here including non-semitic Elamites of the north, Assyrians, Indo-European Lydians, Arameans, from the Syrian or Mesopotamian homeland of Abram. {Gen. 10:1-31—J and P-source.}[21]

In the archaeologically uncovered city of Ebla, c.2300 BCE, Tell Mardikh, 35 miles southwest of Aleppo in modern Syria, approximately 2500 tablets have been uncovered. They mostly deal with economic matters, trading lists for the royal archives, but also some training material for the royal scribes, which include Sumerian vocabulary lists with their Akkadian, (proto-Canaanite) Semitic equivalents.[22] The name of the third king of Ebla was Ebrum or Ebrium, (Eber, grandson of Noah, ancestor of Abraham). Many other names of people and places would be familiar to readers of the Hebrew Bible.[23]

The moral high ground that the "J" historian wishes to emphasize in Genesis is the contrast between the relatively pure and distant non-Semitic neighbors of the ancestors of the Hebrews, Shem and Eber, and the corrupt if momentarily powerful surrounding rivals with whom the Israelites had been in conflict. When the "J" compilers of this tradition, c.950 BCE, were including the story of Noah's post-Flood experience with his sons, they were looking back not merely at an originating relationship with an extraordinary people, the Sumerians, reflected in the etymology of Shem. They were also deeply aware of their own world now populated by peoples from the Aegean, Anatolia, the northern plateaus whence were migrating Assyrians, Medes, possibly Scythians. They had good cause to be aware, for, this world had been and was descending on Israel, Canaan, even on Egypt.

The memory of the Flood, an ancient event of the far north first recorded in Sumerian mythology, was reflected in much of the lore of the Middle East. That it was linked to a son of Noah named Shem (Sumer), and inserted by the writers of Genesis as part of a covenant given by God to Noah and Shem, "the father of all, the children of Eber," is a crucial link in tracing the paths of the patriarchs.

Indo-European Heritage

A great change in the physical characteristics of the Canaanite populations, coinciding with significant cultural changes, occurred by the Middle Bronze period, approximately 2,000 BCE. "… the head is shorter and wider, with a high rounded skull and shorter broader face and nose than in any of the earlier or most of the later populations inhabiting Israel."[24] The new cultural innovations are in the form of building techniques, mortuary practices, pottery style, and general technology. These trends seem to be migrating south through Syria parallel to the wandering Amorite and Hurrian populations.[25]

The new ethnic types reflected in the skeletal evidence at Canaanite burial sites after 2000 BCE seem to indicate a wave of linguistically Indo-European peoples that went south, east, and west, from a presumptive center east of the Don river in Russia. Perhaps it was product of a demographic surge in these northerners, precipitated by good times, followed by "seven" years of hardship. In the Old Testament, written a thousand years later, we can identify the names Hittites and Hivites, the latter referring to Hurrian speakers (also possibly Cilicians from Anatolia), now speakers of a Semitic language, but ruled by Mitanni overlords, the first wave of Indo-Europeans. Soon they would be followed by the Hittites.

Indeed, the flow of peoples south from these originating sources, as with the Egyptians and Sumerians thousands of years earlier, did not have to be always "sanctified" by the monuments of political and military conquest. The flow of peoples, including the incipient male warriors, could have been largely peaceful, as with Abraham, Isaac, and Jacob, moving at a distance into the realm of the indigenous populations in a largely under-populated geography. And usually, because the time frames are so broad here, these movements could have taken place as with dominos. Populations moved in, acculturated themselves with the land and the local residents, learned the language and the holy places and gods of the land, trading, sometimes fighting, always interbreeding with

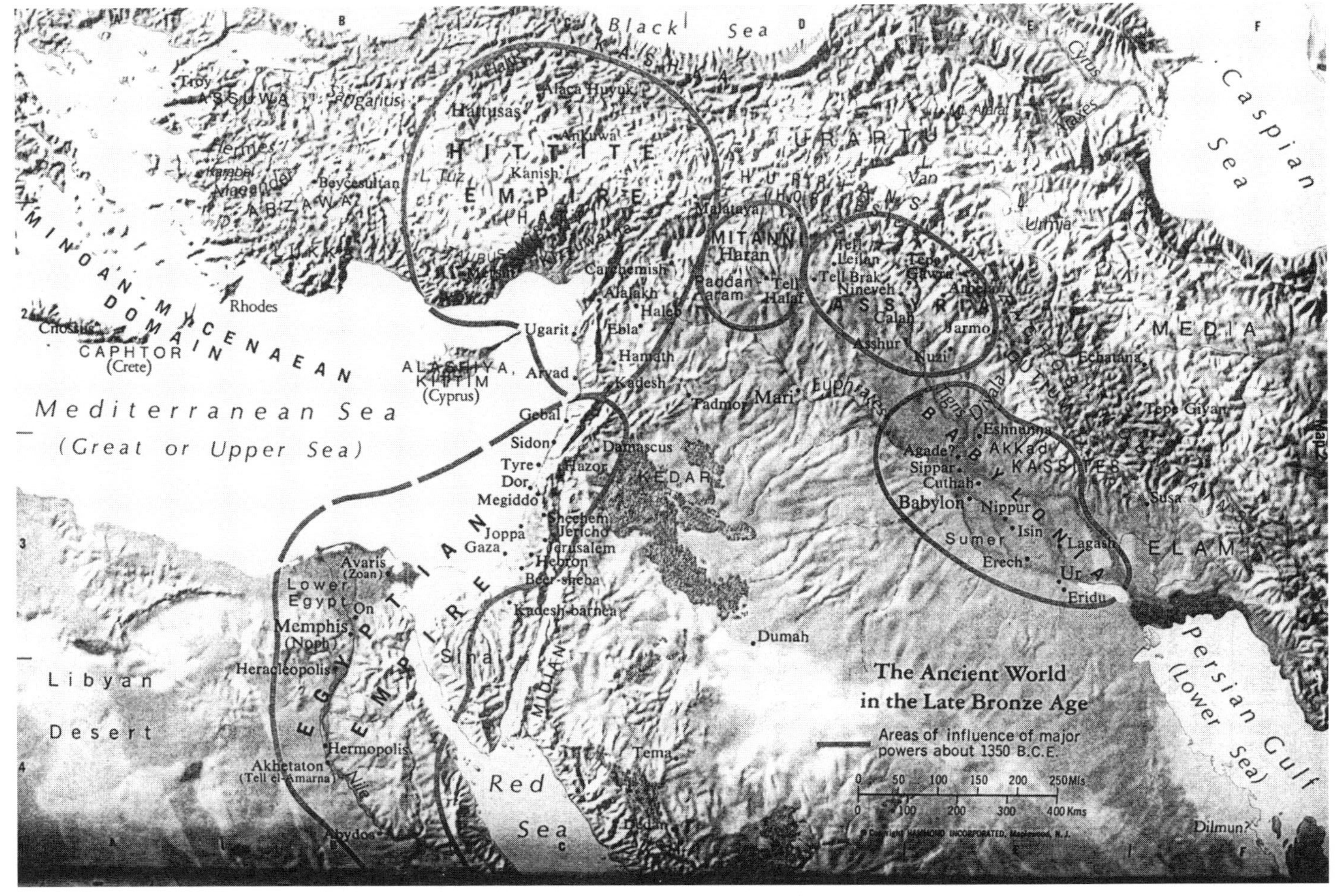

I. The ancient world, in the Late Bronze Age; areas of influence of major powers about 1350 BCE.

them over generations. Their descendants then, moved further south several generations hence.

If you are going to move, go toward the land of "milk and honey." And in the ancient world no land was richer than that of the Nile, Egypt. "Ibsha, the ruler of a foreign country (*Hyksos*), leads a caravan of 37 Asiatics bringing eye paint to Egypt."[26] This is from a tomb painting at Beni Hasan, Upper Egypt, just north of Tel Amarna, on the Nile. Later under Pharaoh Akhenaton, Tel Amarna would become the capital, the center of a new and monotheistic religion of the sun god Aton, c.1350 BCE (see Chapter 5). The above tomb painting dates from c.1890 BCE. It shows both men and women arrayed in "coats of many colours," typical of the Canaanites. {Genesis 37:23, 32—J-source.} The historian J. H. Breasted viewed the physiognomy of these people as Indo-European.[27] "The men carry spears and bows and arrows, thus they are not prisoners. They bring with them gazelles for trade, metal working bellows tied onto donkeys, and musical instruments. {Gen. 4:19-22—J-source.}[28] Breasted sees them, this early in Egyptian history, as having Hittite noses, certainly different from an Egyptian visage, that, more classically flat, if long and straight. [29]

A century and half later, c.1750 BCE, in Thebes, further south along the Nile, an Egyptian household of wealth and power lists 80 servants, of which more than forty are stated to be Asiatics. They are listed by their original Asiatic names, some of which appear to be of Indo-European derivation, along with their new Egyptian names, perhaps, as in Genesis, the Joseph tale, sold into slavery. {Genesis 37:25-26—J-source.} There are many more women in the list than men, the children usually have only an Egyptian name, born into "bondage?" and/or products of concubinage. The women work mostly in the weaving rooms; the male Asiatics are characterized as houseman, cook, brewer, tutor.[30]

' The infiltration north to south of peoples impacts Egypt politically in the founding of the city of Avaris (now Tel ed-Dab'a) in the Nile Delta, c.1850-1750 BCE. Later, adjoining it was Pi-Rameses (now Qantir), the latter built by Rameses II, c.1250 BCE, whose family originated in the Delta. Pi-Rameses is often identified with the city of Israelite enslavement, and possibly the city of Moses' birth. The rule of the Hyksos (he-qaw khasut—rulers from foreign lands) in Avaris came a century after its founding for the Asiatic trade, as the breakdown of dynastic leadership allowed these "Asiatics" to first take control of the Delta, then Memphis and the rest of Egypt, at about 1650 BCE, becoming the 13th Dynasty. Manatho, one of the Hyksos pharaohs claimed that his people had taken over Egypt without a blow.[31] The Hyksos rule of Egypt lasted for 100-150 years, c.1675 (1650)-1550 (1500) BCE. In the thirty-third year of the Hyksos' Pharaoh Apophis, the important Rhind mathematical papyrus was copied out.[32]

Control over all of Egypt inevitably showed itself in monuments and adornments. We find scarabs in Upper and Lower Egypt that reveal new forms of cultic worship, especially of the Syrian deity "Seth." It continued beyond the Hyksos era. Also from this period are one of the earliest alphabetic inscriptions to be found, in a Semitic script, c.1500 BCE, from the Sinai Peninsula.[33] The bringing of chariots to the Delta (by the Hyksos) is further evidence for the Indo-European connection of these people notwithstanding their Canaanite architecture and generally Semitic cultural veneer.

Ahmose, striking out from Thebes, expelled the Hyksos, now wealthy and complacent, from their position of dominance in Egypt after 1550 BCE. The Egyptians, in contradistinction to the coastal areas of Canaan, called the central highland of that area Kharu (Hurru-Hurrians). When Amenhotep II, c.1425 BCE, following up on the Hyksos expulsion, reconquered Canaan/Syria from the indigenous Indo-Europeans/Semites (leftover Hyksos), over 30 percent of his captives were Hurrians.[34]

At the same time the linguistically Indo-European Hittite Empire was encroaching upon the Mitanni-Hurrian syncretic Arian/Semitic civilization in Syria and Northern Iraq. This included the "Nuzi" cities, on the upper Tigris, whose literature throws much light on the intellectual/cultural perspective on life that the Hebrews would later take up in their holy and prophetic writings.

Confirmation of the North

Biblical scholar Baruch Halpern has presented important evidence to support the Indo-European/ Hyksos association of Dynasty 19, Rameses I, 1295-1286, in the Delta. He has also connected the traditions of Genesis, the Joseph story, with this period, as well as an interesting allusion to Exodus and Moses.[35] In {Numbers 13:22—P-source}, the city of Zoan (Hebrew); Djanet (Egyptian); Tanis (Greek), is referred to in association with Hebron (which would become the first royal city of King David. {2 Samuel 5}). {Numbers 13:22—P-source}: "Hebron was built seven years before Zoan in Egypt." Hebron then was an ancient city, going back to the days of the first Hyksos invasions, c.1700 BCE. But, Zoan was relatively new in the eleventh century of King David. The Biblical writers of the seventh or sixth centuries BCE could not have known this. Nor could the people of David's tribe, Judah, have known it, as they themselves were relative newcomers in the area, David's father, Jesse, having been born in Bethlehem. {1 Samuel 16.} They probably were Hebrew (Abram-like) herders, or Moabites from the east across the Salt (Dead) sea, or possibly recent escapees from Egypt.

What confused the writers of the "P"-source was that the stele to the God Seth was relatively new to Zoan. This stele commemorates the inauguration of the worship of this god in Egypt 400 years earlier. It had been originally erected in Pi Rameses by Pharaoh Rameses II, c.1250 BCE, a city of his own construction. Rameses had been born in the Delta of the Nile, and this stele was a recognition of the introduction of this god into Egypt some 400 years earlier by the Hyksos, c.1650 BCE. The god Seth is here portrayed by the artists working for Rameses II dressed as an Asiatic deity. Can we conclude other than that Rameses II himself was aware of his Asiatic, or northern heritage?

Subsequent to the rule of Rameses II, the stele itself was moved by a successor pharaoh to the new inland city of Zoan. This history was unbeknownst to the later Biblical writers. They only recalled the tradition in which the Lord presents an admonition to Abraham that his descendants will be strangers in a land not theirs and will be oppressed for 400 years. {Gen. 15:13-14—"J" source.} Halpern views the Joseph cycle in the Bible as a reinterpretation of the Hyksos period invasion. First, victory, then defeat by a new Egyptian dynasty, perhaps by Ahmose, striking out from Thebes. Then, enslavement. "Israelite tradition associated the descent into Egypt of Joseph and his brothers with the Hyksos period."[36]

Four hundred years for a memory of a tradition! This might strike us as a long span for the holding of ancient ethnic grudges. But remember, Homer wrote in the late ninth century about events that had taken place almost 400 years earlier. The world turneth more slowly in the ancient world, and good stories of great events, natural—as in a great flood, else tragic or glorious in a human way, attracted generation after generation of eager ears and from long distances without.

Rameses II and the Delta pharaohs again figure into the destiny of the Israelites. We will discuss this below.

Mother Nile—Refuge

The movement of Asiatics into Egypt was both fitful and continuous throughout our historical knowledge of the past. The Hebrew Bible is full of references to various personages moving back and forth from Canaan, Israel, Judah, and the northern Syrian and Mesopotamian nations.

Abram is also recorded, in Genesis, as migrating to Egypt, with his wife Sarai, during a famine in Canaan. Wily scoundrel that he was, he sold her off to the Pharaoh, as his sister, and was given protection and wealth in return. The Lord did not like this turn of events. His inflictions on the Pharaoh caused the latter to return Sarai, and rid Egypt of Abram. {Gen. 12:10-20—J-source.} For other Genesis sister-wife incidents, see (now Abraham): {Gen. 20—E-source}; (Isaac): {Gen. 26:6-11—J-source}.

So, too, the seven years of famine that Joseph predicted for the Pharaoh, after the seven years of plenty, allowed Egypt to be prepared for this time of want. But not in Canaan. Thus, Jacob sends his sons to Egypt, without the full sib of Joseph, Benjamin, to purchase grains. There, of course, they are tearfully reunited with the brother who they earlier had sold off into slavery. {Gen. 41:53-57—E-source}; also {Gen. 42:1-6—J and E-source.}

Hadad, King of Edom, also fled to Egypt, from Joab, King David's military commander. He secured safety from the then-Pharaoh, married into the Egyptian royal family, and after David's and Joab's death prepared to return and fight Solomon for control of Edom. {1 Kings 11:14-22.} Edom was founded by Esau, eldest, but despised son of Isaac, dull of mind, outwitted twin brother of Jacob: "Edom—Adam—Esau, red and hairy."

Jeroboam, future first King of the 10 tribes of Israel (Divided Monarchy) deserts his position as head of Solomon's Josephite tribal labor corvee (Hebrew: "missim," what the Hebrews in Egypt suffered under the Pharaoh) when the priest from Shiloh, Ahijah condemns the corruption of Solomon. Pharaoh Shishak takes him in, c.930 BCE. Shishak's predecessor, in an act without precedent, had given Solomon one of his daughters in marriage, and allowed her to live in Jerusalem. At the death of Solomon, Jeroboam will return to lead the northern secession against the son of Solomon, Rehoboam. {1 Kings 11:26-40.}

In the death throes of the monarchy in Judah, in Mizpah just north of now-destroyed Jerusalem, Gedaliah, whom the Babylonian/Chaldeans had placed in charge of a largely devastated Judah, was assassinated. This terrible event caused practically the entire remaining population to flee in fear and panic to Egypt, c.582 BCE, that nation then still independent. Also fleeing was an unwilling Jeremiah, who had been relatively accommodated to Babylonian power, given the moral degeneration of his own people. Jeremiah settled in the northeast Delta town of Tahpanhes. Other Judeans moved down the Nile to Memphis, Migdol (Tel-el-Heir) Pathros. {2 Kings 25:22-26—Deut. 2 writer; Jeremiah 41:17-18; 42; 43; especially 44.}[37]

At the end of the nineteenth century CE, ancient, papyri were discovered that revealed a colony of practicing Jews, if indeed religiously syncretic, at Elephantine, an island in the Nile just north of the first cataract, near today's Aswan. The belief is that these Jews were settled there by the Assyrians after the conquest of Israel (c.720 BCE) as conscripts from Judah and Samaria in the Assyrian employ. The Assyrians then extended their campaign into Egypt. At the time of the Elephantine writings, c.425 BCE, they were now part of a Persian garrison protecting the southern border of an Egypt, now a mere province of Persia.[38]

Joseph is told by an angel to take Mary and Jesus to Egypt to avoid the retribution of King Herod. There they find refuge until Herod dies, and they then return to Israel. {Matthew 2:13-15.}[39]

Egypt Discovers the North-East

The New Kingdom in Egypt developed from 1550-1500 BCE, after the political but not population expulsion of the Hyksos by Ahmose. Egypt now became heavily involved in imperialist designs, making strong forays against the lands from which the Hyksos first entered Egypt, against a Canaanite confederation of independent princes, then moving into Syria to challenge both the Mitanni as well as Hittite empires. The result, after impressive victories by Pharaoh Thutmose III, was a standoff (c.1500-1450 BCE). There is an illustration of his granite portrait and mummy in Breasted, *Ancient Times*. Both of these illustrations reveal Thutmose' Eur-Asian heritage.[40] There were yet limits to Egyptian power. Such a level of expansionary warfare required the pharaohs to employ quantities of non-Egyptian mercenaries—Libyans, Nubians, Sardinians and Sicilians, as well as Asiatics.

So, too, were there massive exchanges of nobility in marriage. For example, C. D. Darlington, the evolutionary botanist, always interested in the genetic destiny of peoples and nations, states that Amenhotep III, 1390-1352 BCE, married the Mitannian, Gilhukhipa, as his fourth wife.[41] She brought with her 317 unmarried ladies (Mitannian and Hurrian), clearly to be subsequently interbred with Egyptian, Theban royalty. His son, Amenhotep IV, who changed his name to Akhenaton, was married to Nefertiti, whom Freud hypothesizes to be a Syrian, but whom Darlington declares to be from the Egyptian-derived priestly governing class of Nubia (Sudan) to the south of Egypt, the second cataract of the Nile. Akhenaton, whom we shall discuss in greater detail (Chapter 5), figures in the mystery of Moses. He was, like his father Amenhotep III, a man of new ideas, stimulated by a cultural and historical awareness of a universe beyond the parochial vision on the Nile.[42]

The New Kingdom's expansionary efforts brought Canaan firmly under the control of Egypt and its bureaucratic organization. Much correspondence and trade took place between the various Egyptian capitals, the vassal kings of the small Canaanite cities as well as treaty nations to the north during the final years of Amenhotep III, the father of Akhenaton (Amenhotep IV) and extending into the first years of the reign of Tutenkhaton, the son-in law of Akhenaton. He was later renamed Tutenkhamon, to fit the now reasserted religious orthodox. Akhenaton's royal progeny were daughters.

It should be remembered that in the heyday of Pharaonic Egypt, the population was in the 4-5 million range. This demographic level held throughout the expansionary period of the Roman Empire. Egypt seems always to have needed more population to exploit her wealth and defend her borders.

The 'Apiru and the Amarna Letters

In 1886-1887, in the capital city that Akhenaton created, Akhetaton (Tel-el-Amarna), a quantity of cuneiform tablets was found These tablets consisted of a series of communications from all parts of the Egyptian empire, up to southern Syria, as well as independent nations to the north, including Alashiya (Cyprus), 350 all told (c.1360-1330 BCE).[43] They were all written in the Akkadian of Syria along with Canaanite "Hurrianisms," with mistakes, as well as colloquial Canaanisms.[44] The vassal kings in Canaan who sent the Amarna letters have mostly Indo-European names.

The Amarna tablets (1360-1330 BCE) are replete with references to marauding 'Apiru (Hebrews?) who are causing havoc by making alliances with various rivals of these vassal monarchs. The requests are for small-scale aid, 50-100 chariots, or corps of archers to put down both rival enemy governors and 'Apiru vagabond raiding groups. (Akkadian: 'Apiru or Habiru is defined as "transients or migrants.").[45] According to W. F. Albright, the term 'Apiru derived from the Egyptian '-p-r, "ship's complement, crew, gang of laborers," this from the 2nd to 6th Dynasty, Old Kingdom, referred to in documents about the trade with Syria.[46] What may have started out as a particular descriptive word, c.2500 BCE, could a thousand years later have turned into a common noun, a colloquial term, just as the word "limey," once referring to English sailors supplied with limes on long journeys to prevent scurvy, now applied to all English people; "Yankee Doodle Dandy," once a New England reference, became "yank," now the descriptive term for all Americans or North Americans.

Gosta Ahlstrom notes its wide-ranging meaning, a social class, refugees, outcasts, fugitives, rebels, slaves, mercenaries, robbers, and raiders. Also, it could include people who were foreigners or immigrants, similar to the Hebrew term *ger*, strangers, or outsiders.[47]

The ruler of Jerusalem during the Amarna period, c.1350 BCE, a "Hurrian" city, was an Indo-European, Abdu-Heba.[48] Ezekiel, in Babylonian exile c.590-580 BCE, says: "Thus says the Lord God to Jerusalem: Your origin and your birth were in the land of the Canaanites: your father was an Amorite, and your mother a Hittite." {Ezekiel 16:3.} In King David's day, c.1000 BCE, Jerusalem was ruled by non-Semitic Jebusites.

Amarna letter from Canaan: " I will say 'Lost are the lands of the king! Do you not hearken to me? All the governors are lost; the king, my lord, does not have a single governor left!' Let the king turn his attention to the archers, and let the king, my lord, send out troops of archers, for the king has no lands left! The 'Apiru plunder all the lands of the king…but if there are no archers here the lands of the king, my lord, will be lost! To the scribe of the king, my lord: Thus "Abdu-Hebda, thy servant. Present eloquent words to the king, my lord.—All the land of the king, my lord, are lost!"[49]

In Genesis we find several referrals to the Israelites in the third person as Hebrews (Habiru). "Then one who had escaped [the abduction of Lot] told Abram the Hebrew living by the oaks [terebinths] of Mamre the Amorite…" {Gen. 14:13—"J" or "E"-source.} Pharaoh's chief cup bearer: "A young Hebrew [Joseph] was there with us, a servant of the captain of the guard." {Genesis 41:12—E-Source.}

Note that the Canaanites' requests for organized corps of archers sufficient to repel the undisciplined raids of the 'Apiru, else chariot warriors who would outclass these vagabond attackers. The first use of chariots in Egyptian military tactics comes into being after the conquest of Egypt by Asiatics (to an important extent Indo-European northerners), the Hyksos, c.1650 BCE. A bit more than one hundred years after the Amarna letters, the Egyptians were still being put to the test by raiding Indo-European sea peoples and their chariots, the latter hoping for succulent pickings from this wealthy but vulnerable treasure trove nation, c.1200 BCE.

In the Amarna letters a plea is also made that regular Egyptian soldiers be sent to protect the Jerusalemites from being looted by mercenary Nubian recruits garrisoned by the Egyptians in the city. Finally there is a suggestive tablet copy sent from the Egyptian royal palace to the local Canaanite vassal, Prince Milkilu (an Indo-European name), of Gezer, (northwest of Jerusalem, in the Shephelah,) to order 40 Asiatic concubines, in exchange for fine and stipulated Egyptian goods totaling 160 deben in value, this calculated as equal to forty shekels of silver per each of "fine unblemished slave girls," destined for the Pharaoh's weaving rooms.[50] Again, we have the characteristic Egyptian tolerance for the constant adding of new blood to its nationality.

As noted above, in the eleventh century, now two hundred and fifty years after the Amarna letters, Jerusalem as well as Gibeah, (El Jib or Tel el-Ful) just to the north of Jerusalem, this latter town the birthplace of King Saul of the tribe of Benjamin, were considered to be "Hurrian" cities. The confluence of the local description of these towns as Hurrian in the Biblical period plus the existence of Indo-European (Amarna letter) ruling classes 250 years earlier, even while writing in Akkadian (not Egyptian), argues the case for the Indo-European Mitanni/Hittite leadership of these people, and therefore a not insignificant Indo-European component in the general Aramaic/Syriac population.

Norman Gottwald sees Abraham and his 318 armed men going out to fight the four kings as an 'Apiru-like campaign. {Gen. 14:13-16.}[51] Thus, it is fair to argue, that the 'Apiru or Habiru, as they appear in the historical record, and even as the writers of the Pentateuch saw their own origins as derived from this wandering social class of Semitic migrants from the north.[52]

The Shasu Nomads

The earliest mention of the Shasu appears in a prisoner-of-war list of Pharaoh Amenhotep II (1453-1419 BCE, connected with his Syrio-Palestine campaigns, cleaning up the remnant Hyksos ruling classes. The largest number of prisoners were Hurrians, next Shasu, then 'Apiru. The list also included Canaanites, Maryannu, the latter, probably remnant Hyksos chariot-riding nobility.[53]

Egyptian texts from c.1355 BCE, the reign of Amenhotep III (from the temple of Amon at Soleb in Nubia), and before the monotheistic revolution of Akhenaton, refer to "the land of the nomads of Yahweh…the land of the nomads of Seir." (Edom-northwest Arabia).[54] At other times these Shasu nomads, often called "plunderers," were subject to extirpation. Seti I, Dynasty 19's second Pharaoh (1294-1280) and father of Rameses II, c.1280 BCE, initiated this struggle because these three distinctive groups, Shasu, 'Apiru, Canaanites, apparently refused to pay tribute to Egypt when using the trade routes to

II. Canaanite gods, one with a "Sea People" feathered crown, c.1800 BCE.

Asia.[55] Seti was mostly involved in defensive action at the Egyptian frontier. He battled the Shasu bedouins in the Sinai, skirmished with 'Apiru (Hebrews?) in Canaan, also defeated a rebellious Canaanite alliance of city-states at Beth-shan. Seti's son and successor, Rameses II, 1279-1213 BCE, one of the great Egyptian leaders, established a new capital in the Delta at Pi-Rameses (the city of Israelite enslavement?), adjacent to the old Hyksos capital, Avaris.

In the minds of the Egyptians there was a distinction to be made between these groups. This struggle might also be the one that is celebrated in the "Song of Deborah" (Judges 4-5), {see Chapter 4), Rameses II (c.1270 BCE), as part of his expansionary efforts in the East, and up against Hittite power, intriguingly refers to "Shasu land, Yahweh," possibly east-central Ammon or Edom.[56]

The iconography of these Delta pharaohs is interesting and important. We have their great stone portraits at Karnak and elsewhere along the Nile. Their mummies were also found, discarded by tomb robbers, early in the twentieth century. Both the mummies of Seti and Rameses II, as well as their stone portraits (Rameses II, at Abu Simbel in Nubia), reveal a typical and recent/historical European visage. For example, the mummy of Rameses II is astonishingly similar to the death mask of Frederick the Great of Prussia.

The plates of the mummies of Seti I and Rameses II, which James Breasted long ago used to illustrate his classic text, *Ancient Times,* reveal an amazing likeness in father and son.[57] Also, in Edition 11 of the *Encyclopedia Britannica,* a number of sculpted portraits of important Egyptian Pharaohs is reproduced—Thutmose III, Seti I, Rameses II (latter two are Indo-European in looks).[58] Interestingly, recent DNA analysis of the mummy of Rameses II indicates that he had red hair. It is highly probable that Delta Dynasty, 19, could have arisen from the remaining Hyksos populations after the reconquest c.1550 BCE, albeit at a remove of c.250 years, when their descendants had become emancipated and integrated Egyptian citizens.

These long-held memories of ethnic origins are reminiscent of the Carthaginian general Hannibal's own awareness of his Greek ancestry (Hannibal was born in Majorca.) His first name is after a Canaanite/Carthaginian god. His last name, Barca, as in Barak—lightning—Hebrew {Judges 4, 5}, was also from the east. Yet in his innovative military tactics against Rome, he attempted to emulate the traditions of his hereditary Hellenic ethnicity.[59]

The northeast delta city of Goshen (Wadi Tumilat), and possibly Kadesh Barnea, the oasis at the southern end of Canaan, where the escaping Israelites from Egypt camped out for 40 years under Moses, were well utilized during this expansive Egyptian dynastic interregnum.

On a later occasion, 1215 BCE, in the reign of Pharaoh Merneptah, (he of Israel stele victory claim—Chapter 4), the Shasu bedouins request admission to Egypt from Edom to water their flocks at Tjeku in the Delta.[60] "We have finished letting the Shasu nomads of Edom pass the fortress…to keep them alive and to keep their cattle alive."[61]

The Shasu are different from the 'Apiru in that they are considered to be less of a brigandage type of people, "pirates of the land," and more generally, wandering herders, partially nomadic. They seem to have then inhabited the Sinai, northern Arabia, and eastern Jordan and Syria. It is possible that there is a relationship here to the tribes of the Judean confederacy (related to David, and even earlier). They figure strongly in the Exodus and impact Moses. Genesis seems to describe the Patriarchs as both Shasu and 'Apiru, but not Canaan urbanites.

Shasu are illustrated in the faience tiles of Pharaoh Rameses III, c.1150 BCE at Medinet Habu, along the Nile, as a distinct people in this monument, along with a Lybian, Syrian, Nubian, Hittite. The delicately-bearded Shasu bedouin wears a feather-like headdress puzzlingly similar to the feathered headdresses of the northern Sea Peoples (Philistines?).[62] Interestingly, David is noted as using for his own personal army Cherethite fighters from the southern desert, the Negeb, who had formerly been allied with the Philistines. {1 Samuel 30:14.} These Cherethites are generally identified as migrants (Sea People) from Crete who had taken to a herding way of life![63] Could it be that these Shasu bedouins illustrated at Medinet Habu were formerly Cretans or Greeks?

Endnotes, Chapter 3

[1] Rosenberg, Joel W. 1993. *The Harper/Collins Study Bible*, New Standard Edition, London: Harper/Collins Publishers, Note, 11:31, p. 20; P. Kyle McCarter, Jr., argues that Haran was the center of a rural Amorite population of Semites (Hammuraubi—Babylonians), who easily could have become the ancestors of the Israelites in their wanderings south: The names of Abram's ancestors, Terah, Nahor, Serug, respectively, his father, grandfather, great-grandfather, were eponymous names after towns near the Balikh River in northern Mesopotamia of Hurrian/Amorite cultural memories. {Genesis 11:22-26—J-source}; "The Patriarchal Age," in Hershel Shanks, ed. 1999. *Ancient Israel,* Washington, D.C.: Biblical Archaeological Society, p. 23.

[2] Smith, Patricia. "People of the Holy Land from Prehistory to the Recent Past," in Levy, Thomas, ed. 1995. *The Archaeology of Society in the Holy Land*, London: Leicester Univ. Press, p. 65.

[3] Bar-Yosef, O. "Earliest Food Producers-Pre Pottery Neolithic (8000-5500)," in Levy, Thomas, ed., *op. cit.,* p. 190.

[4] Smith, Patricia, in Levy, Thomas, ed., *op. cit.,* p. 65.

[5] Diamond, Jared. 1997. *Guns, Germs, and Steel,* N.Y: W. W. Norton, p. 111.

[6] Darlington, C.D. 1969. *The Evolution of Man and Society*, London: George Allen and Unwin, pp. 110-111.

[7] Breasted, James Henry. 1916. *Ancient Times*, Boston: Ginn, Fig. 37, p. 52; Figs. 52, 53, p. 70.

[8] Kramer, S. N. 1963. *The Sumerians,* Chicago: Univ. of Chicago Press, pp. 42-43.

[9] Ibid., pp. 40-41.

[10] Ibid., pp. 42-43.

[11] Ibid., pp. 280-283.

[12] Ibid., p. 268.

[13] Ibid., p. 286.

[14] Ibid., p. 286.

[15] Ibid., p. 275.

[16] Ibid., pp. 291-299.

[17] Translated by E. A. Speiser, in Pritchard, J. B., ed. 1958. *The Ancient Near East*, Princeton, N.J.: Princeton Univ. Press,. pp. 85-86.

[18] Gordis, Robert, "The Bible As a Cultural Monument," in Finkelstein, Louis, ed. 1955. *The Jews, Their History, Culture, and Religion,* 2 vols., N.Y: Harper and Bros., p. 467.

[19] Johnson, Paul. 1987. *A History of the Jews*, N.Y.: Harper and Bros., pp. 8-10.

[20] Kramer, S. N., *The Sumerians, op. cit.,* pp. 298-299.

[21] Rosenberg, Joel W., 1993, in *Harper Collins Study Bible, op. cit.,* Notes, pp. 16-18.

[22] Pitard, Wayne, "Before Israel," in Coogan, Michael D., ed. 1998. *The Oxford History of the Biblical World,* N.Y.: Oxford Univ. Press, pp. 42-44.

[23] Grant, Michael A. 1984. *History of Ancient Israel,* N.Y.: Charles Scribner, pp. 10-11. The Ebla tablets refer to place names: Sinai, Jerusalem, Hazor, Megiddo, Lachish, Acco; Esau, Ismael, David, Saul, Israel. The people called the Mari (Tel el-Harari), in the far north of Mesopotamia, in the 18th century (1700 BCE) under Zimri-Lim, left us 2500 cuneiform tablets containing names such as: Abram-ram, Jacob-el, Levi, Israel. Also listed is an Amorite tribe, Bene-iamina, p. 13.

[24] Smith, Patricia, in Levy, *op. cit.,* p. 69.

[25] Ilan, David, in Levy, *op. cit.,* pp .300-301.

[26] Pritchard, J. B., ed. *The Ancient Near East, op. cit.,* Vol. 1, p. :285; in H. Shanks, ed. *Ancient Israel op. cit.,* Illus., p. 122.

[27] Breasted, J. H., *Ancient Times, op. cit.,* p. 199.

[28] Pritchard , J.B., ed. 1958. *The Ancient Near East* Pritchard, J. B., ed., 3 vols., Princeton, N.J.: Princeton Univ. Press, Vol 1, tr. Matthews and Benjamin, p. 284.

[29] Breasted, J. H., *Ancient Times, op. cit.,* p. 197.

[30] Pritchard, J. B., *The Ancient Near East, op. cit.,* Vol. 1, pp. 87-89, tr. John A. Wilson.

[31] Pitard, Wayne, in Michael D Coogan, ed., *op. cit.,* p. 57.

[32] Poole, R .S. and Griffith, F. L. "Egypt," in *Encyclopedia Britannica,* N.Y.: Cambridge Univ. Press, 11th ed., Vol. 9, p. 83.

[33] Pitard, Wayne, in Coogan, M., ed., *op. cit.,* p. 59.

[34] Bright, J. 1981. *A History of Israel,* 3rd. ed., Philadelphia: Westminster Press, p. 116.

[35] Sarna, Nahm M., "Israel in Egypt," in Shanks, Hershel, *op. cit.*

[36] Ibid., pp. 53-54.

[37] Perdue, Leo. G., 1993, in *Harper/Study Bible, op. cit.,* Notes, p. 1188.

[38] Cogan, Mordechai, "Into Exile," in Coogan, M., ed., *op. cit.,* p. 56.

[39] Redmount, Carol, "Bitter Lives," in Coogan, M., ed., *op. cit.,* p. 100.

[40] Breasted, J. H., *Ancient Times, op cit.,* fig.63, p. 85.

[41] Darlington, C. D. 1969. *The Evolution of Man and Society,* London: George Allen and Unwin, p. 121.

[42] Freud, S. 1939 *Moses and Monotheism,* N.Y.: Knopf, p. 29; Darlington , C. D., *op. cit.,* p. 119.

[43] Pitard, Wayne, in Coogan, M., ed., *op. cit.,* pp. 64-66.

[44] Pritchard, J. B., *The Ancient Near East, op. cit.,* Vol. 1, pp. 262-277.

[45] Rosenberg, Joel ,in *Harper/Collins Study Bible, op. cit.,* Notes, p. 23.

[46] Albright, W. F. 1955. "The Biblical Period," in Finkelstein, ed., *The Jews, Their History, Culture, and Religion, op. cit.,* p. 29.

[47] Ahlstrom, G. W. 1986. *Who Were the Israelites?,* Winona Lake, IN.: Eisenbrauns, p. 13.

[48] Pritchard, J. B., *The Ancient Near East, op. cit.,* Vol 1, p. 269, tr. W. F. Albright and George E. Mendenhall.

[49] Ibid., p. 270.

[50] Ibid., p. 268.

[51] Gottwald, N. K. *The Hebrew Bible, op. cit.,* pp. 72-173.

[52] Grant, Michael, *The History of Ancient Israel, op. cit.*; Anderson, G. W. 1975. *Understanding the Old Testament,* Englewood Cliffs, N.J.: Prentice Hall; Hendel, R. S. 1995. "Finding Historical Memories in the Patriarchal Narratives," *Biblical Archaeological Review* 21/4:52-59; Pritchard, J. B. 1969. *The Ancient Near East in Pictures Relating to the Old Testament, op. cit.,* 3rd. ed.;. Albright, W. F. 1969. *Archaeology and the Religion of Israel,* Garden City, N.Y.: Doubleday; Anderson, G. W. 1966. *The History and Religion of Israel,* N.Y.: Oxford Univ. Press.

[53] cited in Ahlstrom, G. W., *Who Were the Israelites?, op. cit.,* p. 12.

[54] Weinfeld, Moshe, in Seltzer, Robert M., ed. 1989. *Judaism, A People and Its History,* N.Y.: Macmillan, p. 40; Mazar, B., 1977, cited in Moshe Weinfeld, *op. cit.,* p. 40; Gibeon, Raphael,"Les bedouins Shosu des documents egyptiens," Leiden, 1971, Nos. 6a, 16a; Herrmann, S., "Der Name Jhw in den Inschriften von Soleb," *Fourth World Congress of Jewish Studies,* Vol. 1, Jerusalem, 1967, pp. 213-216.

[55] Gottwald, Norman K. 1985. *The Hebrew Bible, A Socio-Literary Introduction,* Philadelphia: Fortress Press, p. 194.

[56] Poole, R. S. and Griffith, F. L. "Egypt," *Encyc. Brit., op. cit.,* 11th ed., Vol. 9, pp. 84-86; Stager, L. E., in Coogan, M., ed., *op. cit.,* p. 145.

[57] Breasted, J. H., *Ancient Times, op. cit.,* Fig. 70-71, pp. 88-89.

[58] *Encyc. Brit., op. cit.,* 11th ed., Vol. 9, Egypt Plate 4, opposite p. 66.

[59] Wormington, B. H. 1960. *Carthage,* London: Hale.

[60] Pritchard, J. B., *The Ancient Near East, op. cit.,* Vol. 1, pp. 183-184.

[61] Papyrus Anastasi VI, quoted from Pritchard, J. B. 1969. *The Ancient Near East in Pictures Relating to the Old Testament,* 3d ed.. Princeton, N.J.: Princeton Univ. Press, p. 259; Moshe Weinfeld, in Seltzer, Robert M., *Judaism, A People and Its History, op. cit.,* p. 42.

[62] Redmount, C. 1998. "Bitter Lives," in Coogan, M., ed., *op. cit.,* pp. 116-118, Illus., p. 118.

[63] Lemaire, Andre, "The United Monarchy," in Shanks, ed., *Ancient Israel, op. cit.,* p. 93.

4

Tribes of Israel

Context

Questions: Did the Israelites fleeing from Egypt with Moses, Aaron, and Joshua, find only Canaanites and their ilk in the lands west of the Jordan River? Did all the Israelites leave Canaan with Jacob/Israel and his sons to join Joseph, their descendants forced to live in bondage in Egypt for four hundred years? {Genesis 15:13}.

Dates/Clues: Saul of Gibeah in Benjamin made King of Israel, c.1025-1005 BCE; David of Bethlehem/Hebron/Jerusalem in Judah made King of Israel, c.1005-965 BCE; Solomon of Jerusalem in Judah made King of Israel, c.965-928 BCE.

Victory stele of the Pharaoh Merneptah, 7.5 ft. tall, made of black granite in Thebes, Egypt, c.1207 BCE: "…Israel is laid waste and his seed is not, Hurru is become a widow because of Egypt."[1] Other conquests carved onto the stele include names such as Ashkelon and Gezer. They are accompanied by written determinatives that indicate citystates. Canaan and Hurru, the latter linked in "marriage" with Israel are characterized as foreign lands. Israel is here described as a foreign people.[2]

Israel=El (God) governs.[3] Israel=El (God) strives.[4]

{Genesis 32:28-29—E-source}: Jacob wrestles with God near the Jabbok River in Ammon (Gilead/Gad). God renames Jacob—Israel. Scholars believe the name Israel might have been brought into Canaan from without.[5]

{Genesis 35:6-10—P-source}: Jacob is told by God in Bethel (House of El/God), in Ephraim, that henceforth, "Israel is thy name." The name Jacob could reflect the movement of an Aramean group from Haran moving into the central highlands of Canaan, the land of Israel, then adopting the place name as their own.[6]

"Jacob-Har," a scarab with this name was found at Shiqmona in Israel, eighteenth century BCE. Later, a Hyksos Pharaoh with this name ruled in Egypt. The tale of Jacob and Joseph and his brothers in Genesis, could derive from this memory. The name Jacob, was common in northern Mesopotamia at this period in history. Later Thutmose II, 1479-1425 BCE, listed a town by the name of Jacob-Har in Central Canaan. The name Jacob was also found in the coastal north Syrian town of Ugarit. (Many Mycenaeans from Greece were then living there.)[7]

Jacob-el=let El protect; Isaac-el=may El smile upon you.

Akhetaton/Tel-El-Amarna, Egypt, c.1360 BCE: Clay tablet letters to the Pharaoh, in Babylonian language, from vassal (Syrian/Phoenician) princes addressing the Pharaoh (Akhenaton?), in homage, as "Ilani," north Semitic version of Canaanite/Israelite, "Elohim" (God).[8] In these tablets there is the repetitive mention of the "robber-like" raids of the 'Apiru/Habiru (Hebrews?) on the Canaanite towns. (See Chapter 3.)

Shasu-land, Yahweh: Egyptian texts, c.1385 BCE, from the reign of Amenhotep III, (temple of Amon at Soleb in Nubia) and before the monotheistic revolution of Akhenaton. Continuing into the fourteenth century BCE, the period of Akhenaton, there are recurring mentions of the Shasu bedouins, who inhabit the Sinai This precedes, by one hundred years, Rameses II, 1270 BCE, (Avaris–Pi-Rameses) where are found intriguing reference to "Shasu land, Yahweh," possible east-central Ammon or Edom.[9] Also, references to "the land of the nomads of Yahweh...the land of the nomads of Seir" (Edomnorthwest Arabia).[10] On a later occasion, c.1215 BCE, under Pharaoh Merneptah, the Shasu request admission to Egypt from Edom to water their flocks at Tjeku in the

Delta.[11] "We have finished letting the Shasu nomads of Edom pass the fortress…to keep them alive and to keep their cattle alive."[12] (See Chapter 3.)

Karnak, Egypt, c.1207 BCE, engraved battle scene, identifies Israelites. Do they appear as Canaanites (Elohim) or Shasu, desert Bedouins (Yahweh)?[13]

Historical Setting

Elohim-Canaan: A break in time of approximately two hundred years occurs between the first mention of Israel in the historical record, by Merneptah, c.1207 BCE, and the crowning of Saul of Gibeah in Benjamin, c.1025 BCE, as King of the Israelite tribes. Certainly they were in existence before the struggle between the Egyptians and the rest of Canaan mentioned in Merneptah's stele. Whether they were the same people ('Apiru/Habiru) that worried the Indo-European vassal states of Canaan 150 years before Merneptah, c.1350 BCE, in the Canaanite appeals to Akhenaton for military aid, we cannot know. In the Old Testament both Abraham and Joseph are referred to in the third person as Hebrews {Genesis 14:13, 39:14—J-source}, {Gen. 41:12—E-source}; also {Gen. 10:21—J-source}, as Eber, son of Shem, (see Ch. 3); also, {Jon 1:9} mid-sixth century BCE. In the book of Samuel, referring to the desperate attempts of King Saul to rally the various Israelite tribes against the conquering Philistines, several referrals are made to the "Hebrews," not Israelites, to join the battle, at the least, to abandon their collaboration with the Philistines. {1 Samuel 13:7, 14:18}.

We should reiterate that, as noted in Chapter 3, the J-source in the Old Testament, originating in Jerusalem, probably during the reign of Solomon, if not soon after, represents a "tribe of Judah" perspective. Here the use of the tetragram YHWH, for the "Lord" is found throughout the Pentateuch. On the other hand, Elohim or El Shaddai are utilized by both the E—source, from the Kingdom of Israel, written not long after J, as well as by "P", the priestly source, either from the late eighth century, or during and after the Babylonian/Chaldean exile. Both the E and P sources begin to refer to the "Lord" as YHWH with the appearance of Moses. This reflects a decisive historical change in the nature of the people of Israel. There is quite a bit of editing by later writers to the Pentateuch, thus many of the attributions to the respective sources are controversial, and inconclusive.

Written Record: In Joshua and Judges we get another dimension of the history of the tribes of Israel, their relationship to the Patriarchs and Moses, as well as the transition, in Samuel 1 and 2, to the historically solidified realities of the United Kingdom. Here, too, the efforts of the so-called Deuteronomist Hisorians, both 1 and 2, (late seventh to late sixth century BCE), have been subject to further emendations. For example, the famous story in {1 Samuel 17:12*ff.*}, of David's slaying of Goliath is largely borrowed and embroidered on from the original, hardly heroic tale in {2 Samuel 21:18-19}. This glorification of David in {1 Samuel 17:12*ff.*}, was added as late or later than the Hasmonean period, c.200 BCE.

By contrast the use of much earlier written material reflecting widespread literacy among the tribes is freely claimed throughout the Old Testament. Recall that in Exodus {17:14—E–source}, the "Lord" tells Moses to write down the details of the victory over Amalek and the Edomite in the Sinai. Gideon, a judge campaigning east of the Jordan River, encounters a "young man, one of the people of Succoth, and questioned him and he listed for him the officials and elders of Succoth, seventy-seven people." {Judges 8:14}.

"The families also of the scribes that lived at Jabez: the Tirathites, the Shimeathites, and the Sucathites. These are the Kenites who came from Hammath, father of the house of Rechab." {1 Chronicles 2:55}. Note that this reference to scribal clans relates to the enigmatic tale, see quote above, of the young boy at Succoth who gives to Gideon a list of the elders of town. {Judges 8:15-16}. It is unclear whether the inhabitants of Succoth, east of the Jordan, were Gileadites or Kenites, possibly the latter blending into the former as Israelites The references to happily literate Kenites places them (see below, re: Rechabites) to the far northeast, in Jabesh-gilead, of their ancient homelands in the south, the Negeb and Sinai.

Such early written documentation is acknowledged, for example: Book of Wars of the Lord, {Numbers 21:14}; Book of Jashar (of the Just), {Joshua 10:13, 2 Samuel, 1:18}; The Song of the Well, {Numbers 21:17,18}; Song of Sihon and Moab, {Numbers 21:27-30}; Song of Lamech, {Genesis 4:23,24}; Song of Moses, {Exodus, 15:1-22}.[14]

The Book of the "Annals of the Kings of Israel" and "Annals of the Kings of Judah" is mentioned over a dozen times by the Deuteronomist Historians, written in the days of the King of Judah, Josiah, c.630 BCE. Also, Chronicles, 5th–4th century BCE uses records of the Prophets, "Nathan, Shemaiah, Iddo" to construct a parallel history of the Israelites. The Chronicler rarely discusses the Kingdom of Israel.[15]

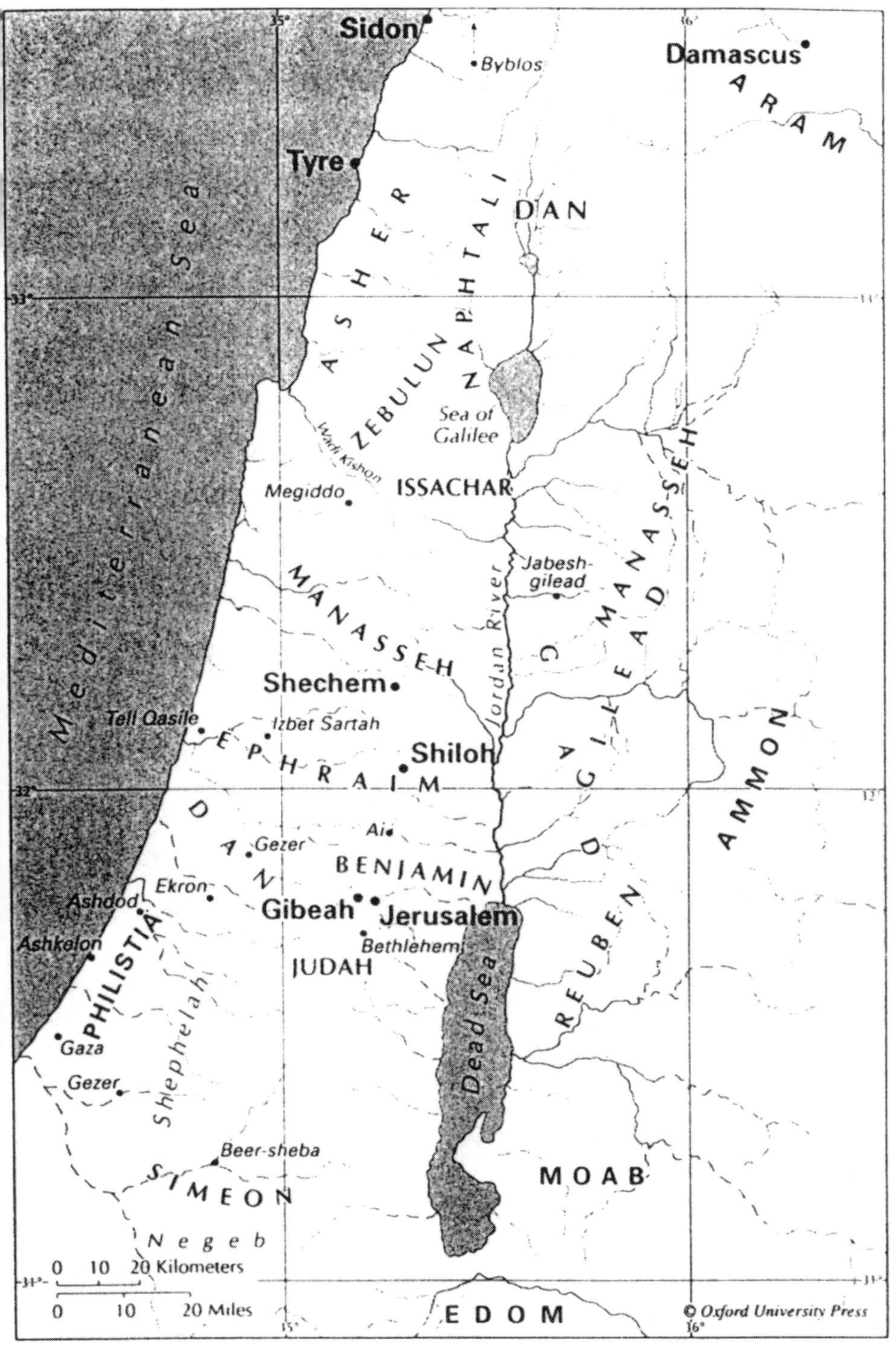

III. Palestine and Transjordan in the early Iron Age, showing the territory assigned
to the twelve tribes of Israel.

A Tough World

It is a probability that the Israelites themselves were relatively late-coming strangers to the land they called Israel. If not urbanites and seafaring traders, like the Greeks, rather, nomadic pastoralists, they found their home in the sweet, wooded uplands of Canaan. Thus Elohim christens Jacob, Israel, when he returns from Paddan-aram for the last time to settle finally in what is now the land of Abraham's God. {Genesis 32:28—J-source; 35:10—P-source}. Earlier in Genesis, Abraham explicitly declares to the Hittite residents of Hebron, (Mamre), {23:4—P-source}. "I am a stranger and alien residing among you" as he seeks the community's agreement to purchase a cave and then a field as a burial place for Sarah.

But, they were, like their neighbors, intensely brutal warriors. Setting our vision deep into the primeval origins of modern human nature in the north, we wonder whether the Cro-Magnons were so intense in war and killing? We have no evidence for widespread murder, genocide, even against their intellectually weaker neighbors, the Neanderthals. That does not mean that they were different from their descendants in the south.

The Judge, Gideon ("Hacker") or Jeruabbaal ("Let Baal Contend"), son of Joash, (at Ophrah in Manasseh, near Shechem) was very prolific. He had seventy sons with many wives. One was a concubine from Shechem. Her son was named Abimelech. The latter persuaded the elders of Shechem to sanction his plan to be head of the town: "He went to his father's house at Ophrah and killed his brothers, seventy men, on one stone..." {Judges 9:5}.

To avert a famine, King David, c.970 BCE took seven innocent grandsons of King Saul, handed them off to the Gibeonites (Amorites/Hivites/Hittites?) in blood-guilt retribution for an undocumented slaughter by Saul against the Gibeonites, ancient residents of the territory of Benjamin: David, "...gave them into the hands of the Gibeonites and they impaled them on .the mountain before the 'LORD.' The seven of them perished together." {2 Samuel 21:9}. By contrast note these verses from what is considered an authentic poem by David, a lament over the death of Saul and Jonathan at the hands of the Philistines: "Oh daughters of Israel, weep over Saul, who clothed you with crimson, in luxury, who put ornaments of gold on your apparel....How the mighty have fallen, and the weapons of war perished." {2 Samuel 1:24, 27}.[16]

Recall the earlier reference to the Judge, Gideon, an ancient campaigner east of the Jordan River. Gideon encountered a "young man of Succoth and questioned him and he

listed for him the officials and elders of Succoth, [Gileadites?] seventy-seven people."
{Judges 8:14}. And because they would not give him additional loaves of bread in his
campaign against the Midianites, Gideon: "...took the elders of the city [seventy-seven]
and he took thorns of the wilderness and briers and with them he trampled the people of
Succoth." {Judges 8:16}.

King Jehu of the Northern Kingdom, Israel, c.841 BCE, gained the throne with the
assistance of the prophet Elisha. Elisha and the northern Yahwists were appalled at the
Baal worship fostered by the previous monarch, Ahab's Phoenician wife, Jezebel. Jehu
wrote to the guardians of the seventy sons of Ahab, after gaining power. "When the letter reached them, they took the King's sons and killed them, seventy persons; they put
their heads in baskets and sent them to him...[Jehu]." {2 Kings 10:7-8}.

Note in the various Old Testament writings, the number seven is a magical number.

The LORD: "When my angel goes in front of you, and brings you to the Amorites,
the Hittites, the Perizzites, the Canaanites, the Hivites, and the Jebusites, and I blot them
out,..." {Exodus 23:23—E-source}; "...and when the LORD your God gives them over
to you and you defeat them, then you must utterly destroy them...show them no mercy."
{Deuteronomy 7:2}.

Sadly, the wars and the killings were and are an integral part of man's search for
meaning in this as yet strange land. Canaan was merely an exemplification of our conjoint alienship in the world. Humans needed to know and understand their place in the
scheme of things. Gods were needed to explain power, weakness, identity, strangeness,
individuality.

The Gods of Israel

From Ugarit, along the coast of northern Syria, south, the great god was El (Elu),
who ruled over 30 lesser gods, including Baal. El was the mighty one, "the lord," creator
of created things, majestic father, king of gods and men. El was also the Bull, mighty in
strength —supreme judge, of justice, charity, hospitality, decency. Monarchs of the
various peoples inhabiting this geography attained their power as representatives, surro-
gates of this divine will. In Hebron—at the terebinth of Mamre, the Amorite, Abraham,
worshipped God as El Shaddai (God on high or almighty). {Gen.17:3—P-source}. The
sacred place of Bethel translates as House of God; Kadesh Barnea, in the Negev, as El
Roi, (El sees me). The god Baal was the son of El (Mightiest Hero, Prince).[17]

For each tribe and its king there was an ethnic god: Milcom (Ammonites), Ashtoreh (Sidonians), Chemosh (Moab), Dagon (Philistines). Solomon's apostasy as his power waxed lay in his desertion of the exclusivity of YHWH to dabble in the corruptions offered by the other gods. {1 King 11:4-7}.[18] El in E-source stories of patriarchs always denotes the location of a god, of the father—related to a wandering family. Jerusalem's god El-'Elyon (the most high), {Gen. 14:18*f*—J-source}; Beersheba—El-Beit, and El Olam (the eternal one) {Gen. 31:13—E-source}; Shechem, El-elohei Yisra'el. {Gen. 33:20—E-source}.[19]

But always in these traditions an attempt is made to explain the world around the people, the path that each person has here on Earth, as well as his/her destiny after life. The human mind finds it difficult to encompass the end of one's own conscious awareness and experience. Life and death must be explained and made significant, sanctified in ritual and myth. Here the priest rises to a position of potential power that mere military success cannot match in the respective claims for the loyalty of the average human. Thus we have in the experiences of the early Hebrews, the Tabernacle and Ark ritually similar to the *mahmal* and the '*otfe*, tent-like structures born aloft in religious processions by ancient and recent Arab tribes. [20] The system of ritual sacrifices in Leviticus {P-source}, along with their explanatory and technical terminology, are also known from contemporary Syrian and Punic documents.

"The festivals and rituals of the Israelites, many of which derived from the customs and celebrations of ancient Near Eastern peoples, especially those of Hittite-Hurrian (Indo-European) origin, underwent a transformation when adapted to the religion of the Israelites."[21] The Canaanite environment contrasted both with the YHWH traditions in the South and East, and Sinai, as well as the Exodus tradition that Moses brought out of Egypt.

The religions of Canaan were characterized by the cyclical nature of the cults, the transitions in nature regarding productivity, the fields, orchards, rivers, flocks. Yahwist religious interpretations do not emphasize nature. More in tune with the harsh realities of nomadic life in the south and eastern borderlands, they are focused on an historical, fiery God leading toward an ordained end.[22] Canaanite myths, festivals, rituals, became annual life-giving dramas; goddesses of fertility and war: Asherah, tree goddess—the tree could be symbolized by a wooden pole or pillar. She was a consort of the male gods. So, too, the god Anath, was an upholder of law and justice, here seen as life-giving forces.

As was then common in Mid-Eastern civic and religious cultism, ritual performance of the sexual act was practiced, symbolizing the society's unification with supernatural powers that embodied the mystery of sex and procreation. This created the "profession" of the Qedeshoth, the female prostitute; Qedeshim, male prostitute. These guilds were state-appointed and sanctified to carry out cult worship of fertility.

In time, 1200-1000 BCE, the Israelites in Canaan learned new technologies, such as the building of stone cisterns on the sides of the hills to catch the water, to be utilized for agricultural production, thus reducing their nomadic dependence on animal husbandry.[23] The Israelites increasingly took over productive lands and made them holy by stone monuments to Baal. El (Ilu) meant lord, owner, husband in Canaanite. Thus Baal could be used for any god and Yahweh became Israel's local Baal, together with the panoply of sensuous Kedeshim and Kedeshoth, Asherah, sacred poles or monuments. {Amos 2:7; Hos 4:13,14; Jer. 2:20-23, 3:6-11; 5:7,8}. The development of a religious syncretism in Hebrew practice continued long into the Monarchy, especially in the reign of Manasseh of Judah, c.650 BCE. King Saul, c.1030 BCE named three of his identified sons after the Canaanite gods. (Ishbaal, Malchishua, Abinadab). {1 Samuel 14:49}. Only Jonathan, the devoted friend of David had a Yahwist name.[24]

Ritual Memories

Under Josiah, c.630 BCE, the Kedeshim and Kedeshoth and the poles of Asherah were banished from the sanctuary of YHWH as it was centralized in Jerusalem. {2 Kings 21:7, 28:7}. Earlier, in the "high places" of Shiloh, Shechem, Bethel, Jerusalem, each had a Yahweh of its own.[25] Ashtoreth, goddess who made cattle and flocks prolific, much revered by the Israelites, was passionately fought by the prophet Hosea, c.730 BCE, in the north. {Hos 2:10}.[26] An eighth-century BCE graffiti drawing on a storage jar at Kuntillet-Ajrud in the Sinai gives a blessing "by Yahweh of Samaria and his asherah." They seem to be dancing to a female accompanist on the lyre.

The upright stone—massebah (Washington monument, Egyptian obelisk), symbol of deity on which blood is smeared, in which the *numen* of the god resided, was part of a deeply embedded ritual in the religious practices of Canaanites and the Shasu nomadic peoples. { Exodus. 24:4-8—J/E-source}. A mound of earth would be raised before the community for a burnt offering. {Exodus 20:24—J/E-source}. This was practiced in "primitive times" as with the Mari, of northern Mesopotamia in the eighteenth century BCE. Later, at Jerusalem or Samaria, an altar of stone or bronze would be erected.

The Asherah could have evolved from holy or revered places, the oak of Morah, near Shechem, and where the Lord commanded the building of an altar, or the oaks of Mamre, near Hebron where Abraham sought shelter and respite, close to where Sarah would be buried {Genesis 12:6—J-Source; 18:1—J-source}; {Gen. 23:17-20—P-source}. A terebinth became a sacred tree, as with "a terebinth of soothsayers" {Judges. 9:37}; the palm tree of Deborah in Ephraim {Judges 4:5}; a tamarisk (eshel) or pomegranate (rimmon) at Migron {Judges 14:2}; the oak of Taborand and the Gibeath-elohim of Saul {1 Samuel 10:3,5}; Gilead's sacred spring at 'Enharod (Mt. Gilboah). {Judges. 7:1}.

How similar these images are to the tradition in northwest Greece of the witch or priestess of Dodona, who resided beneath an ancient oak and showed the wanderers from the north the way south into the heartland.

The *qosem*—soothsayer; *roeh*—seer; *ba-al-obh*—necromancer, possessed by the spirit, were figures all part of the importation of Canaanite religious practices into Israel-Judah. "Before time in Israel, when a Man went to inquire of God, thus he spake, Come and let us go to the seer: for he that is now called a Prophet was beforetime called a Seer"—describing Samuel to Saul. {1 Samuel 9:9-10; 10:5-8}.[27]

Perhaps the most powerful and binding of the Canaanite traditions adopted or originally part of the Israelite Canaanite/Habiru heritage was that of worship in high places. In times of both joy and stress, local families and clans, the *'bet 'ab* and *'bet 'abot*; the villages (*mishpahah*) and their tribes would gather.[28] Geniality and social togetherness in an exhilarating environment on high eventually transformed these sites into holy places. Sacrifices were times of social communion between deity and worshippers. {1 Samuel 9:19-24}.[29]

Samuel invites Saul into his *lishkah*, banqueting chamber, where thirty persons partake of the sacrificial meal—the *'asiph*—festival of ingathering. Such festive opportunities formed the veins and arteries of ancient Hebrew clan and tribal life. And they were powerfully reflected in the debates over the ongoing nature of the people and nations of Israel. {Judges 21:21; 9:27. Amos 1:8*ff.;* Hosea. 9:1*ff;* Jeremiah 31:4; Isaiah 16:10. Jeremiah 48:33. 1 Samuel 9:9}.

Pesah, originally a nomadic holiday, became agricultural in the massoth (unleavened cakes—mazos) celebrated in the Canaanite month of Abib, Shabuhoth (weeks) and Kasir (harvest), held 7 weeks after massoth.[30] In the Canaanite Asiph—ingathering—offerings were made of meal, oil and cakes—massoth, ashishah, kawwan—all part of the

Ashtoreth cult: {Jeremiah 7:18; 44:19; 1 Sam. 21:6}, also for the nomadic water offerings: {1 Sam. 7:6; 2 Sam. 23:16.}. After the c.620 BCE centralization of worship in Jerusalem, the reforms under Josiah, Judahites called this holiday Asiph, *Succoth* (booths, tabernacles). {Leviticus 23:39-43; Zech 14:16-19.}

The Canaanite impress of orgiastic life in these festivals, drunkenness, sexual abandonment, was tangible. {Judges. 9:27; 1 Samuel 14-16; Isaiah 28:7-8.} The primeval Nazarite and Rechabite protest seems to have anticipated, historically, the impact of the Mosaic legislation: {Amos 2:11*ff*.; Judges 13:7,14; 2 Kings 10:15-16; 1 Chronicle 2:55; Numbers 6:1-21}. Not merely did the towns of Shiloh, Shechem, Bethel become important foci for building of holy places, but also Gilgal, Mizpah, and Ramah were added holy places, the circuit of Samuel, a Nazarite himself. He built an altar in the latter locality. {1 Samuel 7:15-17}.

It could be argued that the pathway from the barbarism of the Bronze and early Iron Ages, c.1000 BCE, until the threshold of Hellenic Civilization, can be marked by an ever-intensive obeisance, in ignorance, to the power of nature and its gods, to control the changing and dangerous events and meanings of human existence. It was the barbaric societal behavior of the community under disparate religious impulses, its surrender to the sense of weakness in humans that motivated the work of the Prophets in later Israelite monarchical history, the time of the Exile and then, return to Jerusalem. The rituals of sacrifice tied to the cult of the altar and the temple became central to this transition.

Animal sacrifice was a universal and integral part of the coming into and absorption in Canaan, of the tribes of Israel. Zebah, blood sacrifices, also burnt offerings, kalil, olah, reveal themselves as part of an historical tradition. But behind the sometimes highly specific minutiae of the sacrificial system is an older and more sinister dimension of this human sense of weakness and despair. Life is cheap and with this the concomitant willingness to overstep the brink in order to assuage those all-encompassing powers of life and/or destruction.

Moses quotes the LORD: "Every first born in the land of Egypt shall die, from the first born of Pharaoh who sits on the throne to the first born of the female slave who is behind the handmill, and all the first born of the livestock." {Exodus 11:5—J-source}. "When Pharaoh stubbornly refused to let us go, the LORD killed all the firstborn in the land of Egypt, from human first born to the firstborn of animals. Therefore I sacrifice to the LORD every male that first opens the womb, but every firstborn of my sons I redeem." {Exodus 13:15-E-source}. "All that first opens the womb is mine, all your male livestock, the first born of cow and sheep. The first born of a donkey you shall redeem with a lamb, or if you will not redeem it you shall break its neck. All the firstborn of your sons you shall redeem." {Exodus 34:19—J-source}. "The LORD said to Moses: Consecrate to me all the firstborn; whatever is the first to open the womb among the Israelites, of human beings and animals, is mine." {Exodus 13:1-2—E-source}.

The story by the J source in Genesis, of Cain and Abel, Eve's two sons, is an exemplar. Cain was a tiller of the soil, Abel, the younger, a shepherd. "When they went to sacrifice to Yahweh, Abel brought young lambs, while Cain offered the first products of the fields. Yahweh accepted Abel's gifts but rejected Cain's. Thereupon Cain persuaded his brother to come into the fields—where he put him to death. Yahweh cursed Cain and declared that his land would no longer bear fruit, and that he himself must henceforth wander over the face of the earth, but when Cain protested that anyone whom he encountered would kill him, Yahweh set a protective mark upon him so that this would not happen." {Genesis 4—J-source}.

Thus is recorded the ancient belief recorded in Genesis and Exodus that a man's first fruit or scapegoat was to be given back to the gods. Herewith can be understood in memory of this ancient tradition the rejection of first sons, Cain, Ishmael, Esau, the latter rejected by his mother and sent away from his tribe.[31]Later in the ancient pre-J "Blessing of Jacob," as he approaches death: "Reuben, you are my firstborn, my might and the first fruits of my vigor, excelling in rank and excelling in power. Unstable as water, you shall no longer excel because you went up into your father's bed; then you defiled it—you went up on my couch." {Genesis 49:3-4—J, plus earlier-source}. Reuben had committed sexual intercourse with Jacob's concubine, Bilhah, the mother of his half brothers, Dan and Naphtali. {Genesis 35:22—J-source}.

After the birth of Isaac to Sarah, Abraham expels his Egyptian concubine Hagar and their child Ishmael, his first born. {Genesis 21:8-21—E source}. So, too, "E" shows God (Elohim), commanding Abraham to sacrifice Isaac in the land of Moriah (Jerusalem—Mt. Zion—Temple Mount)[32] : "… offer him there as a burnt offering on one of the mountains that I will show you." {Genesis 22:1-3—E-source}.

Suddenly, the Angel of YHWH intercedes. {Genesis 22:11-12—Redactor}. In the original tribal tale, the sacrifice was probably actually carried out,. now replaced, in the Hebrew Bible by Yahweh's guidance, with animal sacrifices. "So Abraham, returned to his young men, {shepherds} and they arose and went together to Beersheba; and Abraham lived at Beersheba." Seemingly alone, he leaves Mt. Moriah, no mention of Isaac here by E. {Genesis 22:19—E source}.

The Pentateuch is not alone in expressing a tangible memory of this ancient tradition. In Judges, Jephthah, the judge from Gilead vows to the LORD that if he is victorious over the Ammonites, "…whoever comes out of the doors of my house to meet me when I return victorious from the Ammonites, shall be the LORD's to be offered up by me as a burnt offering." Home, victorious, his only child, a daughter, came out to greet him at home in Mizpah, with timbrels and with dancing. Devastated, Jephthah grants her two months of life with her companions on the mountains to bewail her virginity. And the vow was fulfilled. "She had never slept with a man. So there arose an Israelite custom that for four days every year the daughters of Israel would go out and lament the daughter of Jephthah the Gileadite. {Judges 11:29-40}.[33]

In the days of the divided monarchy, Israel was larger and richer, more deeply involved with the tribal nations of the east and north, and, of course, the powerful states of the two rivers, Euphrates and Tigris. About the year 852 BCE, Israel led a united army of Edom, Judah and Israel across the Jordan to the east against the Moabite king, Mesha. This king was hard-pressed. In desperation, after a final counter-attack against the united forces failed: "Then he took his first born son who was to succeed him, and offered him as a burnt offering on the wall. And great wrath [Kemosh/Shemesh] came upon Israel, so they withdrew from him and returned to their own land." {2 Kings 3:27}. Scholars believe the word "Kemosh" (Shemesh) was removed from the original version of {2 Kings 3:27} after "great wrath," {"great indignation" in King James Version}. The implication is that the god Kemosh/Shemesh brought down upon Israel, Judah, Edom, the invaders, a pestilence.[34] The appeasing of divine power in national emergency or in the foundation of a temple or city usually involved the sacrifice of a child, usually, the first-born male.[35]

Tribal Confederation
Documents and Sources

There are only several documents which modern scholarship regards as comprising ancient memories of the earliest tribal confederation. And these are to an extent metaphorical expressions of even more remote associations. Perhaps the earliest is found in {Judges 5}, with a later Deuteronomist commentary in {Judges 4}. It may be that the later prose section was written first and the early "Song (or Victory Hymn) of Deborah,"

IV. Ancient Israel and Environs.

{Judges 5} was added to fill out the commentary. In {Genesis 49—early, used by J-source}, Jacob's farewell, we have a preachment to his twelve sons, with their tribal characterizations which seems also to go back to a period well before the Monarchy.[36] {Deuteronomy 33}: Moses' blessing to his people, edited into Deuteronomy by the Deuteronomist Historian, c.625 BCE, seems to go back 400 years to the Saulide period, c.1050 BCE.[37]

Other descriptions of the tribes of Israel in Joshua, Judges, and elsewhere by the Deuteronomist Historians and their subsequent editors, are compilations made hundreds of years later, but certainly based on writings closer to the time of events, as noted above. "Chronicles," which is an historical summary derived from Deuteronomist research, but also earlier and complementary writings, dates from the time of the Second Temple, in Jerusalem, fifth to fourth century BCE, and thus not too long before the Alexandrian conquest of the Persian Empire, which led to a reestablished Judea.[38]

Robert G. Boling has evaluated Judges, written by the Deuteronomic Historians, Deuteronomy 1 in the reign of King Josiah of Judah, c.620 BCE, and Deuteronomy 2, in exile, c.550 BCE. He views the historical writing as reflecting the pre-Mosaic tribal traditions of Israel under the god, El. The same considerations apply to the ancient poetic rendering of the tribal lists, the "Blessing of Jacob" in {Genesis 49:1-27—J- from earlier sources}.[39] The tenor of the {Book of Judges}, as compared to the {Book of Joshua}, which gives a more triumphal vision of the entrance from Sinai and then the dominating suzerainty of the Israelites over Canaan, is a more equivocal vision of the pre-Monarchic tradition, perhaps to emphasize the need for strong centralized Monarchy, in the rule of Josiah of Judah, 620 BCE. Yet it maintains a balanced historical remembrance through lore and tale, of a time of struggle for Israel.[40] Where and when does this place the Exodus and Moses?

Deep Layers

Wm. F. Albright states: "The book of Joshua does not preserve any tradition regarding the conquest of the land Ephraim and Manasseh, separating Judah from Issachar and Zebulon.. Shiloh, the seat of the tabernacle, before Samuel, Shechem, traditional meeting place of the first Israelite assembly after the conquest, and Timnah, to which Joshua himself retired, are all located in this region." Albright believes that these areas were already occupied by Hebrew clans, which would have made bloody conquest unnecessary. Old Canaanite towns such as Shechem, Hephar, Tirzah were apparently absorbed into Israelite clans easily, so, too, the few fortified towns outside of Shechem, in Ephraim, southern Manasseh between Beth-el and Dothan.[41]

The Jacob tradition is perhaps the core of the historical memory of the people. While Israel later spreads south into Judah and the Negeb, Jacob's life is centered at Shechem and Beth-el.[42] The earliest names in the J-source, in Genesis, Exodus, are "El" names, Israel, Bethuel, Ishmael, hinting at a recognition by the Judeans of different traditions of the northern tribes.[43] It is also possible that the renaming of Jacob, in Bethel, to Israel by YHWH, is a reflection of Jacob's coming down from the north, Trans-Jordan or Paddan-aram (Haran) in Mesopotamia, as an 'Apiru or Hebrew into the lands around Bethel/Shechem, then and now called Israel.

The "Song of Deborah"

This is probably the most ancient Israelite document, written in high archaic Hebrew, twelfth century or possibly earlier. It appears to memorialize an attempt by a group of tribal allies of the Israelites led by the prophetess Deborah ("bee") of Ephraim, along with her chosen but hesitant general Barak ("lightning"), from Naphtali. The alliance probably consisted of Midianites, Edomites, Amalekites, Kenites, as well as Israelite tribes attempting to break a Canaanite blockade led by King Jabin. The hint of who they were, of their 'Apiru/Habiru-like looting: "…the peasantry prospered in Israel, they grew fat on plunder." {Judges, 5:7}. It is possible that such attempts by these 'Apiru tribes are reflected in the documents from the Pharaoh, Seti I, 1294-1279 BCE), sponsoring the Canaanite campaign.[44] Wm. F. Albright hypothesized the enemy to be a later Canaanite and Sea People alliance, c.1125 or—1150-1075, an event 150 years more recent than the archaic qualities of the poem, this later date, on historical and archaeological grounds.[45] See also {Judges:4}, the later version.[46]

Elsewhere in Judges, the 'Apiru/Habiru tradition is seen in the attempt by the lords of Shechem to undermine Abimelech, who had attempted to make himself king. Abimelech was the fratricidal killer of his 70 brothers, and for the moment 'ruler' of Shechem: "…the lords of Shechem set ambushes in the mountain tops. They robbed all who passed by them along that way…" {Judges 9:25}.

Jephthah, son of Gilead by a prostitute, and disowned by his brothers, flees from his inheritance: "Outlaws collected around Jephthah and went raiding with him." {Judges 11:3}. He will thence become a hero and Judge of Israel, only, as noted above, to be forced to sacrifice his daughter to the LORD.

Deborah and Barak sing: "YHWH, when you marched out from Seir, when you marched from the region of Edom, the earth trembled, and the heavens poured, the clouds indeed poured water, the mountains quaked before YHWH, the One of Sinai, before YHWH, the God of Israel." {Judges 5:4-5; also see Deuteronomy 33:1-2}. Ten Israelite tribes are mentioned of which only six join the fight. For some of the 're-fuseniks,' this was their home turf, the southern Galilee, near Mt. Tabor, and also against traditional enemies. Fighting are Issachar, led by their namesake prince, Ephraim (hill-country people), Machir (grandson of Joseph from Manasseh, perhaps meaning Moses— Mosheh, Machir, Manasseh). {Gen. 50:23—E-source}.[47] Benjamin (children of the south), Zebulon {Judges 5:14}, "those who bear the marshall's staff" or "they that handle the pen of the writer"—scribes (King James translation); also, Naphtali (hill-country people). The "refuseniks," Reuben, Dan, Gilead (Gad?), Asher, and Meroz, the latter specifically cursed. Most of the reasons for refusing, as expressed by Deborah, reveal something about their tribal character. In all, ten tribes are mentioned, as allied with other "kindred of Yahweh." But what about Judah, Levi, Joseph, Simeon, (Gad)?

The prophetess Deborah of Ephraim thus attempts to muster the tribes and her general Barak to lead the people to a victory, especially noting the heroism of Zebulon and Naphtali, over the Canaanites, these latter led by the warrior captain, Sisera (an Indo-European name). This battle takes place in the north of Canaan "at Tannach, by the waters of Megiddo," and in the Wadi Kishon. The victory, despite the Canaanites' 900 chariots of iron, which were a specialty of Indo-European/Canaanite/Philistine (the latter are here unmentioned) war tactics. {Judges 4}.

Victory, in {Judges 5}, is assisted by a sudden flash flood in the Kishon, and the abandonment of the chariots by the Canaanites. {Judges 4:15-16; Judges 5:22}: "Then were the horse hoofs broken by the means of the prancings, the prancings of their mighty ones." The Canaanite defeat is culminated as predicted by Deborah, by a woman, Jael, a Kenite clan member (Midianite), wife of Heber, he of "the children of Hobab, the father in law of Moses," (Ruel-Jethro). {Judges 4:11}. Heber had been severed from the Kenites and was now in treaty with the Canaanites. {Judges 4:11-12}. In {Judges 5} no mention is made of a Heber or Hobab. However, Shamgar, son of Anath, a Hurrian (Indo-European name), who is separately listed as a judge, {Judges 3:31} is linked to "the days of Jael." {Judges 5:6}. Jael treacherously agrees to hide and thus succor the now-fleeing Canaanite captain Sisera, in her tent. She soothes him with goat's milk and butter and a blanket. When Sisera is asleep, Jael, hammers a metal tent stake through his skull.[48] The saga ends with Sisera's mother plaintively and hopefully awaiting his return with the booty of "a damsel or two, a prey of diverse colors of needlework…Her wise ladies answered her, yea,…she returned answer to herself, Have they not sped?…." {Judges 5:29-30}.

The tale concludes with a prose epitaph: "So let all thine enemies perish, O LORD but *let* them that love him *be* as the sun when he goeth forth in his might. And the land have rest for forty years." {Judges 5:31}.

Note in this last epitaph, an edited gloss to the more ancient chronicle of Deborah, the reference to the sun as might of the Lord.

Tribal Questions: How Many?

What creates questions is that the total of tribes of Israel (12) usually mentioned in the Old Testament, when added to those here described in the Deborah muster, total 17: Ephraim, Manasseh, Machir, Zebulon, Gad, Gilead, Dan, Benjamin, Levi, Judah, Simeon, Asher, Naphtali, Reuben, Meroz, Issachar, Joseph.

Much later in the history of Israel, the fourth century BCE, and after the ten northern tribes of the nation Israel, now excepting the two, Judah and Simeon, had been deported to Assyria and had vanished (the lost tribes), the Chronicler alters the list, somewhat. {1 Chronicles 2-9}: For the sons of Israel, (Jacob), he includes twelve tribes—Judah, Joseph, Benjamin, Issachar, Levi, Ephraim, Naphtali, Asher, Gad, Reuben, and Simeon. Here excluded, Manasseh, is later in the text included {1 Chronicles 5:23-26; 7:14-19} but hesitantly. The Chronicler states that Manasseh had an Aramean concubine—she bore Manasseh, Machir, father of Gilead. Because of the evil ways of these Israelites, the Assyrians bore away to exile Manasseh, Gad, and Reuben. We now have three more, or fifteen tribes, if we include Machir and Gilead.

The very composition of the various confederations of Israelite tribes that appear in Judges and elsewhere leads one to the view that there was a critical event that united them in both religious as well as military unity This unity was imposed despite disparate tribal traditions. Clearly the omission in the tale of Deborah of Judah, Levi, Simeon, Joseph, Manasseh, and Gad arouses wonder as to whether the first three, Judah, Levi, Simeon existed as social units (mishpahah) at that time, perhaps because of Philistine or other tribal domination. The important role of the Levites, as assigned by Moses in the Exodus, could hint that they were not on the scene as yet.

Tribal Stories

*Ephraim, Naphtali, and Judah (see discussion below): are named as hill-country areas of refuge. {Joshua 20:7}. The prominent role that Ephraim has, as a "blessed" grandson of Jacob/Israel, is probably due to the centrality of this area for the origins of the Israelite confederation. "And he blessed them that day, saying, In thee shall Israel bless, saying God make thee as Ephraim and Mannaseh: and he set Ephraim before Manasseh." {Genesis 48:20—E-source}.

*Bene.yamin=children of the south: "Benjamin is ravenous wolf, in the morning devouring the prey, and at evening dividing the spoil." {Genesis 49:27-J plus earlier source}.The Benjaminites are characterized as left-handers in their battle against the united confederation, after their horrendous gang rape of the concubine of a traveling Ephraimite. {Judges 20:16}. The name Benjamin thus refers to the most southern of the original northern Israelite confederation. In later history, after Saul, Benjamin throws in its fate with Judah. Judah, south of Benjamin and in the ancient days of Deborah, was probably too small a clan to be named.

*Asher: coastal region early named by Egyptians as being located north of the Carmel range, this during the late Bronze Age, 1300-1200 BCE: "A chief of Asher."[49] "Asher sat still at the coast of the sea, settling down by his landings."[50] Asher, was he a male version of the goddess Ashtoreth, signifying a sea-going tribal group converting from the Canaanite cult of Baal to an alliance with the followers of Yahweh? These expanded eastward toward Megiddo, eventually being associated with the Benjaminites. As with Dan, Gad, Naphtali, Asher was the offspring of the handmaidens of Leah and Rachel, not the wives, but the legal concubines of Jacob.[51]

*Manasseh: Regarding the omission of Manasseh from the Song of Deborah, there has been much debate as to whether Machir is a first-stage derivative name from Moses—Mosheh, Machir, Manasseh. The reason that the later and important role of Manasseh in the Old Testament is not yet evident here may derive from the fact that the name had not as yet migrated from its original identification with Moses. The Deuteronomist simply did not know how to handle the "hot" Moses issue *vis à vis* the then-dominant Aaronite priesthood, c.630 BCE.

*Machir: was the grandson of Joseph. {Genesis 50:23—E-source; Numbers 32:39-42—J or P-sources}.[52:] "The descendants of Machir son of Manasseh went to Gilead, captured it and dispossessed the Amorites who were there; so Moses gave Gilead to Machir, son of Manasseh, and he settled there. Jair, son of Manasseh went and captured their villages and renamed them Havvoth-jair." {1 Chronicles 2:21 (Jerusalem c.375 BCE)}. "Afterward Hezron went into the daughter of Machir father of Gilead, whom he married when he was sixty years old…" {1 Chronicles 2:21}. "Then allotment was made to the tribe of Manasseh, for he was the firstborn of Joseph. To Machir the first born of Manasseh, the father of Gilead, were allotted Gilead and Basham, because he was a warrior." {Joshua 17:1}. See also {Numbers 28:26-34; 1 Chronicles 7:14-19}. Clearly the grandson of Joseph, Machir, could not have, 430 years later, sired Gilead as warrior and been part of the post-Mosaic division of the Canaanite lands.

*Gilead—Gad: Gilead and Gad seem to be interchangeable names for the same tribal entity in the same geographic area.[53] Gad, in Hebrew, means "raiders," (Habiru), but there is also a Canaanite deity of fortune by that name.[54] "So he {Jacob} fled with all that he had; starting out he crossed the Euphrates, and set his face toward the hill country of Gilead." {Genesis 31:21—E-source}. "Gilead stayed beyond the Jordan." {Judges 5:17—Song of Deborah}.

*Dan: Most tantalizing mystery. In the ancient tale of the Judge, Deborah, {Judges 4-5} the tribe of Dan is berated for not coming to the aid of other Israelite tribes, under the captain, Barak, then at war with the Canaanites, under the command of an Indo-European, Sisera: "Dan, why did he abide with the ships." {Judges 5:17}.

Historical hints: The Danites could be associated with the Danaans of Homer, else, the Danaoi, who populated the Argolid (Argos-Peloponnesus-Greece), claiming to have come from Egypt after the Hyksos expulsion, c.1550 BCE. Else, they arrived in Canaan after the struggles with Merneptah and Rameses III, c.1207-1185 BCE?[55] The Denyen of Rameses III, at Medinet Habu, c.1175-1150 BCE, are pictured as part of the battle of this Pharaoh with the Sea People on land and sea, c.1188 BCE.[56] A more ancient tradition is that the people known as the Danuna who first arrived in Syria, c.1395 BCE, were their ancestors. Possibly they were the same Danoi under King Mopsos of Colophon, Asia Minor, who is reported to have died in Ashkelon, possibly part of the above-noted Hyksos invasion of Egypt, c.1650 BCE, and then in retreat, 1550-1500 BCE.[57]

The "Sea Peoples"(late-thirteenth century to mid-twelfth century BCE): 1) Philistines: Peleset, Palestine, settled Gaza, Ashkelon, Ashdod, Gath, Ekron; 2) Crete—Cherethites, interior (Negeb), possibly Philistines/Pelethites (see discussion of Judah); 3) Sardinia—Sherden, settled around Acco (Acre); 4) Cyprus—Alashiya, then, when under Greek domination, was renamed the island of Yadanana-Danoi-Denyen-Danunians; 5) Sicilians, Shikalayu, Shekelesh, Tjeker/Sikils, settled at Dor (Haifa).

The Biblical Samson, from the tribe of Dan, in his own time still controlling part of the coast near present-day Ashdod and inland to the Sheppelah, the low hills to the east, (he was born in Zorah, near the border with Judah), was a pre-Monarchical Judge. {Judges 13-16}. "Samson fights his battles alone and performs feats of strength more in the mold of the Greek Heracles than of the Israelite, Gideon. Samson tells riddles, has seven magical locks of hair, and cavorts with Philistine women. His adventures take place on the border between the Israelites and the Philistines. Samson chooses a Philistine bride from the Philistine town of Timnah [always contested for by the Israelites, and later in Jewish history—Jamnia/Yavneh], where Philistine bichromeware is abundant."[58] Note Samson's Nazarite long hair (*nazir*—unpruned vine in Hebrew) "like the rays of the sun," and the mystical powers attributed to it. Hidden in the story an etymological and symbolic resemblance of this Israelite Judge to the Canaanite sun god, Shemesh (Kemosh), Samson=Sunny/Sonny. {Judges 13:24}.[59] Recall that the Philistines had quickly adopted the resident gods from the indigenous Canaanites.[60]

Sometime during this period, as the Biblical chronicle {Judges 18:1-31} tells us, the Danites were uprooted, perhaps displaced (by the Sea Peoples/Philistines) for disloyalty. Possibly, the tribe along with Samson's family had joined the Israelite confederation. Such political fluidity was not uncommon. They left their home territories, were forced to migrate inland and to the far north near the Hula Valley After a scouting expedition reminiscent of Joshua and Caleb, six hundred of their warriors destroyed the citizens of the peaceful Canaanite city of Laish (Lion): "…allied with Zidon, but far from them, unto a people that were at quiet and secure… put them to the sword and burnt down the city….There was no deliverer." {Judges 18:28}.

"Dan shall judge his people as one of the tribes of Israel. Dan shall be a snake by the roadside, a viper along the path, that bites the horse's heels so that its rider falls backward." {Gen. 49:16-17—J plus earlier sources—Jacob/Israel's "Farewell"}.

The story of the tribe of Dan has a bizarre and puzzling conclusion. Migrating north after first scouting out the city of Laish, the Danites had made their way into Ephraim where they encountered Micah, who earlier had offered them hospitality. They then stole from him an idol of cast metal, and a teraphim, both banned in Mosaic Yahwism, {Exodus 20:4-6} also, an ephod, (priestly vestment). The young priest who was serving Micah, (he, clearly a small-time judge), put in his lot with the Danites on their way north. After the destruction of Laish and its people, they set up their idols in the new city, Dan.

Later, under the divided Monarchy, a great sanctuary was established here by Jeroboam, the first king of Israel (also at Bethel). It was maintained until the Assyrians, in 722 BCE, overwhelmed Israel and destroyed its traditional religious shrines. Judges of Deuteronomy 1: "So they maintained as their own, [Dan-Israel], Micah's idol that he had made, as long as the house of God was at Shiloh." {Judges 18:31}. Shiloh historically was the center of pre-Monarchic Yahwism, and remained an ecumenical holy center for both kingdoms until the Assyrian conquest.

Now the puzzle: Micah's young priest had come to Ephraim from his home in Bethlehem, in Judah: "Jonathan son of Gershom, son of Moses, and his sons were priests to the tribe of the Danites until the time the land went into captivity." {Judges 18:30}. Moses has been always associated with Joshua and Ephraim, the latters' tribe. Judah in the later monarchical period, under Solomon, was ministered to by the priest, Zadok, who claimed lineage from the Aaronite opposition. Also, what time frame does a grandson of Moses migrating north with the Danites imply, regarding the time of the entrance of the Israelites into Canaan?[61]

*Meroz: "Song of Deborah": "Curse Meroz, says the angel of YHWH, curse bitterly its inhabitants, because they did not come to the help of YHWH, to the help of YHWH against the mighty." {Judges 5:23}. Other tribes, as we have noted above, did not join in the struggle against the charioted Canaanites: Reuben, "tarrying among the sheepfolds, even as there were great searchings of heart." {Judges 5:16}. Yet, why this terrible and seemingly final "curse"? Meroz is heard from no more in the Old Testament.

*Judah and Yahweh: "From the beginning of his career, David showed himself to be a fervent Yahwist. His religious devotion was confirmed by the presence in his retinue of the priest Abiathar and the prophet Gad. David's devotion to Yahweh probably made it easier for the leaders of Israel to accept him as their king."[62]

This commitment of King David to Yahwism probably was rooted in the ancient tradition among the people of the Judean hill country around the town of Hebron. Nor-

man Gottwald is probably correct in seeing the tribe of Judah as part of an older am-
phyctyony of people who served only one god, YHWH, and this perhaps before the Mosaic period.[63] These included the so-called Jerahmeelites, Simeonites, Calebites Oth-
nielites, Kenites, also the Rechabites.

Jerahmeelites lived in the central Negeb and figure, along with the Kenites, as allies
of David in his campaigns against a variety of the enemies of King Achish of the Philistines. The Philistines were patrons of David, before his accession to the crown of Israel.
{1 Samuel 27:10; 30:29; 1 Chronicles 2:9, 25-27}.[64]

Simeon is first mentioned in Genesis as being in the north-central highlands,
Shechem. {Genesis 34:25, 30-31—J-source}. There, both Simeon and Levi avenge the
rape of Dinah, their sister, by slaughtering the (Canaanite) Shechemites as they are re-
covering from their mass circumcision. In Judges, Simeon is now in the south, along
with his brother Judah, who is the leader. Subsequent to their joining forces, it is Judah
who defeats the giants at Hebron. {Judges 1:1-5}.[65]

Caleb: Is called a Kennizite. {Numbers 32:12}. Kenaz is identified as a descendant
of Esau. {Genesis 36:11, 15—P plus Redactor}. Moses had sent spies to Canaan:
"...from the tribe of *Judah*, [*sic*] Caleb son of Jepphunneh"..."the Kennizite." {Num-
bers 13:6—P-source; Gen. 13:30-33—J-source; Joshua 14:6-15}. On their return, Caleb
and Joshua argue with the elders for an invasion and war, 'let's go up and fight them'.
Moses and Aaron fell on their face before the assembly, to plead for bravery. "But the
whole congregation threatened to stone them" (Joshua and Caleb). {Numbers 14:5-10—
P-source}. Thus, after the conquest, "Hebron was given to Caleb, as Moses had said."
{Judges 1:20}. Caleb had previously been extolled by Moses for his bravery: {Deuter-
onomy 1:36}. Later, Hebron became the capital of David, of Bethlehem.

Othniel: Early in Joshua we find the story of Othniel, where it is revealed that the
Kennizites (Kenites) are the parent tribe of the Calebites. {Joshua 15:13-19}.[66] Othniel,
Caleb's nephew, and friend to the Israelites, goes against Debir, south of Hebron.
{Judges 1:11-15}. Othniel the Kennizite is listed as a Judge of Israel. {Judges 3:7-11}.
He is one of two non-Israelites, the other being Shamgar {Judges 3:31} who is thought
to have been a Hurrian (Indo-European) convert.[67]

Kennizites/Kenites/Cain: These people were the later descendants of Hobab, Moses'
son-in law, peoples also related to the Midianites. It is here recorded that the Kenites
went up from Jericho with the people of Judah to Tel-Arad in the Negeb. Then, oddly,
the Kennizites went and settled with the Amalekites! {Judges 1:16}.[68] They are also

recorded in the "Song of Deborah" as being allied (except for the loyal Kenite Yahwist, Jael) with the Indo-European Sisera as part of the Canaanite campaign against the Israelite/Habiru raids on their trade routes. This campaign brought the Kenites far to the north, near Mt. Tabor.

Rechabites: Another possibly pre-Mosaic Shasu group, are the Rechabites, a nomadic southern tribe mentioned in the Old Testament as worshippers of YHWH. {2 Kings 10:15-16}: "The families of the scribes who lived at Jabez [Jabesh-gilead]: the Tirathites, the Shimeathites, and the Sucathites. These are the Kenites who came from Hammath, father of the house of Rechab." {1Chronicles 2:55}. Then follows a genealogy of the sons of Israel, the tribes and their descendants. Moshe Weinfeld argues that the Rechabites were an associated tribe of the Kenites, and as with the Nabateans, maintained their way of life into the Hellenistic period.[69] "...the Rechabites, like the Nazarites" {Numbers 6:1-21—P-source} (Nazir, unpruned vine in Hebrew, those who are separated or consecrated—they wore their hair long, abstained from wine, did not approach a corpse). Samuel and Samson were Nazarites, considered all aspects of Canaanite culture to be corrupting, and they therefore avoided cultivating land, planting vineyards, and building houses.[70]

Jehonadab, supposedly a son of Rechab, saw an opportunity to help Jehu, c.840 BCE, restore YHWH to the Northern Kingdom. {2 Kings 10:15-16}. Jeremiah has YHWH commend the Rechabites under Jehonadab, son of Rechab, for their faithfulness to YHWH, as compared to the faithless Israelites—Judeans, c.600 BCE. {Jer. 35}. The Rechabites had then taken refuge in Jerusalem, abandoning their tents for fear of the Babylonian/Chaldeans and Amorites.[71]

Ancient Questions

YHWH: In contrast to the agricultural gods of Canaan, the Baals, and Ashtoreth, YHWH was always a fierce warlike god of nature. The radical change, as we shall point out below, came with Moses. We must conclude, based on recent archaeological and historical information, that there was a long-existent tradition of YHWH worship among the more nomadic Shasu-like tribes of the south and east. We are introduced to the LORD and "Jethro, the priest of Midian" early in Exodus. {Exodus 3:1—E-source}. It is there that the LORD gives his name: "I AM WHO I AM—YHWH." {Exodus 3:13-15—E-source}.

A pre-Mosaic exemplification of the "nature power" of YHWH can be seen in the ancient "Song of Deborah": "YHWH, when you went out from Seir, when you marched from the region of Edom, the earth trembled, and the heavens poured, the clouds indeed poured water, the mountains quaked before the YHWH, the One of Sinai, before the YHWH, the God of Israel....The stars fought from heaven, from their courses they fought against Sisera, the torrent Kishon swept them away, the onrushing torrent, the torrent Kishon." {Judges 5:4-5, 20-21}.

Joshua gave thanks to YHWH for his victory over the Amorites. He utters this ancient poetic fragment: "Sun, stand still at Gibeon, and Moon, in the valley of Aijalon, and the sun stood still, and the moon stopped, until the nation took vengeance on their enemies." The Deuteronomist compiler adds, "Is this not written in the Book of Jashar?" {Joshua 10:12-13}.

In the land of the Midianites. A recent discovery of a bronze effigy of a serpent in the land of the Midianites, northwest Arabia and the southern Negeb, recalls the Exodus story of the LORD telling Moses to make a magical serpent of bronze, who would cure the Israelites after they were snake-bitten, by merely gazing at the effigy. {Numbers 21:4-9—J or E source}.[72] Lawrence Stager has long contended that the route of the Exodus was through northwest Arabia, the traditional site of Mt. Seir or Mt. Paran, and that the tradition of Yahwism was well established here when Moses encountered Jethro and his daughters, one of whom, Zipporah, became Moses' wife. Here, in the well-developed communities of Qurrayah, Timna, and Punan, the latter two towns in the Negeb, twelfth to eleventh century BCE, beautiful Midianite pottery was manufactured and traded.[73] The Midianites, like most of the tribes surrounding the Israelites: Kenites, Edomites, Amalekites, are found far from their traditional haunts in the south, in Judges. Gideon from Ophrah in Manasseh routs them in a series of battles in the Jezreel Valley, far to the north of their usual locations. {Judges 7}. And, as noted above, the Kenites are associated with the Gileadites in Jabez and Succoth in Trans-Jordan. {Joshua 8:15-16; 1 Chronicles 2:55}. They too wandered far afield.

Who was David? David hailed from *har yehudah*, the mountain region of Judah. {Joshua 20:7}. Ruth, the Moabite, was the great-grandmother of David. The Judge/Prophet Samuel called upon Jesse of Bethlehem/Judah to interview his sons. David was the seventh and youngest to be paraded before Samuel. "He {Jesse} sent and brought him {David} in. Now he was ruddy and had beautiful eyes and was handsome." {1 Samuel 16:10-12}.[74]

Esau was father of the Edomites. Isaac had married Rebekah daughter of Bethuel the Aramean of Paddan-aram. "When her time to give birth was at hand there were twins in her womb. The first came out red, [Edom] all his body like a hairy mantle [Seir], so they named him Esau." (Edom) {Genesis 24:24-25; 36:1—J-source}. The Edomites themselves were also, in all probability, northerners.[75]

Moses' Testamentary Blessing: "Yahweh came from Sinai, and dawned from Seir upon us; he shone forth from Mt. Paran." {Deut. 33:2}. The J-source of the Pentateuch, written in Jerusalem in the days of Solomon always refers to God as YHWH, never as Elohim or El Shaddai. Could this be a tangible reflection of a tribe's (Judah) historical memory?

Israel before Moses

To the various writers and redactors of the Pentateuch, and Joshua and Judges which follow, it is clear that the Israelites were an intractable people both before and after Moses' flight from Egypt to Canaan. At the Jordan: "Remember and do not forget how you provoked the LORD your God to wrath in the wilderness; you have been rebellious against the LORD from the day you came out of the land of Egypt until you came to this place." {Deut. 9:6-7}. "You have been rebellious against the LORD as long as he has known you." {Deut. 9:23-24}. "For I know well how rebellious and stubborn you are. If you already have been so rebellious toward the LORD while I [Moses] am still alive among you, how much more after my death!" {Deut. 31:27}.

To the E-source writer, Moses is the great divide between the worship of Elohim in Canaan and a new level and form of worship of YHWH, after his arrival and theophany. Elohist history tries to protect God's transcendence and freedom to act; it emphasized fear of God, Elohim, as a motive for vocation and living. In a sense, the E-source is preparing the ground for a more direct assertion of YHWH's transcendent moral power and guidance for a wayward, if chosen people.[76] The emphasis of the E-source on the Covenantal Code, the laws of YHWH, is significant to Richard Friedman. {Exod. 21-23—E-source}.[77]

It is within probability, and here with the consensus view, that: 1) an Israelite confederation in the region of Canaan existed before the Exodus; 2) simultaneously and independently, clans and tribes existed east of the Jordan, in the Negeb, Sinai, and northwest Arabia, that worshipped a nature- and war-god named YHWH. At some point, they came together with the hill-dwelling Canaanite Semites, mostly wandering herders, and sometimes agriculturists. They came together because of a civilizational transition, hardly different from our own time, as the expansive and competitive trading, urban-dwelling Indo-European cosmopolitans, Hittites, Canaanites, Jebusites, Hivites, Sea Peoples, moved east.

The mathematics of migrants, fighting men, slaughtered warriors that abound in the Scriptures are clearly literary in nature. The people in question were too few and far between, though strong in their perception and understanding of events. As with Homeric memory, these tribes had their bards and seers, as noted above. They needed the fascinating tales and events of their past to provide the juice, the *nachas* of living.

They wandered freely, Kenites ranging back and forth from the Sinai to the Jezreel valley, Amalek fighting Moses and the Israelites at Rephidim, in the southern Sinai, (Amalek, a descendant of Esau and Edomites) {Gen. 36:12—P plus-source}.[78] Amale-kites later are seen controlling a city-near Telaim, in southern Judah. {1 Samuel 15:5-8}. Abdon, a Pirathonite, son of Hillel, judged Israel for eight years, had forty sons and thirty nephews that rode on three-score and ten ass colts; he was buried in Pirathon, in the land of Ephraim, "in the mount of the Amalekites!" {Judges 12:13-15}. The back-and-forth migrations of the Patriarchs in Genesis are thus not mere fiction. Travel was hard, but humans had the same exploratory instincts, the need to "move and see," also to survive. Such movement was possible because the land was long empty of humans. In the generations before 1000 BCE, there were real forests east of the Jordan, in Gilead.

"When Gaal son of Ebed moved into Shechem with his kinsfolk, the lords of Shechem put confidence in him." {Judges 9:26}. A new extended family, *mishpahah* moves in, and soon, they "are movers." Note how similar this story is to the earlier one of the migration of Jacob to Shechem. Here Hamor (Indo-European Hivite) (or Semitic Horites), to his eternal regret, invites Jacob/Israel to settle on his land. {Genesis 34—J-source}.

The Israelite tribes constantly engaged in bloody struggles with each other. The tribe of Benjamin was almost made extinct by the confederacy for the terrible gang rape and murder of a country Ephraimite's concubine. Immediately after, Jabesh-gilead is attacked by the same united Israelite confederation because they did not participate in the war against Benjamin. {Judges 19-21}. All men, women, children except four hundred young virgins, were slaughtered—"to the sword." {Judges 21:8-12}.

In {Judges 12:4-6}, Ephraimites escaping from a lost battle with the Gileadites to the east, are caught at the Jordan by their fellow Israelites, the Gileadites. They try to change their identities to avoid capture, but as they attempt to ford the Jordan, they are forced by the Gileadites, one by one, to pronounce the word "Shibboleth." Because in their own pronunciation of Hebrew, they couldn't pronounce "sh," saying "Sibboleth," the Gileadites then and there killed each of them.

The Levite Jonathan, son of Gershom, son of Mosheh, in Bethlehem, of Judah, is revealed to be the priest of Micah in Ephraim. His southern "accent" catches the attention of the Danites moving through Ephraim on their way north to find a new home. The home territory of Dan was just to the northwest of Bethlehem, perhaps one day's walk, and immediately south of Ephraim, another day's walk. Ephraim was just as close to Gilead, over the river Jordan. Why "accent," when these tribes were supposedly neighbors?

The Philistines had conquered the town of Beth-shan that guarded the eastern end of the valley of Jezreel. When the Philistines found Saul and his three sons dead on Mt. Gilboah, they cut off their heads and displayed them in this town. "But when the inhabitants of Jabesh-gilead [on the east of the Jordan] had heard what the Philistines had done to Saul, all the valiant men set out." (Saul had once delivered these Gadites from the Ammonites {1 Samuel 10:27; 11:11})." They traveled all night long, and took the body of Saul and the bodies of his sons from the wall of Beth-shan. "...Then they took their bones and buried them under a tamarisk tree in Jabesh, and fasted seven days." {1 Samuel 31:11-13}.

These tribespeople, worshippers of YHWH or of El/Baal, were a parochial, wild, and barbarous bunch. But it was ignorance and circumstance that made them so. The coming of Moses and his escapees from Egypt changed the entire focus of their energies and their lives. In so doing, Moses reshaped the direction of civilization.

Endnotes, Chapter 4

[1] Callaway/Miller, "The Settlement in Canaan," in Shanks, Hershel, ed. 1999. *Ancient Israel*, Washington, D.C.: Biblical Archaeological Society, p. 77.

[2] Merneptah inscription probably similar in time and description to the tribal roster in Genesis 49. An excellent discussion in:. Boling, Robert G. 1993. *Harper/Collins Study Bible,* New Standard Edition, London: Harper/Collins Publishers, pp. 367-369.

[3] Boling, Robert G., "Introduction to Judges," *Harper/Collins Study Bible, op. cit.,* p. 368.

[4] Rosenberg, Joel W., in *Harper/Collins Study Bible, op. cit.,* Note, p. 50.

[5] McCarter, P. Kyle, Jr., and Hendel, R. S., in Shanks, ed., *Ancient Israel, op. cit.*, pp. 26-27.

[6] Ahlstrom, Gosta. 1986. *Who Were the Israelites?* Winona Lake, IN: Eisenbrauns, p. 17.

[7] McCarter, P. Kyle, Jr., and Hendel, R. S., "The Patriarchal Age," in Shanks, ed., *Ancient Israel, op. cit.*, pp. 25-26; see also Shanks, ed., *op. cit.*, footnote 67, p. 302.

[8] Whitehouse, O. C. 1911."Hebrew Religion," in *Encyclopedia Britannica,* 11th ed., Vol. 13, p. 177.

[9] Poole , R. .S., and Griffith, F. L. 1910. "Egypt," in *Encyc. Brit.*, 11th ed., Vol. 9, pp. 84-86; L. E. Stager, in Coogan, Michael D., *op. cit.*, p. 145.

[10] Weinfeld, Moshe. 1989. "Israelite Religion," in Seltzer, Robert M., ed. 1989. *Judaism, A People and Its History*, N.Y.: Macmillan, p. 40; Mazar, B., 1977, cited in Weinfeld, *op. cit.*, p. 40; Gibeon, Raphael, "Les bedouins Shosu des documents egyptiens," Leiden, 1971, nos. 6a, 16a; Herrmann, S., "Der Name Jhw in den Inschriften von Soleb," *Fourth World Congress of Jewish Studies,* Vol. 1, Jerusalem, 1967 , pp. 213-216.

[11] Pritchard, J. B., ed. 1958. *The Ancient Near East*, 3 vols., Princeton, N.J.: Princeton Univ. Press, Vol. 1, pp. 183-184.

[12] Papyrus Anastasi VI, quoted from Pritchard, 3d ed., 1969, p. 259; also in Weinfeld, Moshe, in Seltzer, ed., *op. cit.*, p. 42.

[13] Stager, Lawrence E., in. Coogan, Michael D., ed. 1998. *The Oxford History of the Biblical World*, N.Y: Oxford Univ. Press, believes that they are dressed as Canaanites;. Rainey, Anson, in Shanks, ed., *op. cit.*, Note 76, p. 310, believes they are identified as Shasu; see also Callaway/Miller, "The Settlement in Canaan," in Shanks, ed., *op. cit.*, Notes 72-75, p. 310.

[14] Cowley, Arthur E., "Hebrew Literature," in *Encyc. Brit.*, *op. cit.*, 11th ed., Vol. 13, p. 169; Gordis, Robert, in Finkelstein, Louis, ed. 1955. *The Jews Their History, Culture, and Religion,* 2 vols., N.Y: Harper and Bros.,Vol. 1, p. 482.

[15] Campbell, Edward F., "A Land Divided," in Coogan, ed., *op. cit.*, p. 276; Cogan, M., "Into Exile," in Coogan, ed., *op. cit.*, p. 347.

[16] McCarter, P. Kyle, Jr., *Harper/Collins Study Bible, op. cit.*, Notes, p. 467.

[17] Grant, Michael A. 1984. *The History of Ancient Israel*, N.Y.: Charles Scribner, pp. 22-23.

[18] Lemaire, Andre, in Shanks, ed., *op. cit.*, p. 112.

[19] Weinfeld, Moshe, "Israelite Religion," in Seltzer, ed., *op. cit.*, p. 39; see Notes p. 61; Weinfeld, on the origins of monotheism, pp. 40*ff.*, good-study.

[20] Gordis, Robert, "The Bible as a Cultural Monument," in Finkelstein, Louis, ed. *The Jews, op. cit.*, Vol. 1, p. 467.

[21] Weinfeld, Moshe, "Israelite Religion,"in Seltzer, ed., *op. cit.*; Weinfeld, Moshe, "Social and Cultic Institutions in the Priestly Source against Their Ancient Near Eastern Background," in Proc. of the Eighth World Congress of Jewish Studies, Jerusalem, 1983, pp. 95-129.

[22] Grant, Michael A., *op. cit.*, p. 24.

[23] Callaway/Miller, "The Settlement in Canaan," in Shanks, ed. *op. cit.*, pp. 74-77.

[24] McCarter, P. Kyle Jr., in *Harper/Collins Study Bible, op. cit.,* Notes, p. 440.

[25] Whitehouse, O. C. 1910. "Hebrew Religion," in *Encyc. Brit.*, p. 180, Vol. 13, following Wellhausen.

[26] Campbell, Edward F., "A Land Divided," in Coogan ed., *op. cit.*, p. 309.

[27] Whitehouse, O. C. "Hebrew Religion," in *Encyc. Brit., op. cit.*

[28] Callaway/Miller, in Shanks, *op. cit.*, p. 83: 'bet 'ab=extended family; -Gottwald, Norman K. 1985. *The Hebrew Bible, A Socio-Literary Introduction*, Philadelphia: Fortress Press, p. 285: bet abot=house of father transitions into mishpahah=clan; see also Gottwald, Norman K. 1979. *The Tribes of Yahweh,* Maryknoll, N.Y.: Orbis Books.

[29] Whitehouse, O. C. "Hebrew Religion," in *Encyc. Brit., op. cit.,* p. 180, following Wellhausen.

[30] Weber, Max. (1917-1918). *Ancient Judaism*, N.Y.: Free Press, p. 34.

[31] Grant, Michael A., *op. cit.,* p. 100.

[32] Ibid.

[33] see discussion by Grant, p. 133.

[34] Whitehouse, O. C. "Hebrew Religion," *Encyc. Brit. op. cit.,* pp. 176, 180.

[35] Grant, Michael A., *op. cit.,* p. 24.

[36] Rosenberg, Joel W., in *Harper/Collins Study Bible, op. cit.,* Notes, p. 73.

[37] McBride, Dean, Jr., *Harper/Collins Study Bible, op. cit.,* Notes, 322S.

[38] Klein, Ralph W., "Introduction" to Chronicles, *Harper/Collins Study Bible, op. cit.,* p. 605.

[39] Boling, Robert G. "Introduction" to Judges," in *HarperCollins Study Bible, op. cit.,* p. 368; Friedman, R. E. 1987-1997. *Who Wrote the Bible?,* N.Y.: The Free Press, p. 258.

[40] Boling, Robert G., "Introduction" to Judges," in *Harper/Collins Study Bible, op. cit.,* pp. 367-369.

[41] Albright, W. F., "The Biblical Period," in Finkelstein, Louis, ed., *The Jews, op. cit.,* p. 17.

[42] McCarter and Hendel, in Shanks, *op. cit.,* p. 13.

[43] Ibid., p. 30.

[44] Gottwald, Norman K., *op. cit.,* p. 194.

[45] Albright, W. F., "The Biblical Period," in Finkelstein, Louis, ed., *The Jews, op. cit.,* p. 20.

[46] Stager, Lawrence E., in Coogan, *op. cit.,* p. 146.

[47] Gottwald Norman. K., *op. cit.,* p. 281.

[48] Stager, Lawrence E., in Coogan, *op. cit.,* pp. 125-127.

[49] Gottwald, Norman K., *op. cit.,* p. 271; McCarter and Hendel, in Shanks, *op. cit.,* p. 19.

[50] Judges 5:17, Song of Deborah.

[51] Ahlstrom, G. W. 1986. *Who Were the Israelites? op. cit.,* pp. 62-65.

[52] Friedman, R. E., *Who Wrote the Bible?, op. cit.,* p. 210.

[53] Gottwald, Norman K., *op. cit.,* p. 281; Whitehouse, in "Hebrew Religion," *Encyc. Brit.,* p. 176.

[54] Rosenberg, Joel W., *Harper/Collins Study Bible, op. cit.*, Notes, p. 74

[55] Darlington, C. D. 1969. *The Evolution of Man and Society*, London: George Allen and Unwin, pp. 154-155, who quotes Wooley, L. 1958. *Art of the World*, London: Methuen; Huxley, G. L. 1966. *The Early Ionians*, London: Faber.

[56] Pritchard, J. B., ed. 1958. *The Ancient Near East, op. cit.*, Vol. 1,.p. 185.

[57] Barnett, R. D. 1953. "Mopsos," *The Journal of Hellenic Studies*, 73:143.

[58] Stager, Lawrence E., "Forging An Identity," in Coogan, *op. cit.*, p. 168.

[59] Boling, Robert G., *Harper/Collins Study Bible*, Notes, p. 393.

[60] Grant, Michael A., *op. cit.*, p. 69.

[61] see Whitehouse, O. C., "Hebrew Religion," in *Encyc. Brit., op. cit.*, Vol. 13, pp. 176, 181; Weinfeld, Moshe, in Seltzer, Robert M., ed., *op. cit.*, p. 39; also, Notes, p. 61; Gottwald, Norman K., *op. cit.*, p. 223; Boling, Robert G., in *Harper/Collins Study Bible, op. cit.*, Notes, p. 401.

[62] Lemaire, Andre, "The United Monarchy," in Shanks, ed., *op. cit.*, p. 103.

[63] Gottwald, N. K., *op. cit.*, p. 281.

[64] McCarter and Hendel, "The Patriarchal Age," in Shanks, *op. cit.*, p. 22.

[65] Robert G. Boling implies that Judges 1:1-36, "Introduction," is by Deuteronomist Historian 2, in *Harper/Collins Study Bible, op. cit.*, Notes, p. 369.

[66] McCarter, P. Kyle, Jr., in *Harper/Collins Study Bible, op. cit.*, Notes, p. 460.

[67] Ibid., Notes, p. 370.

[68] Boling, Robert G., in *Harper/Collins Study Bible, op. cit.*, Notes, p. 370.

[69] Weinfeld, Moshe, "Israelite Religion," in Seltzer, ed., *op. cit.*, p. 41.

[70] Wilson, Robert, in *Harper/Collins Study Bible, op. cit.*, Notes, 2 Kings, p. 576.

[71] Isserlin, B .S. J. 1998. *The Israelites*, London: Thames and Hudson, Ltd., p. 64. Isserlin argues here that the tribe of Judah, and then the Kingdom of Judah incorporated most of the above non-Mushite (Moses) tribes into the Israelite confederation.

[72] Friedman, R. E. *Who Wrote the Bible?, op. cit.*, p. 92.

[73] Stager, Lawrence E., "Forging an Identity: The Emergence of Ancient Israel," in Coogan, *op. cit.*, pp. 147-148.

[74] McCarter, P. Kyle, Jr., in *Harper/Collins Study Bible, op. cit.*, Notes, p. 442; see-also {1 Samuel 16:3}; {Ruth 1:1-5; 4:12, 17-22}; {1 Chronicles 2:3-15}.

[75] Ahlstrom, G. W., *Who Were the Israelites, op. cit.*, p. 60.

[76] Campbell, Edward F., "A Land Divided," in Coogan, *op. cit.*, p. 287.

[77] Friedman, R. E., *Who Wrote the Bible?, op. cit.*, p. 83.

[78] Greenstein, Edward, "Exodus," in *Harper/Collins Study Bible, op. cit.*, Notes, p. 111.

5

Exodus

Was the Exodus Real?

There are those who would argue that because no concrete evidence supports either the Exodus, or the real existence of the person Moses, the foundations of the Hebrew religion stand on a glorified myth, a "just so" story. Indeed, there is no supporting historical or archeological evidence for the epochal events that define and establish the religion of the Hebrews, the Pentateuch, or the *Torah*, the words of Yahweh to the chosen people. However, background historical events described in Exodus and Numbers do support a view that the Exodus and Moses are within the range of historical possibility.

Leviticus is concerned with priestly regulation, by the "P" writers, and other unknown sources, written later in time, to formulize temple practice. Written in part during the Judean monarchy, c.730 BCE, it was completed during the Babylonian/Chaldean exile and then the return to Judah and the building of the second temple, c.539-450 BCE. Deuteronomy 1 and 2, also with composite earlier materials, were probably written during the era of Josiah of Judah, c.640-600 BCE, and later after the fall of Judah to the Chaldean/Babylonians.

The first writing of the events contained in Exodus and Numbers in the Hebrew Bible were probably set down by the "J" writers, at the end of the rule of Solomon, in Jerusalem (c.950 BCE). "E" derived from the Northern Kingdom of Israel, somewhat later (c.850 BCE), there by scribes and Levites, probably at the holy site of Shiloh, in

Ephraim. Almost one hundred and fifty years of intense literary and linguistic analysis, following on the work of the Protestant minister, Julius Wellhausen, c.1870 CE, have revealed layer after layer of additions. First there were subtractions to the "J" and "E" versions, even without having to take into consideration the more traceable edited work of the "P" writers. Then there were the redactions and editions of the Deuteronomic school, itself responsible for the writing of the Book of Deuteronomy.[1]

As we shall point out, the time of the Exodus was roughly between the Pharaonic reign of Rameses II, Dynasty 19, c.1250 BCE, and Rameses III, presumably himself of Asiatic origins, Dynasty 20, c.1150 BCE. The latter date separates itself from the anointing of Saul as King of the Israelite tribes of the north, 1050 BCE, by only one hundred years. Either time frame is possible, putting a gap of 200-300 years between the events of the Exodus and the writings of the "J" source, c.950 BCE, in the Jerusalem of Solomon.

The stories, sagas, tales that we find in Genesis are important beginnings in the self-consciousness of Israel, as a nation and a people. Noah, Abraham, Isaac, and Jacob/Israel are, as we have pointed out in Chapters 3 and 4, part of the rich historical tradition of the peoples of this vast area between the two great rivers and the Nile to the west. The connective tissue between the Patriarchs and the Exodus is, of course, the "novel" of Joseph and his brothers, the progeny of Jacob/Israel, and their transplantation from Canaan to Egypt. It is hardly conceivable that these tales were written down "whole-cloth" and with such relative unanimity of fact and tone by "J" and "E" without the previous existence of a long bardic heritage of oral and written remembrance. As we have noted in earlier chapters, the Hebrew Bible is replete with references to earlier written material, material that the writers thought important as justification for their own compilations.

The earliest transcribers of these events attempted to order the time-line of memory with concrete estimates: "Know this for certain, that your offspring shall be aliens in a land that is not theirs, and shall be slaves there, and they shall be oppressed for four hundred years." {Genesis 15:13—J source + later redactor}. Later in Exodus: "At the end of four hundred thirty years, on that very day, all the companies of the LORD went out from the land of Egypt." {Exodus 12:40—P-source}.[2] These intervals, interestingly, are congruent with the interval of time between the Hyksos Asiatic conquest of Egypt, c.1650 BCE, and the era noted above for the time of the Exodus. Also close by to the above figure in Genesis, the interval for the return is put at four generations. {Genesis

15:16—J-source plus later redactor}.[3] It should be noted that the Samaritan Pentateuch, c.550 BCE, and the Septuagint versions of Exodus (the translation into Greek made for the Alexandrian Jews of Egypt, about 270 BCE) put the time spent in Egypt as 215 years.[4]

With this heritage of oral and written material, originating in the days of the Israel mentioned in the stele of Merneptah, c.1207 BCE, and possibly earlier, we recall the existence of *alphabetic* writing found in the Sinai, at a very early dating, c.1500 BCE. The tradition of writing was by then an ancient and passionate undertaking, by specially gifted scribes and holy people, by guilds existing in practically all the tribes that wanted to establish their historical integrity. Note the references in {Joshua 8 and 1 Chronicles 2:55} that speak of scribes (Kenites and Gileadites) in the lands east of the Jordan River.

Is it realistic to believe that Moses could have been conjured up, as was probably the case with Noah, Abraham, Isaac, Jacob/Israel, as an archetypal prophet and truly the one person that Yahweh had chosen to lead the "chosen people," not merely out of Egyptian slavery but into a permanent homeland under "God?" The struggle by Moses to lead his people into a new future, to a land of "milk and money," to achieve a military/political victory, but also moral goodness, and happiness, was not an easy one. It was *not* crowned by a victory parade of Moses, Aaron, and Joshua through the holy sites of Shechem, Bethel, and Shiloh.

Victory, tragedy, betrayal, faithfulness, miracles, terror, all are in this saga. The tangibles and details in the story of the Exodus are too real to be pushed aside as mere fiction. Moses has a humanness that surmounts his origin as a composite, epitomizing an archetypal tale of the poor, exploited foreigner, saved from death by royalty and then raised as their own. So, too, there is a mythic quality to the unexpected theophany with "God," a transcendental moment when the anointed "one" is consecrated to the task of leading his people out of servitude. The story of Moses and the Exodus reads also as a narrative, both human and concrete, a crucial historic experience that underlies the surface miracles that were needed to astonish naïve listeners, and to raise up its significance.

The story seems too important, a dividing line of history, energizing leading minds, generations down the line, not to have been experienced, at the least by some segments of the Israelite population. The events as they are related by the earliest writers, "J" and "E", seem too personal, direct, and unself-conscious not to have occurred in some form.

"A Stiff-necked People" {Exodus 32:9; 34:9}

The earliest specific reference to the foreign Asiatic element dwelling or attempting to migrate into the Nile Delta area is a text from a ruler of Egypt to his son, "Instruction for Merikare," c.2040 BCE. "The east abounds in foreigners...Now speaking about these foreigners, as for the miserable Asiatic, wretched is the place where he is...Food causes his feet to roam about...[The Delta] gates were opened when I besieged it. I caused the Delta to attack it. I plundered their inhabitants, having captured their cattle. I slaughtered [the people] among them so that the Asiatics abhorred Egypt."[5] Three hundred fifty years later, c.1650 BCE, these "miserable Asiatic wretches," along with newcomers from the north and across the Mediterranean, would become the Hyksos conquerors of all of Egypt, to give the great river civilization a century of peace and prosperity, as well as cultural renewal.

We have noted in Chapter 3 the tomb painting at Beni Hasan, Upper Egypt, just north of Tel Amarna, on the Nile. This tomb painting dates from c.1890 BCE. It shows both men and women, Canaanites, arrayed in many colors, having a Hittite (Indo-European) physiognomy, bringing trade goods to Egypt. In the days of the Pharaoh Akhenaton, 1350 BCE, there ruled an Egyptian high commissioner, a Semite named Yanhamu.[6] During this period, as noted in Chapter 3, the Amarna letters are suffused with appeals from the Indo-European/Canaanite vassals of the Pharaoh, appealing for help against the raids of the 'Apiru/Habiru. Asiatics were an ever-present reality in ancient Egypt.

It is now generally agreed that the terms 'Apiru/Habiru/Ibri/Eber are too close for comfort to the word "Hebrews," not to be in some way linked historically. We have noted in Chapter 4 that Genesis often refers in the first and third person to the Israelite participants as Hebrews. So, too, with Exodus and the early sources "J" and "E". There are many references to the Hebrews. {Exodus 1:16, 19—E-source}; Exodus 2:6, 7—J-source}; {Exodus 3:18—J-source}; {Exodus 5:3—J-source}.[7]

In Pharaoh Merneptah's reign, during the period when he was proclaiming victory over Israel on his stele, c.1212-1202 BCE, frontier officials were instructed to allow Semitic bedouin tribes of Edom to pass through Goshen to "the pools of Per Atum (Biblical Pithom) to keep them alive and to keep their cattle alive."[8] Another translation: "We have finished letting the Shasu nomads of Edom pass the fortress to keep them alive and to keep their cattle alive."[9]

Close in time, also under the reign of Merneptah, the so-called Papyrus Anastasi 5 reports on an attempt by Egyptian officials to track down two escaped slaves sighted near Migdol, an unknown location, but confirming the reality of a possible route of Moses and the Israelites. {Numbers: 33:7—P-source}. "When my letter reaches you, write to me about all that has happened to them. Who found the tracks? Which watch found their tracks? What people are after them?…"[10]

Again in Merneptah's time, c.1210 BCE, the marshal of the court was a Semite named Ben Ozen.[11] Clearly the Semitic Israelites possibly involved in the Exodus during this period were too insignificant to disturb the continuing internationalism that can be found in most of the Egyptian dynasties. These snippets of evidence point to the Delta, Goshen, in Egypt, as containing a polyglot population of Egyptians, Shasu nomads, 'Apiru Semites, as well as a variety of other residents, harking back to the Hyksos invasions and before. An example of this continuing interaction of Egypt and Asia is a Ramasside ostracon of the twelfth century BCE. Here, a father reproaches his son for associating with the Semites of the Delta by eating bread mixed with blood, *i.e.*, making a pact with them. Moshe Weinfeld, who reports this find, states that the blood ritual was found only in Sinaitic ceremonies, which reflects an ancient nomadic realism that adds to the probability of the Mosaic tradition.[12]

Then Moses…said…Take a bunch of hyssop, [a plant used in purification rites] dip it into the blood that is in the basin, [of the lamb] and touch the lintel and the two door posts with the blood in the basin" [Passover rite]. {Exodus 12:21-22—J-source}.[13]

{Exodus 1:11—E-source} speaks of the building of the supply cities "Pithom" and "Rameses." This identifies the Israelites with the enterprise of Merneptah's, father, Rameses II, c.1290-1224 BCE, Pharaoh, c.1270 BCE. In Chapter 3 we noted the stele to the Syrian God, Seth, that Rameses II erected, hinting of an Asiatic interest and his own Hyksos origins. The following description is here given in Exodus of the labor of the Israelites: "Therefore they set taskmasters [*missim*] over them to oppress them with forced labor. They built supply cities, Pithom and Rameses for Pharaoh." {Exodus 1:11—E-source}[14] The next Exodus passage derives from a much later time than the above, c.850 BCE. This is the "Priestly" source {Exodus 1:13-14}, c.500 BCE. The words "…ruthless lives bitter with hard service in mortar and brick and every kind of field labor…" was, hundreds of years later, added as an emphatic description. We cannot be sure that Rameses II was the Pharaoh who increased the misery of the Israelites, since being drafted for the Pharaonic corvée was part of the obligation of the entire population.

Contrast the following directive given with regard to the building of the above city of Pi-Rameses under Rameses II, c.1270 BCE. An Egyptian official in the construction process instructs his foreman to distribute rations to the Habiru: "Distribute grain rations to the soldiers and to the Habiru who transport stones to the great pylon of Rameses."[15]

{Exodus 1:15-21—E-source} tells us about: "Hebrew midwives…Shiphrah and Pua," Semitic names but possibly working for Egyptians, as they are ordered "to kill all [Hebrew] males." The midwives disobeyed, giving the Pharaoh a story that Hebrew women give birth too quickly for the midwives to intercede. "So God dealt well with the midwives; and the people multiplied and became very strong. And because the midwives feared God, he gave them families." {*Harper/Collins Study Bible*} Contrast {Exodus 1:21—E-source, King James translation}, "…he made them houses."

It is debated whether these two midwives were assigned to this large Israelite population. They could have been Habiru, or Asiatic Semites. But we ask, how many women, in an era when fecundity was a high female achievement, could have been reasonably served by two midwives? Then, as now, pregnancy and birth are not without serious complications and many ongoing vicissitudes. Pregnant women often need to consult the wiser and more experienced. Certainly no more than a maximum of five hundred nubile women could be competently handled by these two midwives. What do we reckon the entire population of Hebrews to have been at the crucial moment of revolt, flight, or expulsion? The story of the midwives smacks of legend. But it hints at a demographic reality. This was a small nuclear population of people that had already been set apart. Norman Gottwald reckons the total number of those in flight from Egypt to have been in the hundreds.[16]

The flight from Egypt took place after the terrible Tenth Plague, of the first-born Egyptians, including those of the Pharaoh, the prisoner in the dungeon, of the livestock. {Exodus 12:29—E or J-source} Did the Israelites flee Egypt in fear, because of this horrific act by YHWH, and his agent Moses?

Earlier, in Exodus, God says: "But every woman shall borrow of her neighbor, and of her that sojourneth in her house jewels of silver and jewels of gold, and raiment: and ye shall put *them* upon your sons and upon your daughters; and ye shall spoil the Egyptians." {Exodus 3:22—J-source} Then, "The Lord said unto Moses, Yet will I bring one plague *more* upon Pharaoh, and upon Egypt {Exodus 11:1—J or E—source}.[17] Then,

"Speak now in the ears of the people, and let every man borrow of his neighbor, and every woman of her neighbor jewels of silver, and jewels of gold." {Exodus 11:2-3 J or E source}.[18] "And the children of Israel did according to the word of Moses; and they borrowed of the Egyptians jewels of silver, and jewels of gold and raiment: And the Lord gave the people favor in the sight of the Egyptians, so that they lent unto them such things as they required. And they spoiled the Egyptians." {Exodus 12:35-36—E-source}.[19] See also, "He brought them forth also with silver and gold: and *there was* not one feeble *person* among their tribes." {Psalms 105:37}.

Again, before the Tenth Plague, "The Lord gave the people favor in the sight of the Egyptians. Moreover, Moses himself was a man of great importance in the land of Egypt, in the sight of the Pharaoh's officials and in the sight of the {Egyptian} people." {Exodus 11:3—J- or E-source}.[20]

After the Tenth Plague, "The Egyptians urged the people to hasten their departure from the land, for they said, 'We shall be dead'. So they [Israelites] took their dough before it was leavened, with their kneading bowls wrapped up in their cloaks on their shoulders..." {Exodus 12:33-34—E-source} Then, as above, they took the jewelry of gold and silver, and "spoiled" or plundered the Egyptians. {Exodus 12:35-36—E-source}.

Does this look like an escape from slavery, or an expulsion for plunder? The consensus is that the "E" source believed that the Israelites were expelled from Egypt, and were not in simple flight from the corvée, as with "J".[21]

Later, Moses goes off to Mt. Sinai first with Aaron, Nadab, Abihu, Aaron's sons, and seventy elders (again the magical number seven). They see God, who summons Moses alone to the top of the mountain. He is there a long time, and the people become restless asking Aaron to make gods for them, as "Moses, the man who brought us up out of the land of Egypt, we do not know what has become of him." {Exodus 32:1—E, or Redactor-source}. "And Aaron said unto them, 'Break off the golden earrings which *are* in the ears of your wives, of your sons, and of your daughters, and bring *them* unto me...And all the people brake off the golden earrings which *were* in their ears, and brought *them* unto Aaron." {Exodus 32:2-3—E, or Redactor-source}.

Moses returns from the mountain carrying the two tablets of the covenant agreements with YHWH: *berith*, (covenant-agreement—E-source); *eduth*, (testimony—P-source, except *berith* in Holiness Code, by another "P" writer, in Leviticus, mainly Chapters 17-26).[22] Moses meets Joshua, his assistant, and they observe the "golden calf" that Aaron had made from the loot the Israelites had secured from the Egyptians: "...and he threw the tablets from his hands and broke them at the foot of the mountain." {Exodus 32:19 E-or-Redactor-source} The section dealing with the "golden calf" may be a later redaction/addition that obscures an older "J" section, {Exodus 32:25-29—E-or Redactor-source}. This was seemingly far more indicting of Aaron and the wild Israelites, and translated variably as: When he saw that the people were {"running wild"—"breaking loose"—"naked"}, implying not a mere violation of the second commandment, but more—sexual debauchery, Moses then consecrated the sons of Levi to punish the offending Israelites. This they do, to the tune of three thousand people killed. "Moses said, {to the Levites} 'Today you have ordained yourself for the service of the LORD, each one at the cost of a son or a brother, and so have brought a blessing on yourselves this day.'" {Exodus 32:29—E or Redactor-source}.

"The Israelites journeyed from Rameses to Succoth, about six hundred thousand men on foot, besides children. A mixed crowd also went up with them, and flocks and herds, even very much cattle." {Exodus 12:37-38—E- or J-source}[23] Characterization: "The rabble among them had a strong craving."[24] Or, "And the mixed multitude that was among them fell a lusting."[25] Both are {Numbers 11:4—E-source}.

The move out of Egypt seems to have had several population components: A) A small leadership group under Moses, raised and affiliated with the Pharaonic royal house, but then possibly separated from it by a change in dynastic rule; B) The Hebrews, perhaps represented on the journey through the Sinai by the Levites, of whom Moses was now the leader; C) A larger group of associated Semitic and El-worshipping people wishing to get out from the burden of the corvée, drawn to the rigorous Yahwistic powers and potencies that Moses had brought back from Midian. This new deity might reinvigorate his own Levite/Hebrew clans.

Moses the Person

Moses and Aaron are stated to have been born into a family of Levites. {Exodus 2:1-2—J-source}. The Egyptian name, *Moses* can be translated as Mes (u)=child or son, else, Mashah=one who draws (out of water), possibly related to the Mushite clan of the Levites. {Exodus 6:19—P-source}. With the possible exception of Aaron and Miriam, names derived from the tribes of the Sinai, the Levite names are mostly Egyptian: Merari, Hophni, Phinehas. These Levitical Hebrews/Egyptians are intermixed with numerous El names, among the fleeing children of Israel: Eliezer, Eleazar, Elkanah, Elzaphan,

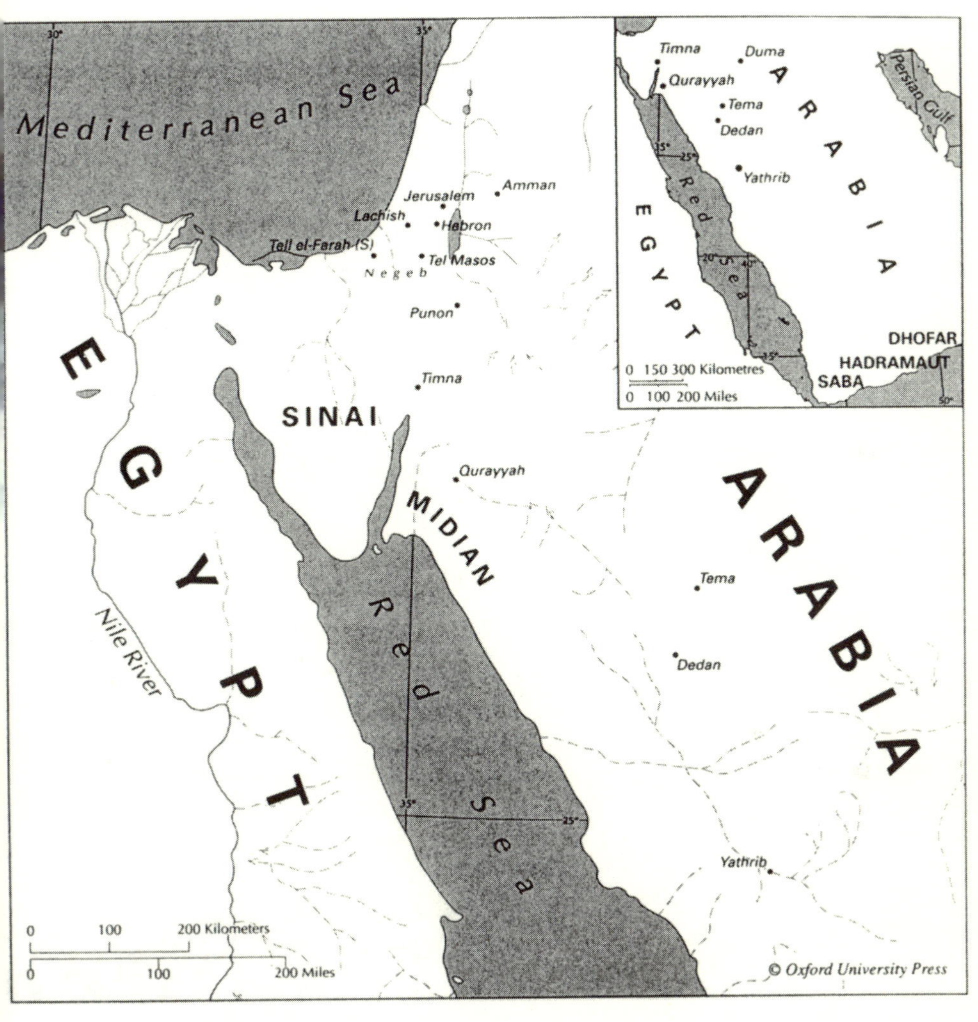

V. Lands of the Exodus: Egypt, Sinai, Arabia, and the Land of Midian.

Elisheba, Putiel, but also the later added, Jochebed (Jahwe), Moses' mother. {Exodus 6:14-25—P-source}.[26]

"And Amram took him Jochabed, his father's [Kohath, son of Levi] sister to wife; and she bare him Aaron and Moses." {Exodus 6:20—P-source}. Miriam is here not mentioned, but included in {Numbers 26:59—also P-source}. This was incest. {Leviticus 18:12—P-source} Isaac also committed incest. {Genesis 20:12—E-source} Jacob married sisters, Leah and Rachel. {Genesis 29:15-30—J-source} This also constitutes incest. {Leviticus 18:18—P-source}.

The tradition of the irregular birth origins of heroic figures is long established, even as with Moses, a descendant of a consecrated clan, the Levites. King David was the descendant of the Moabite, Ruth. Solomon the son of David, was a product of an adulterous procurement of the wife of Uriah, his devoted Hittite associate. David, then had Uriah placed in the front line and thus subsequently killed in battle. {2 Samuel 11:1-26}.

The mythology of Moses' birth, salvation and nurturing amidst Egyptian royalty, so reminiscent of many ancient tales, including that of the Akkadian, King Sargon, (see Chapter 3), is used in Exodus and the Biblical tradition to establish the two worlds in which Moses lived. This was first, as a member of a degraded and enslaved alien group, the Hebrews, second, as an Egyptian, the recipient of the education and potential leadership qualities that attend royalty.

His recognition of kin relationships centers on his murder of an Egyptian overseer who was brutalizing a Hebrew. His subsequent flight to Midian in the wilderness, his gentle considerations at the well to the seven daughters (the sacred number) of the Midian priest, Reuel (friend of God, or ro'eh, shepherd) {J and P—source}, also called Jethro, {E-source} is likewise a typical tale of exile and return to leadership, after having experienced a powerful personal moment. Here, the incident of "the burning bush" and the appearance of YHWH— "I AM THAT I AM" —{Exodus 3:14—E-source, King James Translation} before him to reveal his plan to deliver "my people...from the Egyptians and to bring them out of that land, and to a good and broad land, a land flowing with milk and honey..." (Exodus 3:7-8—J-source). This is the key moment in Moses' joining and then transcending the nomadic theological tradition of the south, of the God of fire and destruction, Yahweh, also and implicitly, the God of Midian {Exodus 18:10-12—E-source}.

The Midianite daughters relate Moses' kindness to their priest father, "An Egyptian helped us against the shepherds." {Exodus 2:19—J-source}. The Midianite Priest,

Jethro, invites Moses, the "Egyptian," into his home and subsequently gives him one of his seven daughters, Zipporah, in marriage. In time, she bears him a son, Gershom ("an alien there" or "drove them away") {Exodus 2:22—J-source}. Jethro, in Judges 4, is identified as being a Kenite, traceable to the nomadic destiny of Cain, and at that later time a group related to the Edomites, descendants of Esau, Jacob's twin brother.[27] These southern tribes seem to be inextricably intertwined with the destiny of the Israelites on their return through the wilderness into Canaan.

Probably the most mysterious insight into the origin of Moses comes from the fragment of an ancient Exodus source inserted into Chapter Four of Exodus. This is the so-called "bridegroom of blood" episode:

"On the way, at a place where they spent the night, YHWH met him and tried to kill him. But Zipporah took a flint and cut off her son's foreskin, touched Moses' feet [genitals] with it and said 'Truly you are a bridegroom of blood to me!' So he {YHWH} let him alone. It was then she said, 'A bridegroom of blood by circumcision.'" {Exodus 4:24-26—J-source}. This circumcision of Moses' son by Zipporah becomes an enigmatic moment in Exodus. A son who is circumcised was often called 'bridegroom of blood' in Semitic tribes. The Hebrew word for father-in-law is "one who circumcises." {Exodus 18:2-6—E-source} In a later incident, both sons of Moses are reintroduced: Gershom and Eliezer (El "my God," ezer "help").

The clear implication here is that Zipporah saved Moses' life by circumcising her son and symbolically circumcising Moses in order to deceive and ward off the wrath of YHWH. Moses had entered into marriage without himself having been circumcised![28]

The next reference to circumcision in Exodus concerns the flight from Egypt. After the Israelites arrived in Succoth, following the Passover sacrifice, which exempted them from the Tenth Plague, the killing of all the first-born of the Egyptians, YHWH gives directions to Moses and Aaron for all subsequent commemorations of the Passover. These require strict observance of the circumcision ritual for all male members of the household, including slaves and resident aliens. {Exodus 12:43-49—P-source}.

The act of circumcision was a typical Yahwist/Shasu tribespeople rite. Too, it was the practice among the royalty of Egypt, but not a Canaanite, nor probably, an Habiru ritual. The contemporary Arabic tradition, of descent from Abraham and Hagar, Abraham's Egyptian slave/wife, through their son Ishmael, continues the ritual of circumcision at age thirteen. This was the age of Ishmael when Abraham and his entire male household underwent the rite at the covenant agreement with God. We have here a "P"-source story added to Genesis, much later in time, c.500 BCE. {Genesis 17—P-source}.

The earliest historical reference to circumcision in the Hebrew Bible occurs in {Genesis 34—J-source}. Here the brothers Simeon and Levi, full brothers of Dinah, from their mother Leah and Jacob/Israel, avenge the rape of their sister by the scion and namesake of the town of Shechem. They kill all the males of the town, still incapacitated from the mass circumcision to which they had agreed, to allow for the marriage of Dinah to Shechem. All the sons of Jacob had beforehand been circumcised. Recall that the "J" source comes from Judah, in the south of Israel.

Moses ostensibly came from a Levite family, and should have been circumcised eight days after his birth. His family did hide him for three months. {Exodus 2:2—J-source} If not a Levite, then the Egyptian tradition of circumcision should have been applicable, circumcision at adolescence, well before the marriageable age. Apparently none of these options took place.

One more possibility is that Moses lived with his family of Levites in the Delta, the place of origin of the largely Indo-European, Asiatic rulers of Egypt, c.1650-1550 BCE. Seti I, and Rameses II, Pharaohs of the 19th Dynasty, brought the capital back to the Delta and "Habiru slaves" built their new cities. Rameses erected a great monument to the Asiatic deity Seth, probably in commemoration of his own family's Hyksos origins. Moses may have been a contemporary, c.1250 BCE. Why not Moses, as a member of this Hyksos commemorating royal family, all uncircumcised?

In the beginning of Exodus, the term "river" is used to describe the a) order of Pharaoh to throw all the "boy" children of the Hebrews into the river, {Exodus 1:22—J-source}, and b) where the daughter of Pharaoh came down to bathe and discovers the basket with Moses. {Exodus 2:3-6—J-source}. Presumably the river is the Nile. This would violate the earlier established context of the enslavement of the Hebrews in the supply cities Pithom and Rameses in the Delta. {Exodus 1:11—P-source}. The significance of this seeming deviation from consistency is as follows.

The Deuteronomist Historian, author of Judges, describes Joshua's arrival west of the Jordan at Gilgal, just north of Jericho. YHWH requires Joshua to make flint knives and circumcise all the Israelite men. The explanation in Judges is that the rite had been lost, that the people, "not having listened to the voice of YHWH," their newborn, en route to the promised land, while wandering in the wilderness, had not been subject to circumcision as had all those who celebrated the first Passover at Succoth. "And YHWH said unto Joshua, This day have I rolled away the reproach of Egypt from you." {Joshua 5:2-9}. The implication here is that while the Egyptians had practiced circumcision, the Hebrews had not, and thus earned for themselves the derision of the ruling classes.[29]

The apparent answer to our question about the origin of Moses would be that he truly descended from the ordinary "rabble" of Habiru (northern Indo-European/Semites) enlisted for the Egyptian corvée. Yet, consider his nurturing within the Pharaonic Egyptian household, that he was held in such high esteem by the Egyptians, {Exodus 11:3—J-source}, being able to confront Pharaoh himself despite, "I am slow of speech and slow of tongue" {Exodus 4:10—J-source} and, "…how then shall Pharaoh hear me who am of uncircumcised lips." {Exodus 6:12,30—E-source}.[30] Also, {Exodus 6:12, 30—P-source}.[31] All this, despite not having been circumcised until Midian.

Another possibility takes us back to the ruling Pharaonic class in the Delta at that time, Dynasty 19, 1275-1200 BCE, including Rameses II, whose ancestors were the Asiatic Hyksos and who built the cities of Pithom and Rameses. His successors were Merneptah, then the 20th Dynasty Pharaohs (1200-1150 BCE) who returned to the Nile and the capital at Thebes, *e.g.,* Rameses III. These latter were of more immediate Asiatic stock. In some way connected to Asiatic traditions, they might have themselves temporarily abandoned the Egyptian circumcision ritual.

YHWH anoints Moses as the prophet of the Israelites, "his" chosen people, redeemed from a life of slavery, but now "enslaved" to the covenantal obligations that Moses will transmit from YHWH. {Leviticus 25:42, 55—P-source}.[32]

An Egyptian, but not an Egyptian, born to privilege, a Levite with a Pharaonic education, hesitant, inhibited, unaware of his potential power, yet quickly, under the persuasions of a higher force, accepting his natural role of prophet and leader. There well could have been an ancient Egyptian underpinning to this entirely new dimension in the experience of the Hebrews, the recreation of YHWH's Covenant with Noah, Abraham, and their descendants. Now, there existed a deeply moral and philosophical sense of community and ethnicity, the law.

Egyptian Heritage: Akhenaton

There were prophets in the historical record of Egypt before Moses. Before 2000 BCE, Ipu-Wer was denouncing evil in Egypt. Nefer-Rohu is said to have foretold punishment and restoration, c.1800 BCE. Prophets in ecstasy, with music, shrieked out their vision in verse, as genuine mouthpieces of the gods. Later in the Yahwist tradition—a nabi, "a person who speaks for {God}," roeh, "same."[33]

About c.2400 BCE, Ptahhotep, 5th Dynasty Vizier, wrote an ethical treatise based on proverbial sayings—how to obtain the good life. As late as 1250 BCE, the "Instruction of Amenmopet" reflects a father giving counsel to his son. Amenmopet advises the son about integrity, honesty, kindliness, and self-control—610 pieces of wisdom. In the Bible, Book of Proverbs, are thirty sayings that echo the thirty chapters of Amenmopet. In Babylonia, the "Poem of the Righteous Sufferer," originally traced to the fifteenth century BCE, is a precursor of the Book of Job. Again, earlier than the Book of Job, we read a Babylonian "Dialogue about Human Misery," c.1000 BCE. Such themes are also found in the literature of the coastal city of Ugarit.[34]

The Pharaoh Akehnaton created an intellectual/religious revolution in Egypt. His father, Amenhotep III, himself a religious experimenter, ruled from 1390 BCE; Akehnaton came to the throne in 1352 BCE and ruled until his death in 1337 BCE. Tutankhaton, son-in-law of Akhenaton, was forced by the then-renewed priesthood to change his name to Tutankhamon. He ruled for nine years, 1336-1327 BCE.

Akhenaton is important for an understanding of the formation of the Jews and Monotheism. Even if one pleads agnosticism concerning Moses' relationship to Egypt, it is clear that a religious revolution was being anticipated by Akhenaton's father, Amenhotep III when he placed the sun god Aton as more important in worship by the Theban priestly class than the worship of Ammon. This constituted an attempt to bring back the tradition of the Sun temple at Heliopolis (On), and elevate to preeminence the role of Maat, the goddess of truth, order, and justice, daughter of the sun god, Re, (the god in human form). The more ancient name of this god, Aton, or Atum, was specially revived by Akhenaton, to be reintroduced less than one hundred years later in the days of Rameses II, c.1270 BCE.

But now the revival by Akhenaton was in the form of a worship of a principle higher than the mere material good that the sun gave to the universe. This exclusive god, this ultimate deity, "was the force by which the Sun made itself felt on earth." Interestingly, in the Tel-el Amarna (Akhetaton) inscriptions are references to "Elohim," the Canaanite expression of God, here used to refer to the Egyptian Pharaoh.[35]

Akhenaton's move of the capitol, and the seat of the new religion, to Tel Amarna, (Akhetaton) north of Thebes, was followed by his savage attempt to extirpate the power of the Egyptian priesthood, and its theological and material influence. The first century

CE Roman writer, Juvenal, reports that the then-priesthood of the god Amon in Thebes, in his own day, still owned, and under benign Roman rule, a tenth of the land of Egypt. Over 90,000 men worked the 433 gardens, 46 workshops, 83 ships; then dominated 65 towns and their lands. The priests owned 400,000 beasts.[36] On Akhenaton's orders, temples were closed, services forbidden. "Ahkenaton flung all these formulas {magic spells} into the fire. Djins, bogies, spirits, monsters, demigods, and Osiris himself with all his court, were swept into the blaze and reduced to ashes."[37] And while iconography reveals Akhenaton and his queen Nefertiti to be under the suasion of the sun and the god, "by a round disk from which emanate rays terminating in human hands," no graven images were permitted.[38] Hugh Thomas affirms that Akhenaton banned the making of all animal deities and destroyed those that did exist.[39]

The "Hymn To The Aton, "supposedly written by Akhenaton to reflect his spiritual commitment to the abstract power of one supreme deity, has long been compared to Psalm 104 in the Hebrew Bible, believed to have been written some 800 years later.[40]

Hymn To The Aton:… "All beasts are content with their pasturage; Trees and plants are flourishing. The birds which fly from their nests, Their wings are stretched to thy *ka*, All beasts spring upon their feet. Whatever flies and alights, They live when thou hast arisen for them. The ships are sailing north and south as well, For every way is open at thy appearance. The fish in the river dart before thy face; Thy rays are in the midst of the great green sea…How manifold it is, what thou hast made! They are hidden from the face of man. O sole god, like whom there is no other! Thou didst create the world according to thy desire, While thou wert alone: All men, cattle, and wild beasts, Whatever is on earth, going upon its feet, And what is on high, flying with its wings."[41]

Psalm 104:10: "He sendeth the springs into the valley, which run among the hills."…Psalm 104:11: "They give drink to every beast of the field: the wild asses quench their thirst."…Psalm 104:12: "By them shall the fowls of the heaven have their habitation, which sing among the branches."…Psalm 104:13: "He watereth the hills from his chambers: the earth is satisfied with the fruit of thy works."…Psalm 104:14: "He causeth the grass to grow for the cattle, and herb for the service of man: that he may bring forth food out of the earth;"…Psalm 104:15: "And wine that maketh glad the heart of man, and oil to make his face to shine, and bread which strengtheneth man's heart."…Psalm 104:21: "The young lions roar after their prey, and seek their meat from God."…Psalm 104:22: "The sun ariseth, they gather themselves together, and lay them down in their dens."…Psalm 104:25: "So is this great and wide sea, wherein are things creeping innumerable, both small and great beasts."...Psalm 104:26: "There go the ships: there is that leviathan, whom thou hast made to play therein."[42]

Son-in law Tutankhamon died c.1327 BCE, being buried with extraordinary luxury of display, symbolic perhaps of the reinstatement of the power and wealth of the Theban priesthood. The death of Tutankhamon officially reestablished this priestly priority during a period of political chaos, perhaps reflected in the probable rule (the record is unclear) of the military usurper Hurmahil, who had married one of Nefertiti's sisters, Mutnedjmet.[43] Then began the literal destruction of the new capital of Akhetaton (el-Amarna), thus doing to Akhenaton what Akhenaton had done to the priests. All evidence of Akhenaton's religion and his kingship was effaced. But *not* the memory of this Pharaoh's vision by his followers.

Is it not ironic that one of the two cities where the Hebrews were engaged in forced labor, "Pithom," is named, persuasively by Rameses II, c.1270 BCE, after the sun god, "Per-Atum," "House of Atum."[44] As with Rameses II, given his probable Hyksos origins, his commitment to an ancient Egyptian Delta tradition, the worship of the Asiatic god, Seth, here memorialized in Tanis (Per-Rameses), the other Delta area city of forced labor, there could have existed other heretical memories reverberating within the world of the Delta. The Delta could have harbored followers of Akhenaton and the one god Aton. After all, it was less than seventy years since this tradition had ended. Between the first deportation of Israelites from Jerusalem and the returns was about fifty-eight years, 597-539 BCE. And they remembered.

The intellectual power of a monotheistic vision of the universe and man's moral position in it has been attested to by history. What it needs to fix itself in the minds and hearts of humans is the proper leadership and a timely historical setting. For a brief moment, this occurred in Egypt. However, the ever slow moving rhythms of the Nile, and the evanescent significance of one human's creative thought, had made heresy impossible to thrive, in Egypt.

By taking a motley crowd of rejects out of this rigid and rooted milieu, and guiding them upon a journey into the wilderness, only the inspired vision of a Moses could have hoped to recreate the passion of commitment to a higher moral law and the one God in whom it was represented. Moses sensed, as few in human history have intuited, how deeply needed was such a covenant/testimony (*berith/eduth*). If established, the discipline of a law of human behavior could be made to penetrate to the deepest stratum of the human heart and mind. It could find its rational and metaphysical roots in the all-encompassing vision of a supreme and jealous moral deity.

The Struggle for Nationhood

The great mysteries of Exodus and Numbers begin only after the flight from Egypt is accomplished. Indeed, the tales of the plagues and the parting of the waters were wondrous and magical. What, in the memory of the participants in this flight or ejection was suppressed in the telling to those generations descended from these refugees? What fascinating stories of life lived at the edge of survival in the ancient world stimulated the artistic symmetry that we now find in this poetic separation from Egypt?

Even greater questions arise regarding the establishment of the Israelites in the wilderness, the attempt to create a nation out of this disparate horde. It is now evident to the scholarly community that the rather clear-cut layers of sources J, E, and P, which contributed to Exodus up to the Israelites' arrival at the wilderness of Sin, can no longer be deciphered so easily. {Exodus 17: J and E-sources}. For now we read about a suddenly aging and wearied Moses being aided in holding up his arms to the "highest" in order to defeat Amalek, as prelude to the ascent of Sinai and the hearing of the "Ten Commandments," the Decalogue. {Exodus 17:12—E-source}.

More than anything else, the various authors of Exodus, Leviticus, Numbers, and Deuteronomy are wrestling with the meaning of Moses' unique imprint. As we attempt to understand the various Books of the Pentateuch dealing with the Mosaic experience, it is clear that not merely Moses and his unique historicity—meaning his break with traditional mid-Eastern life patterns—now comes under scrutiny. But added into the Pentateuchal mix are the then-contemporary realities of Israelite social and political life. These Solomonic or Judaic/Israelite monarchical experiences are being injected ex-post-facto onto this magisterial, often ominous tale.

It is a contradictory and redundant story. The distinct source layers become blurred by rearrangements, untold editing and redacting, as well as seemingly ever more historical additions to the original J and E rendering, c.950-850 BCE. This is added to an already long tradition of oral and written memories. The two early and most distinctive versions of the "Ten Commandments" that in {Exodus 20: 1-17—J and E, ++} and in {Exodus 34:12-26—J and E, ++} are from disparate strands of Israelite history, perhaps echoing fragments of the past.

There seems to be an overriding concern in the second half of the Book of Exodus and in virtually the entire Book of Numbers to go beyond saga. This part of the story of the Exodus also contains priestly material of a more recent historical authorship. Bound together with the older "epic" material of the J and E source time frame, is an almost desperate commitment to create a unique and holy people, under the laws of YHWH.[45] It should be reiterated that Leviticus was completely formulated by the "P" source, partially from the time of King Hezekiah of Judah, c.720 BCE, and mostly from the time of the exile and return, c.586-450 BCE. Deuteronomy, is, of course, a product of the Deuteronomist Historian, in the days of King Josiah of Judah, c.630 BCE.

YHWH: "Thus you shall say to the house of Jacob. And tell the Israelites: You have seen what I did to the Egyptians, and how I bore you on eagles' wings and brought you to myself. Now therefore, if you obey my voice and keep my covenant, you shall be my treasured possession out of all the peoples. Indeed, the whole earth is mine, but you shall be to me a priestly kingdom and a holy nation. These are the words that you shall speak to the Israelites." {Exodus 19:3-6—E and J++ composite source}.[46]

But they are an intransigent lot, the Israelites who are being guided by Moses out of slavery, first in indentured servitude to the Pharaoh's corvée, now toward freedom and a land of milk and honey, promised them by their forefathers. Oddly, it is often those who are closest to Moses who turn out to be turncoats, reverting to the old primeval ways, even after being taught the laws of YHWH.

We have noted above the famous and inexplicable story of the "golden calf," and Aaron's handiwork in creating this apostasy. The sons of Levi were here formed as a military force to kill three thousand Israelites, who may have committed even more terrible actions than to worship "gods of gold." {Exodus 32:25-29, 32—J and E ++}. Long before, Levi and Simeon were the bloody avengers of the rape of their sister, Dinah. {Genesis 34: 25-31—J-source}. We also recall the last words of Jacob regarding his sons Simeon and Levi: "Simeon and Levi are brothers; weapons of violence are their swords. May I never come into their council; may I not be joined to their company—for in their anger they kill men, and in their whim they hamstrung oxen. Cursed be their anger for it is fierce, and their wrath, for it is cruel! I will divide them in Jacob and scatter them in Israel." {Genesis 49:5-7; J or ancient documents}.

Despite their heroic suppression of the insurrection in the "golden calf" incident, the sons of Levi are involved in a treachery against Moses. The entire journey across the wilderness, as they move toward the oasis of Kadesh Barnea, is characterized by one revolt after another against Moses, the lament always being '…why did you take us out of the plenty that was Egypt into the wilderness of hardship, war, and an unknown future?' The revolt of Korah, a Levite leader, and Dathan, and Abiram, leaders of the Reubenites, and pretender holy people, is an example. The latter two address Moses: "Is it too little that you have brought us up out of a land flowing with milk and honey to kill us in the wilderness, that you must also lord it over us?" {Numbers 16:14—P}. The result is that YHWH kills two hundred fifty pretender leaders and their wives and children, as the earth opens and they descend into Sheol. {Numbers 16:1-40—J and P}. Again, in {Numbers 26:10-11—P-source}, the children of Korah, the Levite, do not die. The next day a new revolt by the whole congregation occurs, and YHWH sets a plague upon them in which fourteen thousand seven hundred additional Israelites die, {Numbers 16:41-50—P-source}, and Aaron saved the rest.

In another incident, the scouts Joshua and Caleb are sent out from Kadesh (here Caleb is called "of the tribe of Judah." {Numbers 13:6—P-source}. He is later to be called a Kenizzite. {Numbers 32:12—P-source; Joshua 14:6, 14}. Hoshea is here renamed Joshua, a northerner from the tribe of Ephraim. {Numbers 13:8—P-source}. His inclusion in this tale of scouting and bravery is a later "P" insertion.[47] The report of Joshua and Caleb about the giants that await the Israelites sets off another revolt. The congregation rises up, 'back to Egypt.' {Numbers 14: 1-10—J- and P-source}. They threaten to stone Moses and Aaron, even though Moses and Aaron fall on their faces in front of the entire assembly. {Numbers 14:5-10—P-source}. The LORD threatens the congregation with pestilence and disinheritance, and cries out: "How long shall this wicked congregation complain against me?" {Numbers 14:27—P-source}.

An additional challenge to Moses, from his very own family, is related in the story of the Baal of Peor. {Numbers 25:1-5—J-source; Numbers 25:6-19—P-source}. Here the Israelites are encamped at Shittim (Acacias), presumably on the plain of Moab, across the Jordan from Jericho. They are in close proximity to the Moabites/Midianites. {J and P –sources}. The Israelite men began to have sexual relationships with the other women, attend to their sacrifices, and "bowed down to their gods." {Numbers 25:2—J-source}. A Simeonite, Zimri, brought one of these women, here a Midianite, Cozbi, daughter of a clan chieftain, back to his family (presumably as a wife), but in full sight of Moses and the entire congregation, who at that time were in the midst of a plague. Phinehas, grandson of Aaron, took a spear, went into the Simeonite tent and pierced the two of them, the woman through the belly. Apparently they were in sexual congress.

Moses did not utter a word, presumably because he himself had married a Midianite woman, the daughter of Jethro. This story historically constitutes a later "P" aspersion on the figure of Moses. It purports to benefit the Aaronite priesthood. YHWH here grants the Aaronites "a covenant of perpetual priesthood." Though twenty-four thousand Israelites died of the plague, through the murderous but cleansing act by a scion of Aaron, the plague was miraculously brought to a halt by YHWH.

Perhaps the most famous of the revolts against the rule of Moses, and thus presumably against the laws of YHWH, who communicates to the Israelites through Moses, is that of sister Miriam and Aaron himself. Miriam, she who had saved her brother by ensuring a Pharaonic rescue. {Exodus 2:1-10—J-source}. Miriam, after Moses' song of triumph, {Exodus 15—J+ Earlier-source} sang and danced with tambourine about the miraculous victory of the Israelites against the Egyptians: "Sing to the LORD, for he has triumphed gloriously; horse and rider he has thrown into the sea." {Exodus 15: 20-21— E-source; also see Exodus 18:13-27—E-source}.[48] Miriam and Aaron now, if belatedly, protest against the "Cushite" (Midianite) woman he has married, but also: "Has the LORD spoken only through Moses? Has he not spoken through us also?" {Numbers 12:2—E-source}. "Now the man Moses was very humble, more so than anyone else on the face of the earth." {Numbers 12:3—E-source}. "And the anger of the LORD was kindled against them, and he departed." {Numbers 12:9—E-source}. "Miriam had become leprous, as white as snow." {Numbers 12: 10—E-source}. Aaron begs forgiveness for his sin, Miriam is returned to the camp in seven days. {Numbers 12 1-16—E-source}. Aaron is untouched by YHWH, despite this assault on "His" authority through Moses.

There is another side to the position of Moses in the eyes of the LORD and the people. This is in the role and vision of Moses held by outsiders. First there is the encounter of Moses with the seven daughters of Reuel ("shepherd," "friend of God," also called Jethro), the priest of Midian, at the well in the wilderness. In return for allowing the daughters to draw water into the troughs against the harassment of the shepherds, Moses, as an Egyptian, is invited to their home. Eventually, Jethro gives him one of his daughters in marriage, Zipporah. {Exodus 2:22—J-source}. Zipporah in turn saves Moses' life from an avenging YHWH, when she circumcises their son Gershom and touches Moses' uncircumcised genitals, saying: "A bridegroom of blood by circumcision." {Exodus 4:24-26—J-source}.

Jethro (Reuel) later visits Moses in the wilderness, taking with him Moses' wife and their two children. {Exodus 18: 1-27—E-source}. After a warm reunion, including the giving of burnt offerings and sacrifices to God in the presence of Aaron and the elders, Jethro observes Moses giving advice and judging the people by himself. "What you are doing is not good. You will surely wear yourself out, both you and these people with you. For the task is too heavy for you; you cannot do it alone…. You should represent the people before God and you should bring their cases before God; teach them the statutes and instruction and make known to them the way they are to go and the things they are to do." {Exodus 18: 17-20—E-source}. Jethro counsels Moses to find trustworthy judges so that Moses would hear the important cases only. "Then Moses let his father-in-law depart and he went off to his own country." {Exodus 18:21—E-source}.

In Numbers, Hobab, son-in-law of Reuel, appears in the encampment as the Israelites are about to set out from Sinai. Moses says to him: "…come with us and we will treat you well." Hobab hesitates: "I will go back to my land and to my kindred." He did not. "So they set out from the mount of the LORD…" {Numbers 10:29-33—J-source}.[49]

Caleb is above mentioned as a member of the tribe of Judah. {Numbers 13:6—P-source}. Later, and usually, he is said to be a Kenizzite. {Numbers 32:12—P-source; Joshua 14:6, 14—DH-source}. Commissioned to spy on the Canaanites for Moses, he is singled out by Moses for his heroism and steadfastness: "But my servant Caleb, because he has a different spirit, and has followed me wholeheartedly, I will bring him into the land into which he went, and his descendants shall possess it." {Numbers 14:24—J-source}. Indeed, this was the case, the Calebites probably uniting with Judah.

In Judges 4 and 5, a Kenite woman, whose husband, allied with the Canaanites, was a descendant of the above Hobab, son-in-law of Jethro/Reuel, treacherously kills the Indo-European Canaanite leader Sisera to advance the cause of the Israelite tribal alliance. Her action, under the spirit of YHWH, reflected more faithfully her allegiance to the alliance than did a number of the non-participating Israelite tribes. (See Chapter 4.)

This image of unfaithfulness and weak-hearted support of Moses, as contrasted to the assistance of the outsider, is not complete. Another revolt, and Moses is desperate with frustration and anguish. {Numbers 11:1-3—E-source}. Moses calls out to the LORD, "Why have treated your servant so badly? Why have I not found favor in your sight, that you lay the burden of the people on me? Did I conceive all this people? Did I give birth to them, that you should say to me 'Carry them in your bosom as a nurse carries a suckling child to the land that you promised on oath to their ancestors?'" {Numbers 11:11-12—E-source}. The LORD proposes that he bring seventy elders, "...and I will take some of the spirit that is on you and put it on them; and they shall bear the burden of the people along with you so that you will not bear it all by yourself." {Numbers 11:17—E-source}. The seventy elders gathered themselves outside the tent, and when the spirit rested upon them they prophesied. {Numbers 11:16-30—E-source}. Two elders, Eldad and Medad, stayed in camp to prophesy. Moses was informed that they stayed in camp to prophesy by themselves . On hearing this, Joshua said to Moses: "My lord Moses, stop them! But Moses said to him…Would that all the LORD's people were prophets, and that the LORD would put his spirit on them." {Numbers 11:28-29—E-source}.

To Canaan's Border

For over a century now, researchers have been in agreement that the several ascents to Mt. Sinai/Horab to hear and create the tablets of the Ten Commandments were later additions to the original historical narrative. Both Jebel Musa, (Mt. Sinai) in the south of the peninsula, and Quayyah, in northwestern Arabia seem to be long detours, both in the context of the Biblical narrative, and in terms of the practicalities of the Israelite journey. Although an ancient bronze serpent has been found in one of the encampments excavated in this area, few would agree to the latter itinerary.[50] Whether the mountain of God is known as Horeb {E and D-source} or Sinai {J and P-source}, else from the direction of Mt. Seir or Mt. Paran {Judges 5; Deut.1:2; 32:2}, it is clear that the settlement at Kadesh Barnea, about fifty miles southwest of Beersheba, was where the Israelites long resided, for their cattle and their crops. {Exod. 17:3; 24:5; 34:3; Numbers 20:19}. It was here that the Decalogue was truly revealed and enunciated to the recalcitrant Israelites.[51]

There are several traditions of migration to the borders of Canaan from Kadesh Barnea. The most well-known is toward the south and east in a detour that is thus explained: "God did not lead them by way of the land of the Philistines, although that was nearer; for God thought, 'If the people face war, they may change their minds and return to Egypt' So God led the people by the roundabout way of the wilderness toward the Sea of Reeds." {Exodus 13:17-19—E-source}. Here on the borders of Edom, at the top of Mt Hor, Aaron dies, and his son Eleazar inherits his priestly vestments. {Numbers 20:22-29—J-source}. They thence travel around Edom toward Ezion-Geber (Elath) and up toward the plains of Moab, east of the Jordan and just north of the Dead Sea at Mt. Nebo and Mt. Pisgah, opposite Jericho. {Judges 11:16}.

Moses also commands the people that when they cross the Jordan they are to assemble on Mt Ebal and Mt. Gerizim, both to the northeast in what is the land of Ephraim, of Jacob/Israel, Joseph, and Joshua, there to build altars and make appropriate sacrifices. Indeed, this is where an early document places Joshua, as he renews the covenant of Moses, and, again, before he dies, calls together the tribes of Israel for a final covenantal meeting where they renew their dedication to the Law that Moses had received from YHWH. {Joshua 8: 30-35; 24—DH-1}.

A more southerly route directly into Canaan had already been espied by Caleb and Joshua, including the land of the Anakites, descendants of giants {Numbers 13:21-24— E- and P-sources}. Caleb and Othniel, his nephew, the latter to be a "Kenite" judge of Israel, are given this land in the Negeb, and around Hebron by Joshua. {Joshua 15:13-19; Judges 1:12-15; Judges 3:7-11}. The tribe of Judah is placed further south in Beersheba. And, of course, the first struggles by Joshua against the indigenous peoples takes place in the south.[52] The implication, which harmonizes with archaeological data, is that the highlands of Ephraim were then sparsely populated, as Hamor of Shechem had told Jacob in his invitation to settle there. {Genesis 34; 33:18—J-source}.[53]

The other tradition also describes the arrival from the wilderness east of Jericho and then, later in time, west of the Jordan, at Gilgal, where Joshua has all the male Israelites circumcised before their assault on the Canaanite cities. Moses had been able to establish his people east of the Jordan with a series of victories over the Amorite kings, Sihon of Heshbon and Og of Bashan, "…utterly destroying men, women and children. But all the livestock and the plunder of the towns we kept as spoil for ourselves. {Deuteronomy 3:6-7}.

Moses: "'Oh Lord GOD…Let me cross over to see the good land beyond the Jordan, that good hill country and the Lebanon' But the LORD was angry with me on your account and would not heed me. The LORD said to me, 'Enough from you! Never speak to me of this matter again.'" {Deut. 3:23-26}. YHWH has decreed to Moses: "You shall not cross over this Jordan." {Deut. 30:15-20}. YHWH: "'Ascend this mountain of the Abarim, Mt Nebo, which is in the land of Moab, across from Jericho, and view the land of Canaan, which I am giving to the Israelites as a possession; you shall die there on the mountain that you ascend and shall be gathered to your kin, as your brother Aaron died on Mt. Hor and was gathered to his kin; because both of you broke faith with me among the Israelites at the waters of Meribath-kadesh [Kadesh-Barnea] in the wilderness of Zin, by failing to maintain my holiness among the Israelites. Although you may view the land from a distance, you shall not enter it—the land that I am giving to the Israelites." {Deuteronomy 32: 49-52}.

Here Moses dies, and is buried in a valley opposite Beth-peor, in the land of Moab, "…but no one knows his burial place to this day." {Deuteronomy 34:6}.

The Deuteronomic Historian, from a perspective at least six hundred years into the future, pens this final epitaph to the deliverer of Israel's destiny: "Never since has there arisen a prophet in Israel like Moses, whom the LORD knew face to face. He was unequaled for all the signs and wonders that the LORD sent him to perform in the land of Egypt against Pharaoh and all his servants and his entire land, and for all the mighty deeds and terrifying displays of power that Moses performed in the sight of all Israel" {Deut. 34:10-12}.

Endnotes, Chapter 5

[1] Wellhausen, J. 1957. *Prolegomena to the History of Ancient Israel*, N.Y.: Meridian.

[2] Friedman, R. E. 1987/1997. *Who Wrote the Bible?*, N.Y.: The Free Press, p. 246

[3] Ibid.

[4] Cook, Stanley Arthur, "The Exodus," *Encyclopedia Britannica*, 11th ed., Vol. 10, N.Y.: Cambridge Univ. Press, pp. 77-79.

[5] Papyrus Brooklyn 35, 1446, cited in Shanks, Hershel, ed. 1999. *Ancient Israel*, Washington, D.C.: Biblical Archaeological Society, Note 9, p. 304; Nahum Sarna/Hershel Shanks, "Israel in Egypt," in Shanks, *op. cit.*, p. 39.

[6] Johnson, Paul. 1987. *A History of the Jews*, N.Y.: Harper and Bros., p. 24.

[7] Sarna/Shanks, "Israel in Egypt," in Shanks, ed., *Ancient Israel, op. cit.*, Note 30, p. 305; p. 43.

[8] McCarter, P. Kyle, Jr., "The Patriarchal Age," in Shanks, ed., *op. cit.*, p. 30; Pritchard, J. B., ed. 1958. *The Ancient Near East*, 3 vols., Princeton, N.J.: Princeton Univ. Press, Vol. 1, pp. 183-184.

[9] Papyrus Anastasi VI, quoted from Pritchard, James. 1969. *The Ancient Near East in Pictures Relating to the Old Testament*, 3rd. ed., Princeton, N.J.: Princeton Univ. Press, p. 259; also cited by Weinfeld, Moshe, in Seltzer, Robert M., ed. 1989. *Judaism, A People and Its History*, N.Y.: Macmillan, p. 42.

[10] Pritchard, James. 1969. *Ancient Near East in Pictures, op. cit.*, p. 259; Sarna/Shanks, "Israel in Egypt," in Shanks, ed., *Ancient Israel, op. cit.*, p. 39.

[11] Johnson, Paul, *A History of the Jews, op. cit.*, p. 24.

[12] Weinfeld, Moshe, in Seltzer, Robert M., ed., *op. cit.*, pp. 44-45.

[13] Greenstein, Edward L. 1993. *The Harper/Collins Study Bible*, New Standard Edition, London: Harper/Collins Publishers, Notes, p. 99.

[14] *Harper/Collins Study Bible, op. cit.*

[15] Leiden Papyrus 348, Nahum Sarna/Hershel Shanks, "Israel in Egypt," cited in Shanks, ed., *Ancient Israel, op. cit.*, p. 43; Johnson, Paul, A *History of the Jews op. cit.*, p. 25.

[16] Gottwald, N. K. 1985. *The Hebrew Bible, A Socio-Literary Introduction*, Philadelphia: Fortress Press, p. 224.

[17] Gottwald, N. K., Ibid., p. 182—J-source; Friedman, R. E., *op. cit.*, p. 250—E-source.

[18] Gottwald, N. K., Ibid.; Friedman, R. E., *op. cit.*

[19] Stenning, John Frederick, "Exodus," *Encycl.Brit., op. cit.*, pp. 73-77, E-source; Gottwald, N. K., Ibid; Friedman, R. E., Ibid.

[20] Gottwald, Ibid.; Friedman, R. E., Ibid.

[21] Grant, Michael A. 1984. *History of Ancient Israel,* N.Y.: Charles Scribner, p. 132; Gottwald, N. K., *op. cit.*, p. 199.

[22] Gottwald, N. K., *op. cit.*, pp. 202-203; Milgrim, Jacob, in *Harper/Collins Study Bible, op. cit.*, pp. 151-153.

[23] Friedman, R. E., *op. cit.*,—E-source; Gottwald, N. K., *op. cit.*,—J-source.

[24] *Harper/ Collin Study Bible, op. cit.*, Translation.

[25] King James Translation.

[26] Cook, Stanley Arthur, "Moses," *Encycl. Brit., op. cit.*, 11th ed., Vol. 18, pp. 895-896; Cook, Stanley Arthur, "Aaron," *Encycl. Brit., op. cit .*, 11th ed., Vol. 1, p. 4.

[27] Greenstein, Edward L. in *HarperCollins Study Bible, op. cit.*, Notes, p. 81.

[28] Abrahams, Israel. 1910. "Circumcision," *Encycl. Brit., op. cit.*, 11th ed., Vol. VI, pp. 389-390; Gottwald, N. K., *op. cit.*, p. 218.

[29] Abrahams, Israel, "Circumcision," *op. cit.*

[30] Friedman, R. E., *op. cit.*, p. 250.

[31] Gottwald, N. K., *op. cit.*, p. 185.

[32] Greenstein, E. L., in *Harper/Collins Study Bible, op. cit.*, p. 77.

[33] Grant, M. A., *History of Ancient Israel, op. cit.*, p. 71.

[34] Ibid., pp. 93-94.

[35] Whitehouse, Owen Charles, "Hebrew Religion," *Encycl. Brit., op. cit.*, p. 177.

[36] Quoted in Thomas, Hugh. 1979. *A History of the World*, N.Y.: Harper and Row, p. 132.

[37] Weigall, A. 1923. *The Life and Times of Akhenaton*, N.Y.: Putnam, p. 121.

[38] Freud, S. 1939. *Moses and Monotheism*, N.Y.: Knopf, p. 33.

[39] Thomas, H., *A History of the World, op. cit.*, p. 133.

[40] Breasted, J. H. 1905. *History of Egypt*, N.Y.: Scribner, p. 360; Stager, Lawrence E., in Coogan, Michael D., ed. 1998. *The Oxford History of the Biblical World*, N.Y: Oxford Univ. Press, p. 148.

[41] Pritchard, J.B. 1969 *The Ancient Near East, op. cit.*, Vol. 1, pp. 228-229, tr. John A. Wilson.

[42] King James Version.

[43] Darlington, C. D. 1969. *The Evolution of Man and Society*, London: George Allen and Unwin, p. 119.

[44] Greenstein, E. L. "Introduction to Exodus," in *Harper/Collins Study Bible op. cit.*, pp. 77-78.

[45] Hackett, Jo Ann, "Introduction to Numbers," in *Harper/Collins Study Bible, op. cit.*, pp. 199-200.

[46] Friedman, R. E., *op. cit.*, p. 150—E-source; Gottwald, N. K., *op. cit.*, p. 184—composite.

[47] Hackett, Jo Ann, in *Harper/Collins Study Bible, op. cit.*, Notes, p. 226.

[48] Isserlin, B. S. J. 1998. *The Israelites,* London: Thames and Hudson, Ltd., pp. 205-206; {Exodus 15} is perhaps the most ancient document in the Pentateuch.

[49] Gottwald, N. K., *op. cit.,* p. 200, sees this passage as a repeat of Jethro's family advice to Moses. {Exodus 18:13-27—E-source}. The two passages are thus not doublets.

[50] Stager, L. E., "Forging An Identity," in Coogan, M. D., ed., *op. cit.*, pp. 142-147. Stager argues in favor of the Arabian scenario.

[51] Gottwald, N. K., *op. cit.*, pp. 200-201; Cook, S. A., "Moses," *Encycl. Brit., op. cit.*, Vol. 18, pp. 895-896.

[52] Gottwald, N. K., Ibid., pp. 200-201; Cook, S. A., "Moses," Ibid.

[53] Sarna/Shanks, "Israel in Egypt," in Shanks, ed., *Ancient Israel, op. cit.*, p. 45; Stager, *op. cit.*, pp. 134-136.

6

The Law of Moses

A Teaching Is Preserved

The scenario of conquest and the division of Canaan by the tribes of Israel recounted in the Book of Joshua is today largely discounted by archaeologists and Biblical historians. More likely the gradual movement of the tribes into this land as told in the Book of Judges is closer to historical probability. The people who were guided and inspired by Moses to remain together during their flight from Egypt and the sojourn, mostly at the oasis of Kadesh Barnea, in all likelihood dribbled north, after the repudiation and death of Moses. Joshua, if he existed, was an Ephraimite, and probably moved into this relatively unpopulated highland to join other indigenous dwellers. In the south, the kin of Caleb, Rechab and Hobab, moved directly into the Negeb, toward Beersheba and Hebron. They were part of the so-called "amphycytony" that Norman Gottwald has described as the core of the alliance that later became Judah.[1] Even as these groups may have worshipped YHWH, they were not yet considered part of Israel. This is hinted at in the "Song of Deborah." {Judges 5}. The tribes of Judah, Benjamin, Simeon, as well as Manasseh struggled west of the Jordan from Gilgal to oust the resident peoples, but with only limited success. {Judges 1}. Jebus was not taken, and the grandson of Moses, said to have come from Bethlehem in the tribal area of Judah, wandered north to Ephraim and then Dan. {Judges 17:7; 18:30}.

During this process of gradual incursion and amalgamation, the teachings of Moses must little by little have made their mark among the literate priests of the various clans and tribes. The differentiation of these Yahwist peoples of the hills from peoples of the Baal-worshipping coastal and hill cities (Jebus/Jerusalem), older Semitic populations as well as Hittites/Sea-People and other Indo-Europeans, became sharper as population pressures gradually built up during the early Iron Age, c.1200-1100 BCE.[2] Also, as time went on, ever greater differentiation became evident between the areas that later became Judah, the more arid herding and oases ecologies of the south as compared to the mixed agricultural and cattle raising areas of the more fertile, forested, and wetter Ephraim and the north.

The traditions that were sequentially inspired by the Mosaic vision of Yahwism probably created a variety of interpreted variations of Moses' message. In the "J" traditions of the south, the older nomadic oases, herding and agricultural integration of Yahwism seems to have held steady. In the north, the geographical independence of the various tribal units seems for a time to have supported a variety of holy traditions in Shechem, Shiloh, Bethel, lately brought together in "E".

Two Decalogue expositions are found in the Book of Exodus: A) Exod. 20:2-17—E-source}; B) {Exod. 34:12-26—J-source}. These two covenants have been described as A): the ethical commandments {Exod. 20}, and B): the ritual commandments. {Exod. 34}. Further, it is thought that {Exod. 20} is a product of E, and {Exod. 34}, called the Yahwist Decalogue, the work of the J source. In {Deut. 5:6-21}, another version of the Decalogue is presented. Here Moses convenes the Israelites in order for YHWH to speak directly to them, "face to face." Deuteronomy is closer to {Exod. 20--E-source}, because here there is also an oral communication by YHWH, as it was then for Moses to hear, as he stood between the people and the LORD.

Deuteronomy is already a late document, c.600 BCE, when an established priesthood in Jerusalem was engaged not only in plumbing the historical heritage of Israel, but in purifying the ritualistic character of the faith. It is interesting that the Deuteronomists chose to emphasize a version of the "E" Decalogue, which all now believe to be the philosophically "purer" expression of the laws of YHWH, as given to Moses. For example, in {Exod. 20—E-source}, no mention is made of the tablets and the tempestuous events that anticipate {Exod. 34—J-source}.[3]

In {Exodus 34}, where on close examination twelve laws are enunciated, there is much ritual direction. Considering the ethical content, this seems to reflect an earlier stage in Israel's religious development. For example, there are explicit directives to not marry people having foreign gods; directions for celebrating the festivals of unleavened bread and weeks; how and in what quantity to give the first-born and the fruits of the ground to YHWH; exhortations "not boil a kid in its mother's milk." {Exod. 34: 26—J-source}. Then YHWH commands Moses: "Write these words; in accordance with these words I have made a covenant with you and with Israel. He was there with the LORD forty days and forty nights, he neither ate bread nor drank water. And he wrote on the tablets the words of the covenant, the ten *words* [commandments]." {Exodus 34:27-28—J-source}.

The nineteenth century German scholar Julius Wellhausen saw the {Exod. 20—E-source} Decalogue and the {Exod. 34—J-source} Decalogue as comparable to the eighth century BCE prophet, Amos' deep philosophical understanding of the faith as compared to Amos' contemporaries. Their religion lay solely in the observance of sacred feasts. If, as is clearly the case, the editors of the Book of Exodus, who joined "J" to "E" in building the Pentateuch, introduced {Exod. 34—J-source} from this other source concerning the story of the Exodus, now relating it to {Exodus 20—E-source}, then, Wellhausen opined, "the editor introduced the most serious internal contradiction found in the Old Testament."[4]

One additional and mysterious aspect of the "cutting and pasting" in which the many redactors engaged over the centuries, is seen in a crucial passage in Exodus. J. F. Stenning argued that the "E" writers used the term Elohim in {Exod. 19:9a, 10, 11a—E-source} to describe God's instructions to Moses to consecrate the people for the enunciation of the "Ten Commandments," as in {Exod. 20:2-17—E-source}. Then the "J" term, YHWH, was inserted. {Exod. 19:11b; 18; 20*f.*--J+-source}. Here, in a series of highly edited verses, not only is the older northern Israelite/Canaanite term Elohim, still in use in the redacted "E" Decalogue, but it also shows the "people" as being addressed as the congregation of Israel, rather than the Decalogue being directed to the priesthood, as in the "J" version.[5]

Power and Weakness

The brilliance and power in Moses' vision of the law of YHWH as it pertained to the people of Israel, lay both in historic opportunity, as well as heritage. Indeed, it is a common tradition in the lands between the two great river systems, the Tigris/Euphrates and the Nile, for a ruler to demand an agreement of suzerainty between himself, his nobility, and the people, in a sense, a *berith*, an agreement/covenant, what each shall do for the other in order to maintain the nation, the power, and the culture. It is not accidental that Moses, as part of his covenant with YHWH and the Israelites, promises the land of "milk and honey" as reward for the people's steadfastness in remaining true to the highest sovereign, YHWH. River valley kings, by contrast, used the covenant of allegiance to turn themselves into gods having unlimited power over the lives of the people, to the limits of acceptance and function by the commoners.

If the populace remained "stiff-necked" and were unwilling to fulfill their covenantal vows, then those in power, including a Moses, as in all ancient documents, would spew forth an avalanche of curses and punishments of the most terrible sort. Deuteronomy, speaking already from long Israelite and Judahite experience, is a constant reminder of the horrible deeds practiced by other and unholy nations. We here have many warnings as to what will befall the Israelite imitators of apostasy, and at the hands of YHWH. {Deut. 12:31; 18:9-11}. But there is a difference in the writings of the Hebrew Bible, and in the collective voice of Moses that issues down the ages. The warnings by YHWH do not pertain to the powers of the god/kings, their conquests and ambitions, but to the purity and priest-like holiness of the entire people.

Moses and the intellectual community of priests and prophets face up to the weaknesses in human nature. These must be disciplined if the people are to find favor with the LORD. The future and success in the real world of our congregation will be only determined by its adherence to a covenant of behavior that literally creates out of ordinary mortals, this nation of priests. These warnings are dire, but only because Moses was clearly cognizant of the nature of this and all "stubborn people." {Deuteronomy 9:13}.

The vivid imagery in the following passages was sure to give pause to any contemporary, already accustomed to a world of want and death: If you do not obey the Law, "God will put an iron yoke on your neck until he has destroyed you" {Deut. 28:48}—the memory of Egypt. "In the desperate straits to which the enemy siege reduces you, you will eat the fruit of your womb, the flesh of your own sons and daughters whom the LORD your God has given you. Even the most refined and gentle men amongst you will begrudge food to his own brother, to the wife whom he embraces, and to the last of his remaining children, giving to none of them any of the flesh of the children whom he is eating, because nothing else remains to him, in the desperate straits to which the enemy siege will reduce you in your towns. She who is the most refined and gentle among you, so gentle and refined that she does not venture to set the sole of her foot on the ground,

VI. Moses at the burning bush {Exodus 3:1-61}. Fresco from third century CE synagogue at Dura Europas in Eastern Syria.

will begrudge food to her husband whom she embraces, to her own son, and to her own daughter, begrudging even the after-birth that comes out from between her thighs, and the children that she bears because she is eating them in secret for lack of anything else, in the desperate straits to which the enemy siege will reduce you in your towns." {Deut. 28:53-57}.

This is but an example of the rawness of human nature that comes forth in the lives and destinies of humans in those days. It reveals the extent to which the struggle for survival would dissolve what we think to be some of the most basic forms of human biological and civilizational altruism. What Moses was introducing to the Israelites was a set of laws received from the Highest that would ensure, if obeyed, that this "chosen people" would not have to undergo the horrors that countless people, even their own, had been forced to experience in the past.

But the first and most basic revolution in Moses' mission was to reveal the source of this highest power. The people were not chaining themselves to a king or even a priest who would overlord them with taxes, physical and mental "protection money," (certainly not in E's Decalogue), {Exodus 20:1-17—E-source}. Rather, obedience and the humility of submission were basically expressed in the day-to-day behavior of the individual and the people as a community. The submission was to the ethical principles that constituted their covenant with YHWH, indeed, still and always that fierce and demanding God.

The Emotions of Human Nature

Kings and priests by themselves do not create the institutions that enslave our bodies and our minds. In ignorance, humans readily submit to institutions that exploit their weaknesses and needs. Indeed, when we see how humans genuflect to idols, roar forth in hatred and physical violence at the least precipitate, set all reason aside for the sexual moment, we can only utter in recognition, indeed!

The huge brain with which nature endowed Cro-Magnon in the north many hundreds of thousands of years before the coming of Moses also carried with it an ancient evolutionary message. This ancient primate appurtenance, affect, was linked genetically with the power and selective advantage that cortical intelligence carries with it through the ages. Thus, when, in some mysterious, but purely secular and scientific process, the genes of *Homo* began to propel ever more intelligent humans to the fore, the so-called limbic system and the ancient allo-cortical emotional structures of the brain and nervous system came along for the expansive ride.

Nature did not know that the emotions spewed out into social reality by this now-throbbing brain would act in so many ways as a counter-productive hindrance to the reasoning and ever-ballooning iso-cortex' attempts to find cause and effect. This inquiry into the nature of events, by the iso-cortex would allow us to survive in a dangerous and un-philanthropic world. Yes clearly, over time, the emotional self was mastered by the needs for reason. This was to be, but not without the surges of emotion and the moments of unreason and thoughtlessness that mar the human path forward.

Indeed, magnifying the perspective from individual to group, the institutions established by humans—the sanctuaries, cults, armies, festivals, castles, all that tribes and nations surround themselves with, are testimony to the largeness of this dimension of human nature, the challenge to reason and history. That ancient and recent cultures litter, in decline and decadence, our timeline from the past into the future, fortunately argues for the often fatality of these enthusiasms of power and futility.

When YHWH and Moses constantly refer to the Israelites as "stiff necked" and "stubborn," they are referring to an intransigence created by fear, desire, envy, and all the other emotions that can freeze the mind and blind the body to oncoming danger. That is why nations, whether under the rule of kings, priests, or presidents, immediately and without self-awareness, opportunistically institutionalize these emotions in religious worship, temples, palaces, in the arts, literature, mass entertainments, in coliseums with gladiators, armies with flags and gleaming weaponry.

Woe to those leaders who are completely beholden to the rational brain, who like puritans attempt to suppress or extirpate these human pulsations. These come back, and with a vengeance. The challenge is to elevate them, to channel human emotion through the cortex, to satisfy the sensuous primate brain, but never to allow it to run at cross-purposes with reasons' survival requirements. Here is where we see the greatness of Moses' vision and insight. Here is where we recognize the historical moment that brought together a people, a place, and a man.

History's Opportunity

The Delta of the Nile had always been a swarmy periphery of the Egyptian Empire. It was a place for the armies to gather, provision, and set off on their occasional imperial adventures in Asia. It was a place of refuge for starving and thirsty Asiatics seeking surcease from famine and drought. It was an anonymous refuge for a variety of political and military losers to the east and north. Polyglot is a good word. One exception from this anonymity were the Hyksos, the Indo-Europeans (ethnically, but by then not linguistically), who had drifted in from the north to participate in the wealth and luxury that the Nile brought with it to the shores of the Mediterranean. They stayed to conquer.

In memory of these ancestors, Seti I and Rameses II set out to rebuild its luxury and make it capitol of the nation, perhaps because of, or even in memory of Akhenaton's futile attempt at the new in religion and culture for Egypt. That was attempted at Tel-el-Amarna (Akhetaton), along the placid, eternally flowing Nile. One of their new Delta cities was named after the sun god *Per-Atum* (House of Atum, Pithum), {Exod. 1:11—J-source}.[6] After the death of Rameses II, chaos seems to have overtaken Egypt, in the reign of Merneptah, son of Rameses II, then later, in the twelfth century, c.1150 BCE, under a new dynasty and the rule of Rameses III.

This chaos in the ancient established patterns of control and unity within Egypt, added to the relative emptiness and tribal anarchy in Canaan, provided opportunities for people at the fringes of society. They now could set out on a new time-line of history. The Israelites could move their destiny from one waning center of comfort and hope, Goshen, to a land of ancient memories of wandering and migration, an ancient homeland of milk and honey beyond the intervening wilderness, Canaan.

Then there is the figure of Moses. It is not unlikely, as Sigmund Freud contended, in his *Moses and Monotheism*, and as developed above in Chapter 5, that Moses was an Egyptian.[7] The reign of Akhenaton and then Seti I, who followed in the Delta, was at most seventy-five years. Too short a time for those in alliance with Akhenaton's vision to forget what he so strenuously attempted, a revolution in religious and philosophical thought. Too short a time to lose all those painful allegiances and ideas so pregnant with the future, monotheism.

Recall the stele at Zoan referred to in Chapter 3, which Rameses II had originally erected in his new city, *Per-Rameses*. (The Israelites had had a hand in this city's construction, also.) This stele was erected to celebrate the god Seth, a specifically-designated Asiatic god, one that the Hyksos had taken into Egypt in their conquest four hundred years before the reigns of Seti I and Rameses II.[8] Memories in those days were slow to dissipate. So, too, the memories and allegiance that Akhenaton had established, linked to a truly powerfully intellectual idea, of one god above all the polytheistic, graven images of animal gods. These became linked to a corrupt and venal Theban priesthood. Such memories and intellectual commitments could well have stimulated an aristocrat of once great familial means and power to search out and adopt some of the dispossessed and raucous Asiatics in the Delta.

One God

It is a leap to attempt to impose an ethical religion based on one higher abstract Being onto a motley group of reject peoples in order to bring them into a unified congregation. Indeed, all humans have built into their brain the need to know, to account for the disparities in life and experience, thus to create coherent order. We want to understand the meaning of experience, both for an intrinsic intellectual satisfaction, as well as for the more practical ability to manage our lives so that we will not need to resort to eating our children.

Clearly, Moses was an imposing intellectual. He understood the power of the monotheistic idea, for he had witnessed the abasement of the human intellect in the ritual worship of animal gods. He was fortunate, because in Midian he discovered YHWH, the fiery nature God of the nomads, one God above all their others who seemed to command the awe and the fear of the humble wanderers in the wilderness. Ever facing the imminence of their mortality, the fleeing crowd obeyed. By maintaining Yahweh's fierce judgmental fury, His power over the skies and the forces of nature, and joining it with a high ethical manifesto, Moses could hope to weld these people together, many of them, as we noted above, thieves of Egyptian gold and silver, for the journey into and then the conquest of Canaan.

Moses had to persuade them that obtaining release from the power of Pharaoh did not imply a life of anarchy on this perilous route into the wilderness. No, a force of reason and reality had to exist to discipline their lives, but not a human savior, either king or priest. Their freedom from Pharaoh required the imposition of a higher ruler, unseen, unspoken to, except by Moses, the source of law and its holiness. Without this higher sanction and inner discipline, all would be lost.

Moses took this chance with the Israelites-to-be, because it was his last and perhaps only opportunity to realize the truth and power that lay in man's belief and commitment to the principle of the One. In YHWH lay the mystery of nature's power and the inherent intellectual search of all humans for a rule of law, amidst the chaotic precariousness of physical existence.

Consider, where and when have humans, before and since, been able to freely worship one abstract God of ethical judgment? This, without the paraphernalia of temples, graven images, priests, cultic rituals, and festivals. Indeed, all this eventually came to Israel, but later. In the dimming image of this revolutionary figure, Moses, beyond the memories of seers, editors, and redactors, a kernel of these teachings had to have existed, the elaboration of which allowed the Israelites to seek escape from the perennial human weaknesses of body and the mind.

Strangers and Aliens

Abraham bought the cave of Machpelah from Ephron, the Hittite. He had to secure the approval of "the children of Heth, the people of the land" in order to make the transaction, 400 shekels. "I am a stranger (*nakhri*) and an alien residing among you." {Genesis 23:4—P-source}. The land "was made sure unto Abraham for a possession" by the local people. {Genesis 23:20—P-source}. In Genesis the theme and definition of the Israelite patriarchs is one of alienship, strangers in the land of Canaan. See also {Gen. 12:10—J-source; Gen. 15:13—E- and Redactor; Gen. 19:9—J-source}.[9]

So, too, with Moses, when the LORD tells him that he "will deliver my people from the Egyptians, and bring them up out of *that* [italics added] land to a good and broad land flowing with milk and honey, to the country of the Canaanites, the Hittites, the Amorites, the Perizzites, the Hivites, the Jebusites." {Exod. 3:8—J-source}. Clearly YHWH is telling them that He will take the people of Israel out of one strange land to another. See also {Exod. 3:16-17—J source}.

Indeed, YHWH is the one God of this people and all people, if they will but obey His laws. Here He chooses one people to take them from one place in space and time, to bring them to a new land, occupied by foreign peoples. They will once more come to Canaan as an alien people. Protecting them and ensuring their victory will be YHWH, the one and only God of this people, who has no permanent place of residency, not even Sinai or Horeb. His sole duty is to guide this chosen congregation.

It cannot be otherwise with a truly monotheistic deity. All other gods have their sanctuaries fixed in cities and places. This was the tradition, so that the power that emanated from their gods could flow directly to the city or state that benefited the worshippers of the god. As such, also in Canaan, where the Indo-Europeans, Hittites, and, later, Philistines quickly adopted the existing gods of "place." This was the tradition of the north, in the Aegean, where each city-state had its municipal guardians and the temples that they built for them, example, Athena and the Acropolis (high city) in Athens.

Indeed, the many "high places," local sanctuaries where YHWH was worshipped in the early pre-Mosaic, and later, time of the Judges, in Canaan, testify to the revolutionary democratic potency of the one, abstract and ethical God. Instead of a place god on the heights, YHWH showed the way for a people, perpetual strangers in the physical lands that they occupied.

"And the land is not to be sold in perpetuity, for all land is Mine, because you are strangers and sojourners before me" {Leviticus 25:23—P-source}; "For we are strangers before you, and sojourners like all our forefathers" {1 Chronicles 29:15};"I am a stranger with thee, and a sojourner, as all my fathers were." {Psalm 39:12}.[10]

In the earliest strata of the story of Exodus virtually no mention is made of an established priesthood. Only after the incident of "golden calf" does Moses commission the sons of Levi to slaughter the Israelites, who have violated the covenant, and thereby be "ordained." {Exod. 32:25-29—J-, E-, Redactor-sources}. YHWH requires "only an altar of earth." {Exod. 20:22—J-, E-, Redactor-source}. Moses "sent young men of the people of Israel, who offered burnt offerings and sacrificed oxen as offerings of well-being to the LORD." {Exod. 24:5—E-, Redactor-source}. In the ritual Decalogue, {Exod. 34:10-28—J-source} God's covenant is presented to Moses and then written down on the tablets and read to the people. {Exod. 34:31-35—P-source}. In Judges, the traveling Levite, Jonathan, Moses' grandson, is installed by the wealthy Ephraimite, Micah, to be his priest, a very informal investiture. {Judges 17:18}.

The Pentateuch is a rich composite of a variety of strata, historical, political, and philosophical. And it is clear that monarchical centralization and thus loss of political control over their own destiny ceded the independence of the earliest Israelites, and gave new emphasis to the Temple and the priesthood. This seriously undermined the purity of the monotheistic vision and the sense of alienation/strangeness that supported it. Later, when all was lost, in the tragic destruction of the Second Temple, and the homeland for a second time, a new vision of Israel was formed to carry the monotheistic ideal into the modern era.

The Commandments

The covenant made by Moses and the Israelites to obey one supreme God, YHWH, is amplified in the commandments that are relayed to the people. They are ten in number, largely negative statements of the "thou shalt not" form, easy to communicate and remember on the fingers of both hands. Brief phrases, clear in emphasis. This was a simple people being led by a small elite. The first commandment prohibits the worship of any other god but Yahweh. The second prohibits the worship of, or making of idols representing Yahweh or any other god. These two commandments represent a recognition of the abstract nature of the power and unity of God in the worlds of nature and man.

Placing them first, gives unity to what the LORD says to Moses: "You will not do as they do in the land of Egypt where you lived, and you shall not do as they do in the land of Canaan to which I am bringing you. You shall not follow their statutes." {Leviticus 18:3—P-source}.

These two commandments plus the prohibition not to use the name of Yahweh in magic or as an oath constitute the philosophical base, bringing these humans away from polytheism and anthropomorphism. Such images or utterances degrade our understanding of the abstract workings of deity. It is as if the worshipper requires a picture, an eye to open the mind. {Deut. 7:2-3}.

Caution: The writers of the Pentateuch, starting with J and E, were communicating these ideas and experiences to an increasingly literate population. For YHWH to speak directly to Abraham, Moses, Joshua, and thus, to the congregation of Israel, still extremely naïve in their experiences and knowledge, was the only way these laws and concepts could at that time be communicated, as *Torah*.

The concept of the workings and role of one God, YHWH, was a leap of mind, one that would have long term and dramatic power in sweeping away from history the older forms of religious observance, witness the oncoming triumphs of Christianity and Islam. For believers in his teachings, there is another dimension to the significance of Moses and the commandments. This reflects his deep understanding of human nature.

We are more than thinking beings. There is what Freud called the "superego," the judgmental dimension of our behavior. Such a view goes along with our scientific understanding of what has been called the "postponement" factor in brain and body behavior. Centered in the frontal pre-cortex areas of the brain can be distinguished the "postponement," "privation," "persistence," "practice" dimensions of our human intelligence. These are independent variables from the crucial, yet not sufficient cortex, in describing intelligence, the cognitive abilities of humans. What we mean by the "p"-factor in human behavior is the ability of a human of good intelligence and rational sensibilities to "put off" the importunings of the emotional and affective nature, that primate inheritance of powerfully swelling drive fulfillment needs that can rage against our better judgment.

Indeed, the need to create a plethora of gods, for each emotionally significant occasion, war, fertility, the solstice, ingathering, birth, death, travel, to give these gods form as humans or animals, in image or sculpture, gratifies this deep emotional layering in our social natures. So, too, to create verbal magic rites, for good or evil, utilizing the name of our God constitutes a degradation of His meaning. Such behaviors do not lead upward in thought and action. Quite the contrary, they lead down to rank superstition. Moses and his followers understood this.

It is important to note here how the Covenant is devoid of the mention of the female element. YHWH is a male. Goddesses such as Ashtoreh and Anathoth, female gods of the Canaanites, whose images abound, were rooted in the agricultural traditions of the land. But they were also associated with cultic traditions of female and male prostitution. The fear of the female element, as well as its recognition, in awe and protectiveness, is characteristic of Yahwism, the stringent religion of the wilderness, war, and wandering.

The *no* in the commandments stands as a discipline, 'hold back your more primitive self, act rationally and responsibly, else YHWH will punish you as a lesson for future non-thinkers.' In a more cultured, educated, and stable environment, less direct and raw language might be effective. In the wilderness, the commandments resounded with unspoken force. Yet, in the settlement in Canaan they were to be equally applicable.

The commandment not to commit adultery is an example of awareness that sexuality itself, with its explosive consequences among the young and old, must be contained and directed into socially functional channels. Specificity is spare in this commandment, perhaps that is why Jethro warned Moses that he would wear himself out making judicial decisions for every issue that arose among the Israelites. But it is a commandment that needs specificity. Perhaps in the wilderness, after a few weeks of "real time" experience, YHWH could say to Moses and the Israelites: 'You know what I mean.' After all is it not true that in Genesis, we get a hint of God's view of these matters, and here exemplified in the actions of Abraham and Isaac themselves?

Abraham twice gives Sarai/Sarah away as his sister, not his wife. In the first instance, God afflicts Pharaoh for bringing her into his house. When Pharaoh learns of the true status of Sarai, he sends her back to Abram and tells him to "pack up." {Gen. 12:17-20—J-source}. Now, "Abraham" does this again with Abimelech, King of Gerar. This time, God comes to the king in a dream to warn him of the danger. Sarah is sent back, again with rich rewards for Abraham. {Gen. 20:1-17—E-source}. Isaac, too, tells King Abimelech of Gerar, now identified as a Philistine, that Rebekah is his sister. But Abimelech sees Isaac fondling Rebekah and quickly intuits what is going on. Isaac, as with his father, is the wealthier for the scheme. Abimelech: "What is this you have done to us? One of our people might easily have lain with your wife, and you would have brought guilt upon us." {Gen. 26:1-11—J-source}.

In the original J and E sources in Exodus and Numbers, only two references are made to sexual behavior, rules regarding the seducing of a virgin, {Exod. 22:16-17—J-, E-source} and the treatment of female captives, {Numbers 20:10-14—E-source}, both protective of women.

The enormous range of issues sexual, as they relate to the disciplining of the people, developed in later "P" and "D" sources, as follows below, writings produced during the divided monarchy, the exile, and return to build the Second Temple, are now an integral part of the Pentateuch.[11]

[12]{Leviticus 18:3} Not to do as they do in Egypt and Canaan;

{Leviticus 18: 6 *ff.*} Not to uncover the nakedness—various family relationships;

{Leviticus 19:20-22} Sexual relation with a slave woman not your own;

{Leviticus 19:29} Do not prostitute your daughter;

{Numbers 4:11-31—P-source} Ritual discovery of an unfaithful wife;

(Numbers 25: 6-9—P-source} Marriage to a Midianite woman results in
death;

{Numbers 30—P-source} Vows concerning husband and wife, father and
daughter;

{Deut 5:18} Commandment: not to commit adultery;

{Deut 5:21} Commandment: Neither shall you covet your neighbors wife
Neither shall you covet your neighbor's house, field, donkey, male or
female slave;

{Deut. 22:13-21} Accused bride, not a virgin;

{Deut. 22:22-30} Adultery? A women engaged, is raped in town. She, too,
is to die because she has not called out. But if the woman is raped in the
field, only the man dies;

{Deut. 23:1} "No one whose testicles have been crushed or whose penis is cut off shall be admitted to the assembly of the LORD";

{Deut 23:2} Those born to an illicit union shall not be admitted to the assembly—to the tenth generation;

{Deut. 24:1-4} A bill of divorce after marriage;

{Deut. 24:5} One year exemption for newly married man from going out with the army;

{Deut. 25:5-10} Regulations for marriage to a widow of deceased brother: Levirate marriage;

{Deut. 25:11} "If men get into a fight with one another, and the wife intervenes to rescue her husband from the grip of his opponent by reaching out and seizing his genitals, you shall cut off her hand; show no pity";

{Deut. 27:20-23} At Mt. Ebal in Ephraim covenant sanctions are again repeated as antiphonal curses led by Levites. Sexual offenses are again dealt with: Whoever lies with whom, humans and animals, etc., as curses from the Levites;

{Deut. 28:30} Curses for disobedience to the commandments and decrees. "You shall become engaged to a woman, but another man shall lie with her."

A Holy People

The commandments to uphold the Sabbath and the other regulations concerning the seventh day of rest are the pivot around which the Israelites can claim their special relationship with their one God, YHWH. {Exod. 20:8—J-, E-, P-source; Exod. 31:12-17—P-source; Exod. 34:21—J-, Redactor-source; Exod. 35:1-3—P-source; Leviticus 19:30—P-source; Deut. 5:12-15; Deut. 15:1-3}.

While the number seven was significant in all mid-Eastern cultures at that time, it is linked in the "P" source {Gen. 2:2-3—P-source}, to God resting on the seventh day, after creating the world and man. It now becomes a crucial element in the ultimate discipline of the Israelites. They must put aside one day of the week to pray and worship God. The injunction by Moses in {Exod. 31:14-15—P-source} that a violation of the Sabbath subjects the individual to death by the community is pointedly carried out, when a man is found gathering sticks in the wilderness on the Sabbath. "The whole congregation brought him outside the camp and stoned him to death just as YHWH had commanded Moses." {Numbers 15:32-36—P-source}. It is this discipline of peoplehood, wherein not a fire must burn, nor a harvest may be cut on the Sabbath, that sharply demarcates the holy people.

Circumcision, too, becomes a special differentiating ritual, though it did not have the unique impact of difference and holiness in the original Exodus. Abraham's covenant with El Shaddai is an historically later addition. "Any uncircumcised male who is not circumcised in the flesh of his foreskin shall be cut off from his people; he has broken my covenant." {Gen. 17:10-14—P-source}. It seems to have been an inheritance from the Egyptians, and an important differentiating characteristic of the nomadic Semites from the Indo-Europeans, *i.e.*, Philistines. Joshua's injunction to the Israelite men to be circumcised before the invasion of Canaan is a reflection of the tradition of "warrior asceticism" that Max Weber saw as its origin.[13] The manner in which kings of Israel, when they fought nations with foreign gods would cut off the foreskins of their slain enemy is reminiscent of Native Americans scalping their victims, sometimes when the victims were still alive.

The importance of both rituals, circumcision and the rigorous Sabbath, commandments from YHWH, is that both became critical symbols of the separation of Christianity from Judaism. Conversion to Christianity by pagans was made much easier, by omitting both.[14] Yet the seeming strenuousness of the Sabbath day of freedom from labor is belied by the joyousness of Sabbath immersion in study, family, and friendship. It has certainly been an essential and harmonic part of the glue of the Israelite people, especially as they settled into a more sedentary agricultural life. We do not read such details of a Sabbath with the subsequent festive richness in either "J" or "E", for then, the memory of the nomadic course of the Exodus was still warm.

Insofar as the Exodus is concerned, the great concentration of effort in bringing this rag-tag assemblage through so many near-fatal external as well as internal challenges kept Moses' attention to the basic festive dimensions of social life to a minimum. We have the sacrificial tradition, which probably roots itself in the ancient tribal sacrifice of the first-born male to the deity, a propitiation for the survival of the family and the clan. The slaying of the first-born of the Egyptians, both human and animal, reflects this tradition. So, too, is: "The LORD said to Moses: Consecrate to me all the firstborn; whatever is the first to open the womb among the Israelites, of human beings and animals is mine." {Exod. 13:1-2—E-source}.

In a passage that is a ritual ratification of the covenant, the ethical commandments given in {Exod. 20:1-17—E-, Redactor-source}, the LORD beckons Moses, Aaron, the latter's' two eldest sons, Nadab and Abihu, and seventy elders to "come up to the LORD." {Exod. 24:1-3—E-source}. But only Moses could approach and hear the LORD. Moses again wrote down the words of YHWH, and repeated these ordinances, the Ten Commandments to the people, which they in turn affirmed that they would obey. Then Moses "rose early in the morning, and built an altar at the foot of the mountain, and set up twelve pillars, corresponding to the twelve tribes of Israel. He sent young men of the people of Israel, who offered burnt offerings and sacrificed oxen as offerings of well being to the LORD. Moses took half of the blood and put it in basins and half of the blood he dashed against the altar. Then he took the book of the covenant, and read it in the hearing of the people; and they said, 'All that the LORD has spoken we will do, and we will be obedient.' Moses took the blood and dashed it on the people and said, 'See the blood of the covenant that the LORD has made with you in accordance with these words.'" {Exod. 24:3-8—E-, Redactor-sources}.

This form of ritual was the first and most basic form of what later was to cause the building of the Ark of the Covenant, the Tabernacle, and then the institution of holy days, of worship, festivities and sacrifices. No national religion could hope to be maintained without adding these dimensions of human psychological need. In the setting of the Exodus, however, only the primal roots of what would later become a great cultural/civilizational edifice could hope to be established.

It is ironic that the cruelties and conflict that characterize this difficult journey consumed many of the established leadership. Later, the two eldest of Aaron's four sons, Nadab and Abihu, above mentioned in Exodus, "offered unholy fire before the LORD…And fire came out from the presence of the LORD and consumed them and they died before the LORD." {Leviticus 10: 1-2—P-source}. The other sons of Aaron were named Eleazar and Ithamar. {Exod. 6:23—P-source}. And, indeed, both Aaron and Moses die before they reach the Holy Land of milk and honey. Moses himself is severely chastised by YHWH because he failed to save the people of Israel from their sinfulness, their violation of the laws of God, his commandments. {Deut. 32:48-52}.

Dimensions of the Faith

There are three primeval human dimensions to this Mosaic religious creation: A) the intellectual/philosophical vision of an abstract God; B) a series of ethical commandments, prohibitions on behavior, without which civilized life is impossible; C) the ritual, festive, symbolic dimension that contribute the emotional juices needed for us to nourish our ancient mammalian/primate heritage.

A) "Since you saw no form when the LORD spoke to you at Horeb out of the fire, take care and watch yourself closely, so that you do not act corruptly by making an idol for yourselves, in the form of any figure—the likeness of male or female, the likeness of any animal that is on the earth, the likeness of any winged bird that flies in the air, the likeness of anything that creeps on the ground, the likeness of any fish that is in the water under the earth. And when you look up to the heavens and see the sun, the moon, and the stars, all the host of heaven, do not be led astray and bow down to them and serve them, things that the LORD your God has allotted to all the peoples everywhere under heaven. But the LORD has taken and brought you out of the iron-smelter, out of Egypt, to become a people of his very own possession, as you are now." {Deut. 4: 15-20}.

B) "You shall put these words of mine in your heart and soul, and you shall bind them as a sign on your hand, and fix them as an emblem on your forehead. Teach them to your children, talking about them when you are at home and when you are away, when you lie down and when you rise. Write them on the doorposts of your house and on your gates, so that your days and the days of your children may be multiplied in the land that the LORD swore to your ancestors to give them, as long as the heavens are above the earth." {Deut. 11:18-21}.

C) "You shall keep the festival of Succoth for seven days, when you have gathered in the produce from the threshing floor and your wine press. Rejoice during your festival, you and your sons and your daughters, your male and female slaves, as well as the Levites, the strangers, the orphans, and the widows resident in your towns. Seven days you shall keep the festival for the LORD your God at the place that the LORD will choose; for the LORD your God will bless you in all your undertakings, and you shall surely celebrate." {Deut. 16:13-15}.

Endnotes, Chapter 6

[1] Gottwald, Norman K. 1985. *The Hebrew Bible, A Socio-Literary Introduction*, Philadelphia: Fortress Press, pp. 280-281.

[2] Coogan, Michael D., ed. 1998. *The Oxford History of the Biblical World*, N.Y: Oxford Univ. Press, pp. 598-599.

[3] Smith, W. Robertson, Stanley Arthur Cook. 1910. "Decalogue," *Encyclopedia Britannica,* 11th ed., Vol. 7, N.Y.: Cambridge Univ. Press, pp. 907-909.

[4] Smith, W. Robertson, "Old Testament in the Jewish Church," p. 335, cited in W. R. Smith, S. A. Cook, "Decalogue," *Encycl. Britann.*, 11th ed., Vol. 7, *op. cit.*, pp. 907-909.

[5] Stenning, John Frederick. 1910. "Exodus," *Encycl. Brit., op. cit.*, 11th ed., Vol. X, p. 96.

[6] Redmount, Carol, "Bitter Lives," in Coogan, M., ed., *The Oxford History of the Biblical World, op. cit.*, p. 88; see also Greenstein, Edward L. 1993. "Introduction to Exodus," in *The Harper/Collins Study Bible*, New Standard Edition, London: Harper/Collins Publishers, pp. 77-78.

[7] Freud, Sigmund. 1939. *Moses and Monotheism,* N.Y.: Knopf.

[8] Sarna, N. M., and Shanks, H. 1999. "Israel in Egypt," in Shanks, Hershel, ed. *Ancient Israel*, Washington, D.C.: Biblical Archaeological Society, pp. 52-53.

[9] Johnson, Paul. 1987. *A History of the Jews*, N.Y.: Harper and Bros., p. 8; Weber, Max, 1952 (1917-1919) *Ancient Judaism,* N.Y.: The Free Press. pp. 247, 342.

[10] see Paul Johnson, *A History of the Jews, op. cit.*, p. 19.

[11] Gottwald, N. K. 1985 *The Hebrew Bible*, A *Socio-Literary Introduction*, Philadelphia: Fortress Press, pp. 10-16.

[12] These are the locations for the Biblical texts.

[13] Weber, Max. 1952. *Ancient Judaism,* (1917-1919), *op. cit.*, pp. 92-93.

[14] Noss, J. B. 1949. *Man's Religions,* N.Y.: Macmillan, pp. 609-610.

7

In the Family of Nations

Dislocated Worlds

The *Iliad* and *Odyssey,* written in the north Aegean by the Greek, Homer, c.800 BCE, bring together bardic tales reflecting an earlier time, c.1200 BCE, of turmoil and migration in the Mediterranean. It was not merely the Achaean Greeks setting forth to Troy to avenge a tribal wrong. It was a massive dislocation perhaps caused by a time of famine, a volcanic explosion on the island of Santorini in the Aegean, or more likely the adventurous press of northerly peoples advancing on a series of quiet, stable, and soft civilizations along the Mediterranean littoral.

This movement of peoples from the north, to both the east and south of the Mediterranean coastline was not limited to the end of the second millennium, c.1300-1000 BCE. The Minoans on Crete had long had commercial intercourse with both Egypt and the East, c.2000 BCE, so, too, the Sumerians before them, through overland as well as routes out of the Persian Gulf. Two bronze Canaanite deities were found dating from about 1800 BCE, one is a Baal figure, a warrior, decorated with a feathered crown, quite similar to those of the "Sea People" warriors from the northern Mediterranean, battling Egypt, as illustrated at Medinet Habu, by Rameses III, c.1150 BCE.[1]

Indeed, Rameses II, in his description of his conquests in Asia, refers to his defeat of the (Indo-European) Hittites of Ashkelon, c.1260 BCE, later, c.1100 BCE, a Philistine redoubt.[2] There is no doubt that these in-migrating peoples quickly took on the religion and much of the culture of the resident peoples, as do most newcomers when they come to a new land in small numbers. Even the Philistines, from the north maintained this tradition: In Egyptian: "p-r-s-t" = Peleset, Purasati; in Assyrian: Palestu (Palestine), Pilitsu.

At Deir el-Balah, southwest of Gaza, Egyptian styled anthropoid clay coffins of the late Bronze Age have been found dating to c.1300 BCE, 100-200 years before the Sea People supposedly arrived. The controversy is whether these coffins contained locals, because Egyptians preferred to be buried in the homeland, or "Egyptians who were buried abroad in their own tradition." This "does not mean an early arrival of Sea People and their adopted Egyptian style of burial."[3] However, similar coffins, at nearby Lachish, were found to contain the feathered headdresses of the Sea Peoples.

The classic research by Stanley Arthur Cook argued that the Philistines occupied the five-city area before Merneptah's stele, c.1209 BCE, which contradicts recent claims by Finkelstein and Silberman. Philistines were quickly "semiticized" in language and religion, even given the recent discoveries of Aegean style of art work.[4] The black and red bi-chrome pottery found in the various Philistine cities along the coast, c.1100-1000 BCE, testify to a highly-developed culture of fine aesthetic realization, which does not correspond to the pejorative Biblical description of these warrior people.

Egypt also took a "hit" from this time of social and economic chaos. The iconographic renderings by the Egyptians at Pharaoh Merneptah's steles, 1210-1209 BCE, in Thebes, celebrating the defeat of the "Lybians and their Sea People allies," as well as the faience tiles decorated by the Egyptians, at Medinet Habu, Thebes, by Rameses III, 1184-1153 BCE, reveal a whole new stage in Egypt's weakened control of its own destiny and that of the Mediterranean world. The inscribed stele, and wall reliefs of Pharaoh Merneptah, c.1209 BCE, reflects an invasion by the same ethnic groups that were on the move in the Homeric tales, and includes "Israel" as one of the conquered people of Asia. The Medinet Habu faience tiles shows the five people of this new international awareness: Lybian, Nubian (Negroid), Syrian (Canaanite), Hittite (beardless—Greek), Shasu (bedouin). While the Sea-People are illustrated as being similar to the Hittites (all Indo-European northerners), without beards, the lightly-bearded Shasu bedouins wear a Sea People-like headdress.[5]

Homer's *Odyssey* refers to the Lybians as active players in the then-politics and trade in the Mediterranean. The Sea Peoples (Philistines/Pelethites) settled Gaza, Ashkelon, Ashdod, Gath, Ekron; Crete—Cherethites—interior—Negeb (King David's Israelite mercenaries); Sardinia—Sherden—settled around Acco; Sicilians Tjeker/Sikils—ultimately settled around Dor; Cypriot Greeks, now the isle of Yadanana/Danoi/Denyen/Danunians.

Note the phrase in {1 Samuel 30:14}: "the Negeb of the Cherethites."[6] Cherethites...are probably to be identified with Cretans, a contingent of the Philistines ("Pelethites") who had settled in the semiarid Negeb. {1 Samuel 30:14; 2 Samuel 8:18; 15:18; 1 Kings 1:38}. The as-yet unidentified Weshesh (Ekuesh—Achaeans) from Merneptah's various documents are now identified as coming from north Mediterranean and/or Aegean sites, or from Anatolia, the coastal areas of present Asiatic Turkey.

The Shikalayu (Shekelesh/Sikils) in seven ships, scouted, then raided the important city of Ugarit, then under Hittite suzerainty. This event was reported by the king of Ugarit, Ammurapi, in c.1185 BCE. Ugarit was a prosperous city of about 25,000 including its hinterlands. The Hittites were nominally the suzerains, and the local garrison and ships were off in Hittite Lycia (Anatolia). But the locals could not raise a force to fend off the 200-300 Sikil fighters aboard that small flotilla. We should thus be extremely careful, if not skeptical, about large numbers boasted about in the wars of this era, those of Egypt, as well as the Hebrew Bible.[7]

Pharaoh Merneptah managed to defeat his northern and Asiatic enemies using a melange of mercenaries, including some of "his own Sea Peoples." These groups were for the most part free-lance pirates or warriors forced away from their own homelands, now ready to exploit the weaker but wealthy south and east, as they had just done with Troy, c.1200 BCE. The Philistines, who figure so large in the Biblical histories along the present southern half of Israel and the Gaza strip, probably dribbled onto the land, along with the other Sea Peoples from the northeastern Mediterranean coast, for several centuries before these events, but in fits and starts.[8]

{Exodus 13:17—E-source}: "And it came to pass, when Pharaoh had let the people go. That God led them not through the way of the Philistines, although that was near; for God said, Lest peradventure the people repent when they see war, and they return to Egypt":

{Gen. 21:22-34—E-source}: Abraham and King Abimelech of Gerar (Philistine); {Gen. 26:12-33—J-source}: Isaac and Abimelech, King of Gerar, are here linked. This may be indicative that the stories were part of a joint "J" and "E" tradition, redacted and spliced into a continuous narrative, c.950-850 BCE.

The struggle was soon renewed. And though Pharaoh Rameses III was able to repel the Sea Peoples, again not without the help of former enemies, and then to celebrate his triumph with revealingly decorated tiles at Medinet Habu, the days of unquestioned Egyptian dominance and glory were behind it. Here, perhaps, in these decorative tiles we encounter, contemporary with the silent slipping away of Moses and his followers, a celebration of the ethnic world that Egypt has now met, conflicted with, absorbed, and finally come to terms with.[9]

Freedom Lost

Shortly after the arrival into Canaan/Israel of the fleeing vagabonds from Egypt, now led by Joshua, absorbed by the resident Yahwists, but establishing for this religious tradition a new intellectual priesthood and thus, leadership, the dynamics set forth above, began to make their impact. In the Books of Samuel, we read about the ferment that requires new visions, new solutions of these hereditary soothsayers/seers/prophets.

"In those days there was no king in Israel; all the people did what was right in their own eyes." {Judges 21:25}. These enigmatic words from a period long into the future conclude the Book of Judges, commenting both on the chaos of the tribal era, as well as its need to maintain an internal system of ethics and values in tune with the laws of God. The gradual disintegration of the life of tribal freedom is earlier mourned in this same book in the story of the usurper Abimelech (*sic*), son of an Ephraimite concubine of the Judge Gideon of Manasseh.

Gideon (Hacker), or Jerubbaal (Let Baal Contend), son of Joash (the LORD has given), owner of the oak at Ophrah, in Manasseh, wins many great victories over the Midianites. {Judges 6:11-8:21}. "Then the Israelites said to Gideon, 'Rule over us, you and your son and your grandson also; for you have delivered us from out of the hand of Midian.'" Gideon /or/ Jerubbaal had seventy sons from his many wives. He also had a concubine in Shechem (Ephraim) who bore him a son, Abimelech. Abimelech went to the lords of Shechem to convince them that one leader was preferable to seventy. They agreed and allowed him to hire "worthless and reckless fellows" who assisted him in killing all seventy of his half brothers, less one, Jotham, who hid himself.

Abimelech was eventually done in after he attempted to burn down the fortress/temple tower at the town of Thebez. Here, as Abimelech was setting the fire, a certain unnamed women threw an upper millstone on Abimelech's head, and crushed his skull. {Judges 9:53}. This passage is reminiscent of the female Kenite, Jael, who, in an

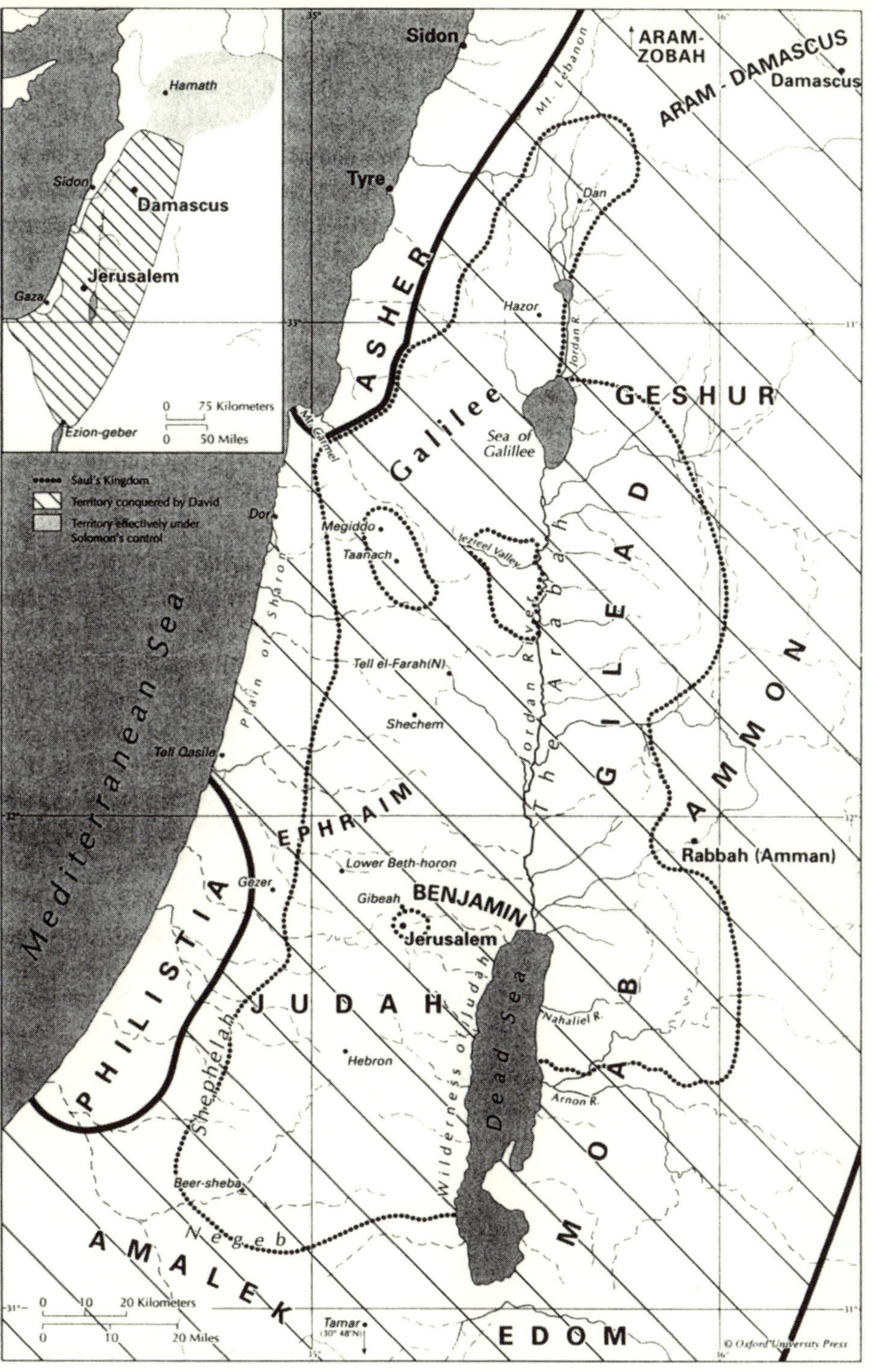

VII. The Kingdoms of Saul, David, and Solomon.

act of treachery against her husband, but with the tribes of Israel, hammers a tent peg through the skull of the Indo-European Canaanite captain, Sisera. Also, there is here a parallel to the death of King Saul. Abimelech requests that his sword-bearer "thrust him through" that he should not be thought to have been killed by a woman. {Judges 9:54-57}. Wounded by arrows, Saul asks his armor bearer to thrust him through so "that these uncircumcised [the Philistines] may not come and thrust me through and make sport of me" But the armor bearer, terrified, was unwilling. "So Saul took his own sword and fell upon it." {1 Samuel 31:1-7}. His three sons in battle had already been killed by the Philistines.

However, after the death of his brothers at the hand of the gang of Abimelech:

Jotham "…stood at the top of Mt. Gerizim and cried aloud to the lords of Shechem, so that God may listen…The trees once went out to anoint a king over themselves. So they said to the olive tree, 'Reign over us'. The olive tree answered them, 'Shall I stop producing my rich oil by which gods and mortals are honored, and go sway over the trees? Then the trees said to the fig tree, 'You come and reign over us.' But the fig tree answered them, 'Shall I stop producing my sweetness and my delicious fruit and go to sway over the trees?' Then the trees said to the vine, 'You come and reign over us.' But the vine said to them, 'Shall I stop producing my wine that cheers gods and mortals and go to sway over the trees?' So all the trees said to the bramble, 'You come and reign over us.' And the bramble said to the trees, 'If in good faith you are anointing me king over you, then come and take refuge in my shade; but if not, let fire come out of the bramble and devour the cedars of Lebanon.'" {Judges 9:7-15}.

Thus Jotham cries out, shall we cede the rich oils and sweet fruit of our liberty for the bramble of control and power that a king will exercise over us, and for what?

The priest Eli of Shiloh seems to have been a descendant of the Mushites, of the Levitical heritage of Moses.[10] His two corrupt priest/sons, Hophni, and Phinehas, (note the Egyptian-Levitical name, as in Exodus), were doomed by YHWH for their evil ways. YHWH accepted Eli, who in turn adopts the sainted Nazarite, Samuel, as his successor. {1 Samuel 2:11-36}. The war with the Philistines was becoming intense as the latter extended their domain further into the Israelite hill countries. At Ebenezer, east of modern Tel Aviv, the Israelites brought the Ark of the Covenant, and this to a mighty war cry that echoed in the Israelite camp. Nevertheless the Philistines defeated them, the Ark of God was captured, and Hophni and Phinehas, and thousands of "Hebrews" died.

The sons of Samuel, Joel and Abijah, became judges in Beer-sheba. But, as with Eli's sons, they perverted justice and took bribes. Growing older, Samuel still went on his circuit to judge Israel at Bethel, Gilgal, Mizpah, and then at his home in Ramah, there to build an altar to YHWH.

{1 Samuel 8:4}: " Then all the elders of Israel gathered together and came to Samuel at Ramah, [south of Bethel] and said to him, 'You are old and your sons do not follow in your ways; appoint for us, then, a king to govern us like other nations'. But the thing displeased Samuel when they said, 'Give us a king to govern us.' Samuel prayed to YHWH, and YHWH said to Samuel, 'Listen to the voice of the people in all that they say to you; for they have not rejected you, but they have rejected me from being king over them. Just as they have done [to me], from the day I brought them out of Egypt to this day, forsaking me and serving other gods, so also they are doing to you. Now then, listen to their voice, only—you shall solemnly warn them, and show them the ways of the king who shall reign over them.'

{10} "So Samuel reported all the words of YHWH to the people who were asking him for a king. He said, 'These will be the ways of the king who will reign over you: he will take your sons and appoint them to his chariots and to be his horsemen, and to run before his chariots; and he will appoint for himself commanders of thousands and commanders of fifties, and some to plow his ground and to reap his harvest, and to make his implements of war and the equipment of his chariots. He will take your daughters to be perfumers and cooks and bakers. He will take the best of your fields and vineyards and olive orchards and give them to his courtiers. He will take one-tenth of your grain and of your vineyards and give it to his officers and his courtiers. He will take your male and female slaves, and the best of your cattle [goodliest young men—Heb. and King James] and donkeys and put them to his work. He will take one tenth of your flocks, and you shall be his slaves. And in that day you will cry out because of your king, whom you have chosen for yourselves; but YHWH will not answer you in that day.'

{19} "But the people refused to listen to the voice of Samuel; they said, 'No! but we are determined to have a king over us so that we also may be like other nations, and that our king may govern us and go out before us and fight our battles.' When Samuel had heard all the words of the people, he repeated them in the ears of YHWH. YHWH said to Samuel, 'Listen to their voice and set a king over them'. Samuel then said to the people of Israel, 'Each of you return home.'" {1 Samuel 8:4-22}.

Samuel was the last Judge of Israel before his appointment of Saul as King of the tribes of Israel. Samuel poured oil on the head of Saul, of Gibeah in Benjamin. "…that when he had turned his back to go from Samuel, God gave Saul another heart…a company of prophets met him; and the spirit of God came upon him and he prophesized among them." {1 Samuel 10:9-10}. "The people asked, 'Is Saul also among the prophets?'…And when he made an end of prophesizing, he came to the high place." {1 Samuel 10:12-13}. "Samuel told the people the rights and duties of the kingship, and he wrote them in a book and laid it up before the LORD." {1 Samuel 10:25}. And Israel had its kings.

These tales were written by the Deuteronomistic Historian in the days of Josiah, King of Judah, c.630 BCE, 100 years after the destruction of the Northern Kingdom of Israel, in 722 BCE, by the Assyrians.

Sadness of the Hebrews

Saul: "There was not a man among the people of Israel more handsome than he; he stood head and shoulders above everyone else." {1 Samuel 9:2}. Saul was called to battle while tending his cattle in the field. He sent out twelve pieces (tribes) of a slaughtered ox to summon the people of Israel to battle against the Ammonites, and he was victorious. He was a talented, charismatic individual, ruling the nation from under a tamarisk tree in Gibeah. He was extremely suspicious, perhaps paranoiac (consulting the medium at Endor) {1 Samuel 28:3-25}, in his justified fear of the charisma of David. The LORD rejected Saul for impure sacrifices, and for having given mercy to the Amalekite, King Agog. However, his beloved son Jonathan was a "soul" companion of David, and Saul gave his youngest daughter, Michal, with pleasure, to David as wife. Despite these relationships: "Saul was still more afraid of David." {1 Samuel 18:17-29}. His victories, even lacking the means for iron armaments, were many, perhaps in the end contributing to his final death on Mt. Gilboah, by a Philistine arrow, in the battle of the Jezreel Valley. {1 Samuel 3:19-22; 1 Samuel 31}. His violent and unbalanced tendencies reveal themselves in his renewed prophetic frenzies {1 Samuel 19:23-24} and his savage ordering of his Israelite servants to kill the priests from Nob. They refuse, his Edomite servant Doeg slaughtering "eighty-five who wore the linen ephod." {1 Samuel 22:18}. A classical tragedy of a talented, but flawed man.

David: "...and the women came out of all the towns of Israel, singing and dancing to meet King Saul, with tambourines, with songs of joy, and with triangles. And the women sang to one another as they made merry, 'Saul has killed his thousands, and David his ten thousands.'" {1 Samuel 18:6-7}. Extremely shrewd and steady, David was more astute than Saul in kingly wiles. He had long been a vassal of the Philistine, King Achish, in Judah and the Negeb areas. {1 Samuel 27}. The roster of David's private guard of thirty included Uriah, the Hittite husband of Bathsheba; an Ammonite, Othnielite; a Hagrite, all non-Israelites. {2 Samuel 23:8-39}. His personal army of Cherethites (Cretans), Pelethites (Philistines), Gittites (from Ziklag and Gath), all non-Israelites, protected him from conspiracies within Israel. This private army achieved a victory not given to Joshua, the sneak attack up the water shaft of Jebus, even as the Indo-.European Jebusites taunted his men from above as being of the "lame and the blind." {2 Samuel 5:5-10}. David moved his capital from Hebron to Jerusalem, a far more impregnable city.

When the ark of God is brought to Jerusalem: "David and all the house of Israel were dancing before the LORD with all their might, on instruments made from fir wood, even on lyres and harps and tambourines and castanets and cymbals." {2 Samuel 6:5}. "David danced before the LORD with all his might; David was girded with a linen ephod. So David and all the house of Israel brought up the ark of the LORD with shouting, and with the sound of the trumpet." {2 Samuel 6:14-15}. Michal, daughter of Saul, was already aware of the many other wives and concubines David had brought from Hebron to Jerusalem. {2 Samuel 5:13-15}. Michal: "'How the king of Israel honored himself today uncovering himself today before the eyes of his servants' maids, as any vulgar fellow might shamelessly uncover himself.'" David: "'I will make myself yet more contemptible than this, and I will be abased in my own eyes; but by the maids of whom you have spoken, by them I shall be held in honor.' And Michal the daughter of Saul had no child to the day of her death." {2 Samuel 6:21-23}.

David, proud with the prerogatives of kingship has a house of cedar built for himself. But the ark of God remains in a tent in Jerusalem The prophet Nathan receives the word of the LORD to be told to David: "I took you from the pasture, from following the sheep to be prince over my people, Israel. When your days are fulfilled and you lie down with your ancestors, I will raise up your offspring after you, who shall come forth from your body, and I will establish his kingdom...But I will not take my steadfast love from him, as I took it from Saul, whom I put away from before you. Your house and your

VIII. The Kingdoms of Israel and Judah.

kingdom shall be made sure forever before me; your throne shall be established forever." {2 Samuel 7:8-16}.

David sins immeasurably, seducing Bathsheba, having caused her husband's death at the hands of the Ammonites. He sees the various sins committed by his sons—the rape of a daughter, Tamar, by her half-brother, Amnon; the killing of this perpetrator by Tamar's full brother, Absalom; the revolt of Absalom against his father; Absalom's violation of David's ten concubines left in Jerusalem to care for his house; the death of rebellious Absalom; the shutting up in "widowhood," but not death, of the violated concubines; revolt after revolt by Israelites, but military victory after military victory, and the expansion of Israel over its neighbors—typical vicissitudes and intrigues of the now-imperial life, in Moses' "land of milk and honey."

Solomon: Struggle for succession. David to Bathsheba: "Your son Solomon shall succeed me as king, and he will sit on my throne in my place." {1 Kings 1:30}. Solomon was clever at the first. When Adonijah, the eldest son of David who rightfully should have become king, asked of Bathsheba that she request of Solomon, for Adonijah, the hand in marriage of Abishag, the virgin who warmed David in his last days, Solomon quickly saw into the scheme to usurp his position, as Bathsheba had not, and had Adonijah killed. The latter's priest, Abiathar, (Jether or Jethro?), a representative of the Mosaic Levitical wing, was exiled to Anatoth (named after a Canaanite god), just outside Jerusalem, home of his descendant, Jeremiah. {1 Chronicles 4:17—descendant of Judah}.[11] The Levitical Aaronite priest Zadok then came into power.

Solomon maintained the empire that his father David had conquered, divided into twelve administrative districts, not for the tribes of Israel, whose lands were now broken up, but for the yearly tithe that each district would pay in succeeding months. The building of the temple in Jerusalem required forced labor, slavery for non-Israelites, the corvée (*missim*) for the Israelites. Labor was needed in the thousands to transport material from Lebanon, and then in shifts in Jerusalem. {1 Kings 5:13-18; 9:15-22}. Not being able to pay for this massive building program, not including a more professional army, Solomon ceded twenty towns in the Galilee to Tyre. The rich soils of the tribe of Asher were now reverted to the goddess Ashtoreth. {1 Kings 9:10-14}.

"Solomon made a marriage alliance with Pharaoh king of Egypt; he took Pharaoh's daughter and brought her into the city of David." She could not have left the Nile in Egypt's heyday. "The people were sacrificing at the high places, however, because no house had yet been built for the name of the LORD…Solomon…sacrificed and offered incense at the high places." {1 Kings 3:1-4}. "King Solomon loved many foreign women along with the daughter of Pharaoh: Moabite, Ammonite, Edomite, Sidonian, Hittite, …Solomon clung to these in love…For Solomon followed Astarte the goddess of the Sidonians, and Milcom the abomination of the Ammonites. So Solomon did what was evil in the sight of the LORD, and did not completely follow the LORD, as his father David had done. Then Solomon built a high place for Chemosh the abomination of Moab, and for Moloch the abomination of the Ammonites on the mountain east of Jerusalem. He did the same for all his foreign wives, who offered incense and sacrificed to their gods." {1 Kings 11:1-8}. David's wives and concubines had all been worshippers of Yahweh, including Beersheba.

The Israelite kings were to be feared. Hadad, the Edomite fled to Egypt, from David's sword, when a young boy. Rezon, of Zobah, east of Mt. Hermon in Lebanon, fled to Damascus. Jeroboam, of the tribe of Joseph in the north of the kingdom, he, too, fled to Egypt, this time from Solomon. {2 Kings 11:14-25}. Jeroboam was the head taskmaster of the Josephite tribal corvée under Solomon. One day Ahijah, the priest of Shiloh, informed him that YHWH, the God of Israel, would rend the monarchy because of Solomon's evil ways, "I will give Israel to you…I will punish the descendants of David, but not forever." Solomon learned of this prophecy, and sought to kill Jeroboam, who found refuge in Egypt. He awaited the death of the powerful King. {1 Kings 11:38-40}.

Rehoboam: He became King of the United Monarchy, c 925 BCE, one hundred years after the accession of Saul to be King of the Hebrews, c.1025 BCE. Rehoboam traveled to Shechem to be anointed. The Israelites who had assembled there said to him: "Your father [Solomon] made our yoke heavy. Now therefore lighten the hard service of your father and his heavy yoke that he placed on us and we will serve you." {1 Kings 12:4-5}. Rehoboam, the son of an Ammonite wife of Solomon, withdrew for consultation. The older men urged him to agree to this request and "…they will be your servants forever." The younger men who had grown up with Rehoboam urged the following: "My little finger is thicker than my father's loins [sexual organ]. Now whereas my father laid on you a heavy yoke, I will add to your yoke. My father disciplined you with whips, but I will discipline you with scorpions." The people answered: "To your tents, O Israel!

Look now to your own house, O David." The people stoned to death Adoram, the task-master of the corvée.

Jeroboam, within the year, c.925 BCE, was called back to lead the ten northern tribes in Shechem and Penuel, east of the Jordan. He set up golden calves as footstools of the altar in Bethel and Dan, the latter where Moses' grandson had been priest, apparently appointing non-Levites as priests in the northern monarchy of Israel. Was he attempting to amalgamate the worship of YHWH with a more ancient Israelite/Canaanite tradition of the worship of the bull, the god El and his lesser associate, Baal?

"Judah [under Rehoboam] did what was evil in the sight of the LORD; they provoked him to jealousy with their sins that they committed, more than all their ancestors had done. For they also built for themselves high places, pillars, and Asherim on every high hill and under every green tree; there were also male temple prostitutes in the land. They committed all the abominations of the nations that the LORD drove out before the people of Israel." {1 Kings 14:21-24}.

Israel under Omri and Ahab: Jeroboam had transferred the capital from Shechem to Tirzah, seven miles northeast of Shechem. Omri then reigned from 876-869. After six years in Tirzah, Omri "bought the hill of Samaria from Shemer for two talents of silver; he fortified the hill, and called the city that he built, Samaria, after the name Shemer, the owner of the hill." {1 Kings 16:24}. His son Ahab, when King of Israel, coveted a vineyard close to the palace in Samaria, that belonged to Naboth the Jezreelite. Jezebel, his Sidonian, Baal-worshipping Queen, conspired to have Naboth stoned to death. The LORD, knowing of this thing, told the Prophet Elijah to meet Ahab, saying: "In the place where dogs licked up the blood of Naboth, dogs will also lick up your blood... Because you have sold yourself to do what is evil in the sight of the LORD, I will bring disaster on you..." {2 Kings 21:19-20}.

One King of Israel acts with modesty and probity to honor the seller of his land to the kingdom for a capital. His son, also a King of Israel, uses his power with greed and evil. Does the difference attribute itself to the wife who profanes in worship?

Ahab: Son of Omri, he ruled Israel for twenty-two years beginning in 869 BCE. He married the Sidonian princess Jezebel and worshipped Baal in Samaria. The prophet

Elijah, the Tishbite from Gilead, warred against Ahab in a sacred conflict. {1 Kings 17-22}. "And so the king [Ahab, wounded by an Aramite arrow] died, and was brought to Samaria; they buried the king in Samaria. They washed the chariot [of the king] by the pool of Samaria; the dogs licked up his blood, and the prostitutes washed themselves in it, according to the word of the LORD that he had spoken." {1 Kings 22:29-40}. At the behest of Elijah and his prophetic warning about the fate of the house of Ahab {1 Kings 21:21-22, 24}, Jehu has had killed Ahab's seventy sons, slaughtered the worshippers of Baal. "Then they demolished the pillar of Baal, and destroyed the temple of Baal, and made it into a latrine to this day." {2 Kings 10:18-27}.

King Mesha of Moab: In the days of Elisha the prophet, c.840 BCE. The kings of Judah, Israel, and Edom unite against Moab. Elisha agrees to help Israel because of his regard for Judah "'...get me a musician' And then while the musician was playing the power of the LORD came over him." There would be water in the wilderness for their animals. The allied armies were defeating Mesha of Moab. "Then Mesha took his first born son who was to succeed him, and offered him as a burnt offering on the wall. And great wrath came upon Israel, so they withdrew from him, and returned to their own land." {2 Kings 3:15-27}. "Omri, king of Israel, humbled Moab many days because Chemosh was angry at his land. And his son, [Omri] succeeded him, and he also said, 'I too will humble Moab'. During my days he said this, but I have triumphed over him and his house, and Israel has perished forever" (Moabite Stone of King Mesha).[12]

A Solomonic dilemma: Samaria/Israel, later, under King Jehoahaz, c.800 BCE, during the siege by Ben-hadad of Syria. Starvation ensued, and even a donkey's head sold for eighty shekels of silver. A woman cried out to the king of Israel who walked on the city wall. "'Help, my lord king!'.... 'How can I help you'...'This woman said to me, Give up your son; we will eat him today, and we will eat my son tomorrow. So we cooked my son and ate him.'" The next day the woman said to her, "'Give up your son and we will eat him.'" But the other woman had hidden her son. "When the king heard the words of the woman he tore his clothes..." {2 Kings 6:26-30}. Curse: "In the desperate straits to which the enemy siege reduces you, you will eat the fruit of your womb, the flesh of your own sons and daughters whom the LORD your God has given you." {Deut. 28:53}.

IX. Jehu, son of Omri, presenting tribute to Shalmaneser III. On the black obelisk in Assyrian Nimrud, c.820 BCE.

Ahaz: King of Judah, he reigned for sixteen years in Jerusalem, 743-727 BCE. "He did not do what was right in the sight of the LORD his God, as his ancestor David had done....He even made his son pass through the fire....He sacrificed and made offerings on the high places, on the hills and under every green tree." {2 Kings 16:1-4}. He sacrificed his son in the Valley of Hinnom, south of Jerusalem, for the god Moloch.

"With what shall I come before the LORD, and bow myself before God on high? Shall I come before him with burnt offerings, with calves a year old? Will the LORD be pleased with thousands of rams, with ten thousands of rivers of oil? Shall I give my firstborn for my transgression, the fruit of my body for the sin of my soul?" {Micah 6:6-7}.

Hezekiah, son of Ahaz, reigned for twenty-nine years in Jerusalem, 727-698 BCE. "He removed the high places, broke down the pillars, and cut down the Asherah. He broke in pieces the bronze serpent that Moses had made {Numbers 21:4-9}, for until those days the people of Israel had made offerings to it; it was called Nahushtan. He trusted in YHWH, the God of Israel." {2 Kings 18:4-5}.

"Hezekiah sent word to all Israel and Judah, and wrote letters also to Ephraim and Manasseh [now under Assyrian rule], that they should come to the house of the LORD at Jerusalem, to keep the Passover to the LORD, the God of Israel....So [the King and the assembly] decreed to make a proclamation throughout Israel, from Beersheba to Dan...Do not be like your ancestors and your kindred, who were faithless to the LORD God of their ancestors, so that he made them a desolation as you see. Do not be stiff-necked as your ancestors were. For as you return to the LORD, your kindred and your children will find compassion with their captors, and return to this land...So the courtiers went from city to city through the country of Ephraim and Manasseh, and then as far as Zebulon; but they laughed them to scorn and mocked them. Only a few from Asher, Manasseh, Zebulon humbled themselves and came to Jerusalem...the Levites had to slaughter the Passover lamb for everyone who was not clean, to make it holy to the LORD. For a multitude of the people many of them from Ephraim, Manasseh, Issachar, and Zebulon had not cleansed themselves yet they ate the Passover otherwise than as prescribed." {2 Chronicles 30:1, *passim*}.

Manasseh, son of Hezekiah, ruled for "fifty-five years in Judah" (OT), c.698-642. Building on the success of his father in placating and-or/repelling the Assyrians from

Jerusalem, he remembered the fate of both Israel and Judah's Lachish, in fighting Assyria. The priests could not explain how the good Hezekiah could have lost Lachish and the Sheppalah, now given back to the Philistines, a land of devotion and prosperity. Hezekiah had also tolerated the extortion of the wealth of the Temple that was given to the Assyrians to send them away from Jerusalem. {2 Kings 18:14-16}. Instead, Judah now prospered as a vassal of Assyria under Manasseh. In Sennacherib's palace at Nineveh in Assyria, the commemoration of their victory over Hezekiah's Judah at Lachish, shows Judean soldiers being led away to Assyria as prisoners. But the women and children along with their belongings were allowed to sit upon oxen drawn carts![13]

The Deuteronomists hated this son of the holy Hezekiah, despite the latter's surrender of much of Judah. Manasseh: "…rebuilt the high places that his father Hezekiah had destroyed; he erected altars for Baal, made an Asherah, as King Ahab of Israel had done, worshipped all the host of heaven, and served them. He built altars in the house of the LORD, of which the LORD had said, 'In Jerusalem I will put my name.' He built altars for the host of heaven in the two courts of the house of the LORD. He made his son pass through fire; he practiced soothsaying and augury, and dealt with mediums and wizards….The carved image of Asherah that he had made he set in the house of which the LORD said to David and to his son Solomon, 'In this house and in Jerusalem, which I have chosen out of all the tribes of Israel, I will put my name forever.'" {2 Kings 21:1-8}.

Corruption: Solomon accessed the throne of the United Monarchy in c.970 BCE. Thence, for three hundred years, Jerusalem and Judah disdained the Mosaic teachings.

Josiah, esteemed grandson of Manasseh, ruled, 639-609 BCE. "The king [Josiah] commanded the high priest Hilkiah, the priests of the second order, and the guardian of the threshold, to bring out of the temple of the LORD all the vessels made for Baal, for Asherah, and for all the hosts of heaven; he burned them outside Jerusalem in the fields of the Kidron, and carried their ashes to Bethel. He deposed the idolatrous priests whom the kings of Judah had ordained to make offerings in the high places at the cities of Judah and around Jerusalem; those who made offerings to Baal, to the sun, the moon, the constellations, and all the host of the heavens. He brought out the image of Asherah from the house of the LORD, outside Jerusalem to the Wadi Kidron, burned it at the Wadi Kidron, beat it to dust and threw the dust of it upon the graves of the common people. He broke down the houses of the male prostitutes that were in the house of the LORD, where the women did the weaving for Asherah. He brought all the priests out of the towns of Judah, and defiled the high places where the priests had made offerings, from Geba to Beer-sheba; …He defiled Topheth, which is in the valley of Ben-hinnom, so that no one would make a son or a daughter pass through fire as an offering to Molech." {2 Kings 23:4-10}.

Memory: Jephthah's Offering to YHWH. In the ancient pre-monarchical days of the Judges of Israel, Jephthah asked the assistance of YHWH against the Ammonites. "If you will give the Ammonites into my hand, then whoever comes out of the doors of my house to meet me when I return victorious from the Ammonites, shall be YHWH's, to be offered up by me as a burnt offering." YHWH made him victorious. When he returned home, out of his house to meet him "with timbrels and with dancing" was his only child, a daughter. The vow to YHWH had to be fulfilled. His daughter said to Jephthah: "Grant me two months, so that I may go and wander on the mountains, and bewail my virginity, my companions and I….She had never slept with a man. So there arose an Israelite custom that for four days every year the daughters of Israel would go out to lament the daughter of Jephthah the Gileadite." {Judges 11:29-40}.

Torah: "You shall not delay to make offerings from the fullness of your harvest and from the outflow of your presses. The firstborn of your sons you shall give to me. You shall do the same with your oxen and with your sheep: seven days it shall remain with its mother; on the eighth day you shall give it to me." {Exodus 22:29-30—J/E- or E-source}.

Prophets: The Heritage of Moses:

Jotham {Judges 9:7-15} and Samuel {1 Samuel 8:4-22} had warned about kingship and power as they accompanied the strivings for nationhood and safety in a precarious world of social conflict. The prophets came into historical consequence as a peripheral group of intellectual and moral visionaries carrying with them the dream of the force of Mosaic law for good under an all-encompassing abstract God, YHWH. It was expected that devotion to the principles enunciated by this all-powerful creator and guide for a forlorn and confused people would result in their happiness and prosperity. But this was not to be under kingship and nationhood.

Power and war, modernity, urbanism, and class struggle were to be the fruits of life in Israel and Judah. More tragically, a tribal people of equals was now undergoing exploitation. The religion of YHWH was itself being corrupted by the needs of the flesh, in the temple in Jerusalem, in the high places, in the valleys where terrible and barbaric rituals were being celebrated in deference to ancient and foreign gods.

These prophets often were traveling solace givers, in bands or groups, some opportunistically supping at a heathen Jezebel's table. Others claimed to have access to the wishes of the Deity, Yahweh, having insight into divine displeasure and human disillusionment. The thinkers among them, in reverence to the Mosaic Law, urged good governance, pursuit of justice for the people, as well as the reinvigoration of individual moral behavior, loyalty to YHWH and the national heritage.[14]

Elijah and Elisha, in Israel, mid-ninth century, c.850 BCE. Ahab, son of Omri, King of Israel, marries Jezebel, princess of Phoenician Sidon. Ahab worships Baal.[15] Ahab and Jezebel thereby unleash the wrath of the mystic magician Elijah, the Tishbite from Gilead. On Mt. Carmel Elijah confronts four hundred and fifty prophets of Baal and four hundred prophets of Asherah. {1 Kings, 18, 19}. Elijah then flees to Mt. Horeb, (in the spirit of Moses), where he mourns his sense of failure to convert the heathen: "Yet I will leave seven thousand in Israel, all the knees that have not bowed to Baal, and every mouth that has not kissed him." {1 Kings 19:15-18}. YHWH tells Elijah, the Tishbite from Gilead, that his successor is to be Elisha son of Shaphat of Abelmeholah "as prophet in your place." {1 Kings 19:16}. Elisha becomes Elijah's disciple. {1 Kings 19:19-21}.

Later, after Elijah had inflicted punishment on the Baal-worshipping Ahab and his successor, Ahaziah, and performed many miracles, Elijah and Elisha travel from Gilgal to Bethel, thence to Jericho and the Jordan River. On their way, the sons of prophets announced to Elisha that YHWH was to take Elijah. The Jordan parted, Elijah walked across, and a chariot of fire and horses of fire, in a whirlwind took him up to heaven. "Father, father! The chariots of Israel and its horsemen!" {2 Kings 2:12}. Elisha had requested of Elijah a double or, first son's share of Elijah's spirit, which YHWH granted.

Elisha parted the waters of the Jordan and returned to the waiting sons of prophets on the other side of Jericho. {2 Kings 2}. Elisha would thence perform many more miracles, including the destruction of Jezebel and the seventy sons of Ahab by Jehu, with the support of the fundamentalist non-Israelite, nomadic Yahwist Rechabites {2 Kings 9-10}, a fulfillment of Elijah's prophesy. {1 Kings 21:21-22; 24}. Alas, Jehu, too, "…did not turn from the sins of Jeroboam [first King of Israel], which he caused Israel to commit." {2 Kings 10:31}.

Amos, from Tekoa, south of Bethlehem, in Judah, from a landed family, aims at the world of Ephraim and Bethel, the luxury and corruption of Samaria, c.760-750 BCE.[16] Amos claims to be "a herdsman and dresser of sycamore trees." {Amos 7:14}.[17] Amos travels north to preach: about social injustice, the break-up of the old tribal and family system of ownership, leading to class divisions (similar to Greece at the beginning of coinage, c.625 BCE). {Amos 2:6; 4:1; 5:11-12}. He is challenged by the northern priests of the golden calves, at Bethel. {Amos 7:1}. Amos rails against unfair trade practices {Amos 2:6}; the fines and levees on poor {Amos 2:8, 11}; the violation of legal rights, bearing false witness {Amos 5:10}; the high living {Amos 6:4-7}; and hollow religiosity. {Amos 4:4-5}.

Amaziah, priest of Bethel, to Amos: "O seer, go, flee away to the land of Judah, earn your bread there, and prophesy there; but never again prophesy at Bethel, for it is the king's sanctuary, [Jeroboam II] and it is a temple of the kingdom [Israel]." {Amos 7:12-13}.

How crass is the lavish use of ivory in eighth century Samaria: houses decorated by Phoenician craftsmen taken from elephants hunted in the Syrian river valleys. "Alas for those who lie on beds of ivory, and lounge on their couches and eat lambs from the flock and calves from the stall; who sing idle songs to the sound of the harp, and like David improvise on instruments of music; who drink wine from bowls, and anoint themselves with the finest oils, but are not grieved over the ruin of Joseph! [the tribal nation of Joseph's sons, Manasseh and Ephraim]. Therefore they shall now be the first to go into exile, and the revelry of the loungers shall pass away. The Lord God has sworn by himself (says the LORD, the God of hosts): I abhor the pride of Jacob and hate his strongholds; and I will deliver up the city and all that is in it." {Amos 6:4-8}.

"Hear this word that the LORD has spoken against you, O people of Israel, against the whole family that I brought up out of the land of Egypt: You only have I known of all the families of the earth; therefore I will punish you for all your iniquities." {Amos 3:1-2}.

Hosea, from the north, c.750-722 BCE, reflects on the war of Israel and Syria against Judah to create an anti-Assyrian alliance and the consequent rebellion against Assyria that ultimately caused the defeat of Israel. The metaphor of Hosea's marriage to Gomer, a whore, by whom he had children, after which he then purchased an adulteress, all reflect Israel's relation to YHWH. Hosea evinces broad learning and considerable rhetorical skills.[18] He rails against the corrupt northern priests. {Hosea 4:4-10; 5:1-2; 6:9}. He utterly rejects the calf of Samaria: "The calf of Samaria [golden bull of Bethel] shall go up in flames. For they sow the wind and they shall reap the whirlwind." {Hosea 8:6-7}. Hosea's writings are a metaphor for the return to holy purity by the people of Israel and Judah, back into the wilderness, for a new covenant, a second history of reconciliation and regeneration.[19] "The LORD said to me again, 'Go, love a woman who has a lover and is an adulteress, just as the LORD loves the people of Israel, though they turn to other gods and love raisin cakes'. So I bought her for fifteen shekels of silver and a homer of barley and a measure of wine. And I said to her, 'You must remain as mine for many days; you shall not play the whore, you shall not have intercourse with a man, nor I with you' For the Israelites shall remain many days without a king or prince, without sacrifice or pillar, without ephod or teraphim. Afterwards the Israelites shall return and seek the LORD their God, and David their king; they shall come in awe to the LORD and to his goodness in the latter days." {Hosea 3}.

"Like grapes in the wilderness I found Israel. Like the first fruit on the fig tree in its first season, I saw your ancestors. But they came to Baal-peor and consecrated themselves to a thing of shame [Baal], and became detestable like the thing they loved. Ephraim's glory [honor] shall fly away like a bird—no birth, no pregnancy, no conception!" {Hosea 9:10-11}.

Micah, c.725-700, in Judah, from Moresheth-gath, 25 miles southwest of Jerusalem, in the Shephelah, from the laboring classes. Micah did not espouse the David-Zion tradition of Hezekiah's Judah, nor the inviolability of Jerusalem. He seemed to favor the Moses/Sinai tradition of Jacob/Joseph and the Northern Kingdom, with its emphasis on the Exodus, Moses and Joshua.[20]

"Hear this, you rulers of the house of Jacob and chiefs of the house of Israel, who abhor justice and pervert all equity, who build Zion with blood and Jerusalem with wrong! Its rulers give judgment for a bribe, its priests teach for a price, its prophets give oracles for money; yet they lean upon the LORD and say, 'Surely the LORD is with us!

No harm shall come upon us.' Therefore because of you Zion shall be plowed as a field; Jerusalem shall become a heap of ruins, and the mountain of the house a wooded height." {Micah 3:9-12}.

Micah on the tragedy of Lachish and the Shephelah, his Judean homeland, after its siege and destruction by the Assyrians under Sennacherib in 701 BCE.[21] "Harness the steeds [Larekesh—Heb.] to the chariots, inhabitants of Lachish; it was the beginning of sin to daughters of Zion, for in you were found the transgressions of Israel". {Micah 1:13}. "Do not rejoice over me, O my enemy; when I fall, I shall rise; when I sit in darkness, the LORD will be a light for me." {Micah 7:8}.

Isaiah 1, 738-c.690 BCE). Oracular visions of the tragic afflictions to be imposed upon Jerusalem, God's city. A morally purified city led by good kings of the Davidic tradition would save it from external as well as internal enemies.[22] Isaiah 1 is a counselor to the kings of Judah, dreams of a more moral future, a greater king, Hezekiah?

Isaiah has a following in Judah. He speaks both to the corrupt, if wily Ahaz, but also to his pure son, Hezekiah. To Ahaz of the "House of David," he sends a message in the name of Isaiah's son's, Shearjashub: "a remnant shall return/only a remnant shall return." To whatever reasonable extent possible do not cooperate with the conspiracy in the north by the kings of Syria and Israel against the Assyrians, which will not succeed. {Isaiah 7-11}.[23] The house of David will be protected: "Therefore the LORD himself shall give you a sign; Behold a virgin shall conceive and bear a son, and shall call his name Immanuel." {Isaiah 7:14} (King James Version) (Immanuel=El is with us).

Oracle of hope for the coronation of Hezekiah of Judah, as the Assyrian dismemberment of evil Israel continues:

"The people that walked in darkness have seen a great light: they that dwell in the land of the shadow of death, upon them hath the light shined. Thou hast multiplied the nation, and not increased the joy: they joy before thee according to the joy of the harvest, and as men rejoice when they divide the spoil. For thou hast broken the yoke of his burden, and the staff on his shoulder, the rod of his oppressor, as in the day of Midian. For every battle of the warrior is with confused noise, and garments rolled in blood; but this shall be with burning and fuel of fire. For unto us a child is born, unto us a son is given: and the government shall be upon his shoulder: and his name shall be called Wonderful, Counselor, The mighty God, The everlasting Father, The Prince of Peace. Of the increase of his government there shall be no end, upon the throne of David, and upon his kingdom, to order it, and to establish it with judgment and with justice from henceforth even for ever. The zeal of the LORD of hosts will perform this." {Isaiah 9:2-7} (King James Version).

End of Nationhood: Israel

Discovered in 1910, and recorded between 779 and 771 BCE, in the reign of Jeroboam II of Israel, imprinted "ostraca" were found near the palace in Samaria.[24] These were records of agricultural taxes and support of the palace activities by various estates in Israel. A number of names carried a Baal element. It is possible that the naming of a child after Baal was a tradition, as with most of the sons of King Saul, else an "epithet for Yahweh in this period, since Baal means 'Lord.'" {Hosea 2:16}.[25]

However, the number of Yahwistic names outnumbers the Baal names by 11 to 7. Also, since many of the Baal names could have been of Phoenician businessmen, active in the economic life of Israel, it is possible that the Yahwist majority was even greater.[26] These ostraca were found together with the large quantity of ivory that supposedly comprised the "ivory house" or "beds of ivory" about which the prophet Amos complained {Amos 6:4}. This dated from the end of the Omri/Ahab/Jehu period, much inlaid furniture, the ivory imported from valleys near Damascus in Syria, where wild elephants then roamed, (also near Carthage in the days of Hannibal, c.200 BCE). The furniture was then fabricated by Phoenician craftsmen. It reveals the wealth and power of Israel, as compared to Judah in the ninth and eighth century BCE.[27]

At a site in the northeastern Sinai peninsula, called Kuntillet 'Ajrud, a way-station between Beersheba and Elath on the Red Sea, in the late ninth to eighth centuries BCE, a discovery was made of a number of ancient Hebrew inscriptions on the walls and on pottery jars. One of the pottery jars has a painting depicting two standing figures. Behind them, seated, is a musician with a harp. The inscription: "I have blessed you by Yahweh of Samaria and his Asherah." The figures: The forward figure is a man with a bovine face, horns, and a tail. Behind him, the figure has a human body, breasts, a bovine face, and a tail. The writings found throughout the excavated site are in the Judean as well as Israelite dialects of written Hebrew.[28]

The name of God is always referred to as a place name, "Yahweh of Samaria," "Yahweh of Teman"—southland, as in the town and mountains of northern Arabia. This practice was similar to the place names of El, in the ancient Canaanite traditions. Always it is Yahweh and his consort Asherah, signifying as with the female figure that a joint

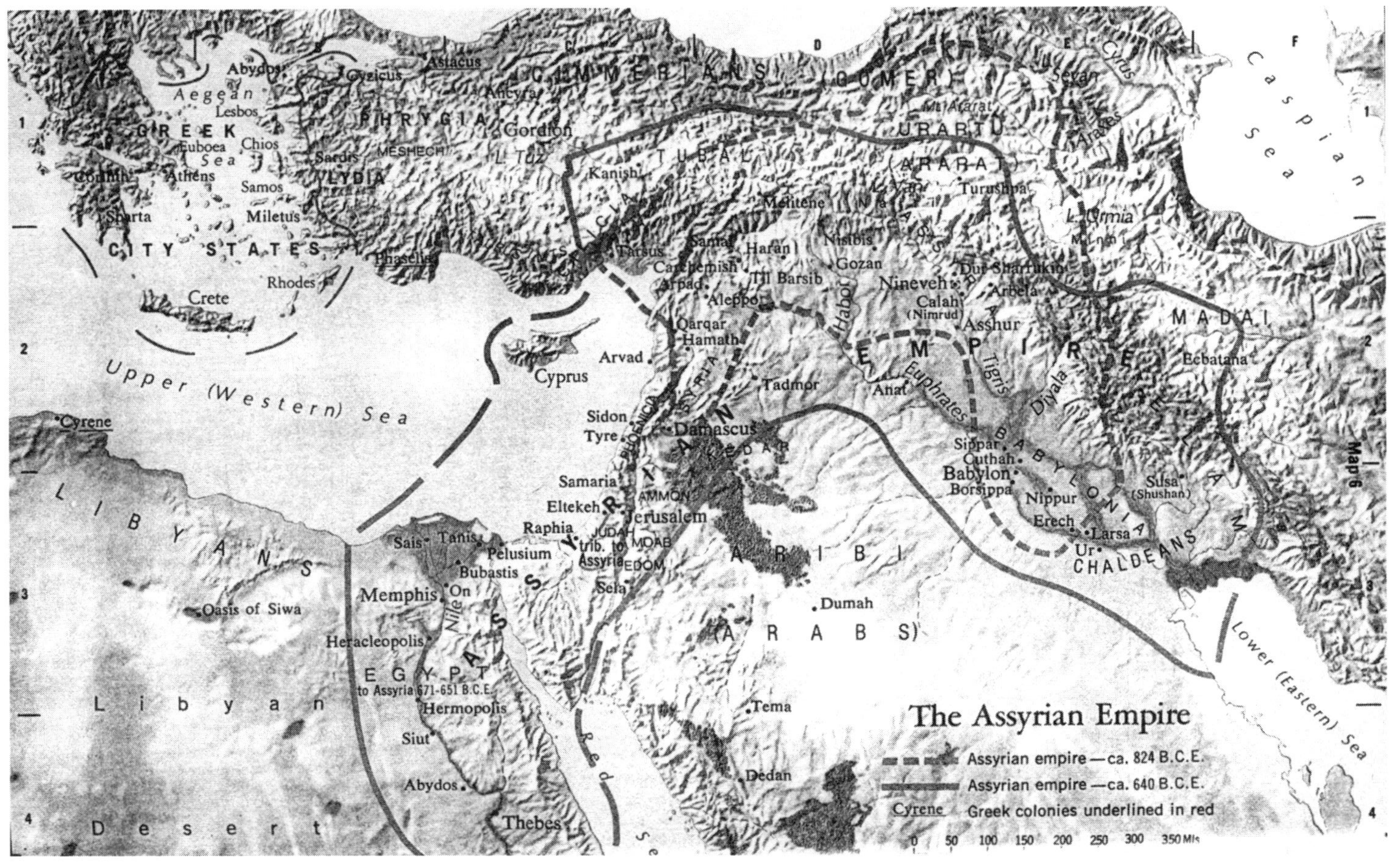

X. The Assyrian Empire.

syncretic amalgam regarding the Yahwist religion has now taken place among the ordinary people of Israel and Judah in the south. The depiction of both gods with bovine characteristics hints at the use of the bull motif ensconced in Bethel and Dan, by Jeroboam I, much to the horror of the prophets and the Judean reformers, the Kings, Hezekiah and Josiah. Here we have in the living traditions of ordinary people the violation of the high commandments imposed by Moses.

During this period, and down through the reign of Josiah, 639-609 BCE, especially in Judah, many fertility figurines have been found in excavations. The typical figurine has enormous breasts; her pillar-shaped body may represent the Canaanite goddess Asherah as a tree, "terebinth."[29]

The inclusion of references to YHWH and his Asherah all over the Judean Shephelah, including Lachish, is widely recognized. Cult objects seen being taken out of Lachish by Assyrians as booty testify to the existence of religious cults in Lachish, even after Hezekiah's Judean reforms. Hezekiah died in Jerusalem in 698 BCE, three years after the destruction of Lachish by the Assyrian, Sennacherib in 701 BCE.[30]

We must recall that in the construction of the first temple, Solomon used golden cherubs for the "footstool" of the throne platform in the temple. These cherubs were related to the Canaanite traditions of the god El.[31] Thus at the very beginning of the united monarchy there was already a bending of the Second Commandment of Moses.

The fate of the nation of Israel hung in the balance at the close of the reign of the Yahwist usurper Jehu, and then, apostate to the faith, and his royal descendants. Nominally a vassal of Shalmaneser III of Assyria, Aram/Damascus/Syria another client state, nevertheless pressed Israel hard, c.815-788 BCE. Jeroboam II, 788-747 BCE, brought Israelite power to its height in both political-territorial and economic terms. His death set off a chaotic period in Israel's monarchical structure, with assassination after assassination.

Usurpation of the throne was more common in Israel than in Judah, as its monarchy was charismatic, whereas Judah's was hereditary within the line of the descendants of David. The delicate political situation in Israel corresponded with another surge from the Assyrian north under Tiglath-Pileser who saw the wealth of the Mediterranean states as opportune for the maintenance of his unruly empire. Not merely vassalage, but now utter conquest was fated for the fat Phoenician states, Aram/Syria and Israel.

Between 738-727 BCE, Tiglath-Pileser conquered Dor, Megiddo, the Jezreel valley, Galilee, Hazor, Dan, and Gezer, near the coast. He deported about 13,500 people, especially from the Galilee, as per policy, where the opposition was heavy, importing immigrants from other sections of the empire. "The land of Bit-Umria [Omri], all of whose cities I leveled to the ground in my former campaigns…I plundered its livestock, and I spared only isolated Samaria." [32] Shalmaneser V succeeded Tiglath-Pileser, only to be succeeded by Sargon II, who related the final chronicle of Israel's extermination in 722 BCE, consequence of more intrigues by the Israelite kings, attempting to bring Egypt back into the fray. After a three-year siege Samaria finally fell. This time 27,280 people are listed as deportees. The totals, about 40,000 deportees of the approximate population of 200,000 in Israel, were scattered around the Assyrian empire. The largest number, from the capital of Israel, Samaria, were probably the most Judaized segment of the population. But theirs was still a syncretic Yahwism, and it is unlikely that in a narrow, if opportunistic militarized culture, their strength of belief in the ancient Mosaic tradition could have maintained itself outside the homeland. The urban elite of the ten tribes thus disappeared into the northern fastness. Yet Sargon II was practical. "I formed a unit with 200 of their [Israel's] chariots for my royal force."[33] We shall note the possible ramifications of this action later in Judah's history.

Transferred into Israelite cities by the Assyrians was a polyglot population of Syrians and Babylonians. Many of them were settled near the border with Judah, at the sacred town of Bethel. Up until now Judah had kept its peace with Assyria, c.722-715 BCE.[34]

The new population did not know the governing religious reality of the territory and needed instruction from the indigenous priesthood, because of the God-induced depredations of lions among them, and no God of Israel to protect them. {2 Kings 17:24-26}. "Then the king of Assyria commanded, saying, Carry thither one of the priests whom ye brought from thence; and let them go and dwell there, and let him teach them the manner of the God of the land" or "He taught them how they should worship the Lord." But they worshipped their own gods in the high places of Samaria. {2 Kings 17:24-33}.[35] Here began the long-to-be separation of the Judahite Yahwist elite with their Samarian/Israelite confreres. The memory was long that these so-called worshippers of the land of the God of Israel were foreigners who still "served their carved images." {2 Kings 17:41}.

Judah's Final Agony

Archaeological evidence exists of Judah's growth during the generation, c.738-715 BCE, during which Israel suffered her final humiliation. No doubt, prior to the re-population of the province of what was by then Samaria and its outlying districts by the Assyrians, many Yahwists fled to Judah. The western parts of Jerusalem especially seem to have grown. Now an estimated total population of 15,000 people of the Judean capital resided within the newly walled sections. The construction of the Siloam tunnel, which brought water from the Gihon spring within the walls of the city, stands as a verifiable and wondrous achievement of King Hezekiah.

Between the death of Saigon II and the full installation of Sennacherib in power in Assyria, Hezekiah took a gamble, feeling that the new strength of Judah, enhanced by internal Yahwist patriotic support and much trade with Egypt and Arabia, would enable him to throw off Assyrian vassalage, perhaps even to reclaim parts of the old Israelite homeland. In 701 BCE the armies of Sennacherib descended on Judah, sweeping down along the Phoenician coast to deny all separatist national claims, destroying well-fortified Lachish in the Judean Sheppalah. Next, his armies arrived at the walls of Jerusalem. And in a colloquy worthy of the Athenian historian, Thucydides, c.420 BCE,[36] the Assyrian emissary, the Tartan (Viceroy—second in command) along with both the Rabshakeh (Chief Butler—ran the royal court) and Rebsaris (Chief Eunuch—led the armies) address the representatives of King Hezekiah.[37] Rabshakeh: "See, you are relying now on Egypt, that broken reed of a staff, which will pierce the hand of anyone who leans on it."

"Then Eliakim son of Hilkiah, [in charge of the palace] and Shebnah [the secretary] and Joah [the recorder], said to Rabshakeh, 'Please speak to your servants in the Aramaic language, for we understand it; do not speak to us in the language of Judah within the hearing of the people who are on the wall.' But the Rabshakeh said to them, 'Has my master sent me to speak these words to you, and not to the people sitting on the wall, who are doomed with you to eat their own dung and to drink their own urine?' Then the Rabshakeh stood and called out in the language of Judah, 'Hear the words of the great king, the King of Assyria! Thus says the king: 'Do not let Hezekiah deceive you, for he will not be able to deliver you out of my hand. Do not let Hezekiah make you rely on the LORD by saying, The LORD will surely deliver us….Come now, make a wager with my master, the king of Assyria: I will give you two thousand horses, if you are able on your own part to set riders on them. How then can you repulse a single captain among the least of my master's servants, when you rely on Egypt for chariots and horsemen?" {2 Kings 18}.

The Assyrians withdrew, either the angel of the LORD struck them down, else Hezekiah bribed them with more silver and gold than he had earlier given. Else they tired of an unsuccessful siege, Siloam tunnel bringing water to besieged Jerusalem. In the end the salvation may been due to Sennacherib's indolent generalship.[38] Isaiah has the LORD say to the Assyrians: "Because you have raged against me and your arrogance has come to my ears, I will put my hook in your nose and my bit in your mouth; I will turn you back on the by which you came." {2 Kings 19:28}. The reward for a holy king, Hezekiah.

Mystery. Who was this Rabshakeh, Tartan/Viceroy and Hebrew-literate representative of the Assyrian king? Could he have been one of those deported Israelites enlisted like the charioteers into Assyrian hegemony? Was the relief of Jerusalem due to the secret intervention of a Yahwist lieutenant of an incompetent king?

Manasseh, son of Hezekiah, ruled for almost fifty five years, 698-642 BCE, maneuvering between a declining Assyria and an Egypt who with the Anatolian Lydians under Gyges had helped Egypt reclaim its independence in 660 BCE. The Assyrian king, Assurbanipal, had died in 668. The Assyrian empire was now unraveling, invaders from the west, east, north and south exposing its now-exhausted manpower and will power. The political/military vacuum was of extreme benefit for the economic and social fortunes of Judah, but now again in reversion to religious and moral apostasy. Manasseh sacrificed his eldest son to the fires of Hinnom. New population movements seem to be evidenced in the archaeological record: Arab people in Jerusalem; Greeks (Lydians?) in the Beersheba valley and along the coast north of Philistia; Yahwist Judeans at work in the Philistine cities.[39]

Amon, a surviving son of Manasseh, was murdered after his father's death, and Amon's son, the eight-year-old Josiah, became King of Judah, c.639-609 BCE. Eighteen years into his reign during repairs for the Temple, a scroll was found by the high priest, Hilkiah. It was the Deuteronomist History. Josiah quickly understood that the ancient laws of the LORD enunciated to the people of Israel had been violated by the rulers of Israel. A prophetess, Hulda, interpreted the meaning of these ancient laws: "Thus says the LORD, I will indeed bring disaster on this place and on its inhabitants—all the words of the book that the king of Judah, has read. Because they have abandoned me and have made offerings to other gods, so that they have provoked me to anger with all the work of their hands, therefore my wrath will be kindled against this place, and it will not be quenched." {2 Kings 22:16-17}.

Of course, this document, and others that were brought into Judah from scribes and priests fleeing Israel a century earlier, was to be used by the priestly intellectuals then, and in the exile to come, as documentary grist for their reinterpretation of the history of the Hebrews. And, as noted above, Josiah undertook, for political as well as moral/religious reasons, to destroy the non-Yahwist religious superstructure in Judah {2 Kings 23:4-10}, even reoccupying the ancient Ephraimite shrine at Bethel in Israel.

But the LORD was not placated. "…I will reject this city which I have chosen, Jerusalem, and the house of which I said, My name shall be there." {2 Kings 23:27}. Josiah went out to meet Pharaoh Neco, the latter now allied with the Assyrians for fear of the new power of Chaldea/Babylonia. "…But when Pharaoh Neco met him at Megiddo [in the north of Israel], he killed Josiah." {2 Kings 23:28-30}.

Jeremiah, from Anathoth, in Benjamin, was a descendant of Abiathar, rival to Zadok as head of the Jerusalem priesthood. Abiathar had been banished to Anathoth by Solomon when Adonijah, Abiathar's candidate for the throne of David, failed and was later killed. Jeremiah may have seen his Levitical inheritance from Abiathar as representing the Mosaic tradition, not the political Aaronites of the Temple. He was active from c.627 BCE.[40] There is, similar to Micah, a deeply critical outlook in the prophetic commitment of Jeremiah. Jeremiah came to Jerusalem after Josiah's death.

It is clear that the reforms of Josiah were only "skin deep" in the lives and behavior of ordinary Judahites as well as those in power. Return to ancestral faith, Jeremiah preaches. {Jeremiah 3}. He rejects the false sacrifices of the Temple. {Jeremiah 7:26}. Also, similar to the prophet Hosea, Jeremiah makes use of the unfaithful wife metaphor and the word "repent, *shuv*." {Jeremiah 3}.[41]

"Do you not see what they are doing in the towns of Judah and in the streets of Jerusalem? The children gather wood, the fathers kindle fire, and the women knead dough to make cakes for the queen of heaven [Ishtar]; and they pour out drink offerings to other gods, to provoke me to anger. Is it I whom they provoke? Says the LORD. Is it not themselves, to their own hurt." {Jeremiah 7:17-19}.

"For the people of Judah have done evil in my sight, says the LORD: they have set their abominations in the house that is called by my name, defiling it. And they go on building the high places of Topheth [fireplace-shame], which is in the valley of the Hinnom, to burn their sons and daughters in the fire—which I did not command, nor did it come into my mind. Therefore the days are coming, says the LORD, when it will no more be called Topheth, or the valley of the son of Hinnom [Gehenna], but the valley of murder: for they will bury in Topheth until there is no more room. The corpses of this people will be food for the birds of the air, and for the animals of the earth; and no one will frighten them away. And I will bring to an end the sound of mirth and gladness, the voice of the bride and bridegroom in the cities of Judah and in the streets of Jerusalem; for the land shall become a waste." {Jeremiah 7:30-34}.

The death of Josiah coincides with Egypt moving into the Assyrian vacuum. Josiah's son Jehoahaz rules for three months and is then exiled by the Pharaoh. The next son of Josiah, Jehoiakim becomes a loyal vassal of Egypt, amid the steady disintegration of Judah's internal character. The Egyptians were defeated by Chaldean/Babylonians at Carchemish in the north and, again, in retreat, at Hamath in southern Syria, a futile attempt to aid a disintegrating Assyria. Judah now in the Egyptian camp was in deep panic as Jeremiah rejoiced: "Go up to Gilead and take balm [from the balsam tree] O virgin daughter of Egypt! In vain you have used many medicines; there is no healing for you. The nations have heard of your shame and the earth is full of your cry; for warrior has stumbled against warrior; both have fallen together." {Jeremiah 46:11-12}.

The Chaldeans were coming. Formerly, rough and ready Semites from the swampy confluence of the two rivers, perhaps migrants from Arabia, they were now devoted to the ancient and holy Babylonian cultural tradition. The Assyrians themselves in their final generations of power, from Sennercherib to Assurbanipal, were surprisingly and increasingly under the sway of this ancient intellectualism. The twin brother of Assurbanipal, Samas-sam-yukim, was made viceroy of Babylon. He even attempted to reinstate the Sumerian language as the official tongue in that ancient province. This action reminds us of the efforts of Julian the Apostate, Emperor of Rome, as he tried to turn back the clock on Christianity by re-introducing the pagan religions as orthodox in waning Rome, c.363 CE. Julian suddenly died two years later. Samas-sam-yukim was killed as he revolted against his brother. These dreams ended in failure. The vision of Jeremiah for the reinstallation of the Mosaic covenant in Jerusalem under the Chaldean/Babylonians would likewise dissolve before his own eyes. {Jeremiah 21}.

Jeremiah prophesizes/envisions the final debacle. The LORD then sends him to a colony of Rechabites now encamped within the walls of Jerusalem. These non-Hebrew Yahwist nomads of the eastern desert had fled both from the Arameans and Babylonians now ravaging cities of Judah, Lachish, and Azekah. In a chamber of the temple of the

LORD, Jeremiah offers them wine. They refuse, citing their ancient covenant of abstinence, as it contrasts sharply with Jerusalem's inhabitants: "We have obeyed the charge of our ancestors….to drink no wine all our days, ourselves, our wives, our sons, or our daughters, and not to build houses to live in. We have no vineyard or field or seed, but we have lived in tents…" {Jeremiah 35}.

Between December 598 and March 597 BCE, Jerusalem was under the first Babylonian/Chaldean siege. Egypt had now withdrawn to Gaza and the Sinai. Jehoiakim mysteriously died during the siege and his son, Jehoiachin became king and surrendered to Nebuchadresser, the Babylonian king. {Jeremiah 36}. Nebuchadresser took 10,000 Judahites to Babylon, including Jehoiachin {2 Kings 24:14-16}, consisting of 7,000 soldiers, 1000 craftsmen and smiths. Zedekiah, son of Josiah, uncle of Jehoiachin, became the vassal of Nebuchadresser.

"In the seventh year, the month of Kislev, the king of Akkad mustered his troops to the Hatti-land, [*sic*], and encamped against the City of Judah…" [Babylonian Chronicle].[42]

There was agitation from free Moab, Edom, Sidon, Ammon, Tyre, for Zedekiah to revolt, with ever more conspiracies from 597 to 587. Jeremiah, preaching strenuously in favor of accommodation, walked the streets of Jerusalem wearing a yoke of oxen, demonstrating his vassalage to Babylon and urging it on the approximately 15,000 Jerusalemites and 75,000 additional Judahites who had seen their country again devastated in the initial Babylonian advance. {Jeremiah 27}. Prophet Hananiah from Gibeon (also a Benjaminite), in opposition to Jeremiah, removed the yoke from Jeremiah, enunciating that God would do the same for Judah against the Babylonians. Within two years. Hananiah dies. {Jeremiah 28}. Zedekiah does revolt under the influence of resurgent Egyptians, but Egypt, "a broken reed of a staff," does not return to the fray. {2 Kings 18:21}. Jerusalem was under siege from January 587 BCE- to the summer of 586 BCE; "severe hunger."[43]

Zedekiah was captured after the demise of Jerusalem, all his officers were executed; at age thirty-one, he saw his two young sons killed before his eyes, then his own eyes gouged out, and he was taken away in captivity. {Jeremiah 52}. Jeremiah stated that the total deported to exile were 4,600. Of these, 3,023 in 597 BCE; in 586 BCE, 832, including deserters. {2 Kings 25:11}. There was a third deportation of 745 ranking Jews from Judah in 582 BCE.

In August of 586 BCE, Nebuzaradan, the captain of the bodyguard of the king of the Babylonians, "came to Jerusalem. He burned the house of the LORD, the king's house, and all the houses of Jerusalem; every great house he burned down"…and… "broke down the walls around Jerusalem." {2 Kings 25:8-10}.

Poor Jews were allowed to remain so as to continue the grape harvest for the making of wine, as Jerusalem was recaptured in 586 BCE during the wine harvest. "But the captain of the guard left some of the poorest people of the land to be vinedressers and tillers of the soil" (the *am ha arez*). {2 Kings 25:12}.

Albright believes Negeb towns with Judean populations escaped destruction, separated from Judea when Jehoiachin was taken into exile in 597 BCE, Edomites (Idumeans) having taking over Hebron and Dura. Large Israelite populations still remained in the north and east, Ephraim, Galilee, Ammon, Beth-El, and Samaria, under Babylonian control before 589, remained intact.[44] Benjaminites who submitted before 587 BCE were not exiled and their cities of Bethel, Gibeon, Mizpah, Anatoth were left intact after Jerusalem was sacked and the Temple destroyed, after the "traitorous" revolt of Zedekiah in 587-586 BCE.[45]

A retrospective view of Jerusalem by "Jeremiah" during its final siege, from the distance of the Babylonian exile or later, by the Biblical editors of *Jeremiah*[46]:

"Then the cities of Judah and the inhabitants of Jerusalem will go and cry out to the gods to whom they make offerings but they will never save them in the time of their troubles. For your gods have become as many as your towns, O Judah; and as many as the streets of Jerusalem are the altars you have set up to shame, altars to make offerings to Baal….Because the people have forsaken me, and have profaned this place by making offerings in it to other gods whom neither they nor their ancestors have known; and because they have filled this place with the blood of the innocent, and gone on building the high places of Baal to burn their children in the fire as burnt offerings to Baal, which I did not decree, nor did it enter my mind….And I will make them eat the flesh of their sons and the flesh of their daughters, and all shall eat the flesh of their neighbors in the siege, and in the distress with which their enemies and those who seek their life afflict them." {Jeremiah 11:12-13; 19:4-9}.

The following oracle of salvation almost duplicates {Jeremiah 30:10-11}. It is also similar to Isaiah 2 {Isaiah 41:8-14}:

"But as for you, have no fear, my servant Jacob, and do not be dismayed. O Israel; for I am going to save you from far away, and your offspring from the land of their captivity. Jacob shall return and have quiet and ease, and no one shall make him afraid. As for you, have no fear, my servant Jacob, says the LORD, for I am with you. I will make an end of all the nations among which I have banished you, but I will not make an end of you! I will chastise you in just measure, and I will by no means leave you unpunished." {Jeremiah 46:27-28; 52:28-30}.

Epilogue

Nebuchadresser appointed Gedaliah, son of Ahikam, as administrator of Judah, in Mizpah, in Benjamin, eight miles north of Jerusalem. This is the same Gedaliah who freed Jeremiah from imprisonment during the reign of Jehoiakim, c.608 BCE. {Jeremiah 26:7-24}. Gedaliah's family line extended back to his grandfather Shaphan, the scribe, to King Josiah. In 582 BCE, a conspiracy was hatched by armed remnants of the Davidic royal house, now variously ensconced in Moab, Ammon, and Edom. They came to Mizpah and treacherously assassinated Gedaliah while sharing his bread, killed the other Judeans with Gedaliah, as well as the Chaldean guards. {Jeremiah 41:1-3}.

"On the day after the murder of Gedaliah before anyone knew of it, eighty men arrived from Shechem, and Shiloh, and Samaria, with their beards shaved and their clothes torn, and their bodies gashed, bringing grain offerings and incense to present at the temple of the LORD" [Jerusalem]. {Jeremiah 41:4-5}. The same men who assassinated Gedaliah, caught them and slaughtered all but ten, who pleaded: "Do not kill us, for we have stores of wheat, barley, oil, and honey hidden in the fields." {Jeremiah 41:8}. Clearly many Yahwist peasants of Israel/Ephraim had recovered their economy and wealth in the 140 years since the Assyrian and Babylonian/Chaldean occupations.

The remaining Judeans were now afraid of further retribution by the Babylonian/Chaldeans. They determined to set off for Egypt, the legendary place of refuge. Jeremiah resisted, urging them to remain: "The LORD has said to you, O remnant of Judah, Do not go to Egypt." {Jeremiah 42:19}. Johanan, son of Kareah, and the few commanders, took the remaining people of Judah (745 persons), "also the prophet Jeremiah and Baruch [his scribe], son of Neriah. And they came into the land of Egypt, for they did not obey the voice of the LORD. And they arrived at Tahpanhes." {Jeremiah 43:*passim*}.

Endnotes, Chapter 7

[1] see Color Plate 2 in Coogan, Michael D., ed. 1998. *The Oxford History of the Biblical World*, N.Y: Oxford Univ. Press.

[2] Cook, Stanley Arthur (Cambridge University). 1911. "Philistines," in *Encyclopedia Britannica*, 11th ed., Vol. 21, N.Y.: Cambridge Univ. Press, pp. 401-404.

[3] Stager, Lawrence E., in Coogan, ed., *The Oxford History of the Biblical World, op. cit.*, p. 160.

[4] Cook, S. A., "Philistines," in *Encyc.. Brit., op. cit.*, pp. 401-404; see in Coogan, M., ed., *op. cit.,* Plates 6, 11, Cypriot and Philistine ceramics; see also in Shanks, Hershel, ed. 1999. *Ancient Israel*, Washington, D.C.: Biblical Archaeological Society, Plate 3, Philistine Bi-Chrome-ware; Finkelstein, I., and Silberman, N. A.. 2001. *The Bible Unearthed*, N.Y.: The Free Press, p. 89; see also Roddy, Nicolae, review critique of Finkelstein and Silberman, in *Journal of Religion* and *Society*, Vol. 3, 2001, "Archaeology's 'New Vision' or Myopia?" 9 pp.

[5] see Redmount, Carol, 1998 in Coogan, M., ed., *The Oxford History of the Biblical World,. op. cit.*, p. 118; also Hackett, Jo-Ann, in Coogan, M., ed., 1998. *op. cit.*, p. 203.

[6] McCarter, P. Kyle, Jr. 1996. *Harper/Collins Study Bible,* New Standard Edition, London: Harper/Collins Publishers, Notes, p. 463, Cherethites and Philistines from Crete; Stager, L. E., "Forging An Identity," in Coogan, M., ed., *op. cit.*, pp. 167-168.

[7] Stager, L. E., in Coogan, M., ed., *op. cit.*, pp. 156-158.

[8] Ibid., p. 156.

[9] Redmount, C., in Coogan, M., ed., *op. cit.*, p. 118; Stager, L. E., in Coogan, M. ed., *op. cit.*, p. 168; Pritchard, James B., ed. 1958. *Ancient Near East,* Illustrated, 3 vols., Princeton, N.J.: Princeton Univ. Press, Vol. 1, p. 7; Breasted, James H. 1916. *Ancient Times.* Boston: Ginn and Co., Fig. 146, p. 240; Fig. 148, p. 243.

[10] McCarter,. P. Kyle, Jr., *Harper/Collins Study Bible, op. cit.*, in Notes, p. 421.

[11] Cook, S. A., "Jews," *Encyc. Brit.*, 11 ed., 1910, Vol. 15, *op. cit.*, p. 387.

[12] Campbell, E. F., Jr. 1998. "A Land Divided," in Coogan, M., ed., *op. cit.*, pp. 299-300.

[13] Isserlin, B. S .J. 1998. *The Israelites,* London: Thames and Hudson, Illustration 33.

[14] Ibid., pp. 310-311.

[15] Ibid., pp. 292-293.

[16] Ibid., pp. 309*ff*

[17] says Campbell, *op cit.*, pp. 299-300; see comments of Tucker, Gene M., *Harper/Collins Study Bible, op. cit.*, pp. 1355-1357.

[18] Mays, James L. 1993. *Harper/Collins Study Bible, op. cit.*, p. 1329.

[19] Ibid., pp. 1329-1331.

[20] King, Philip J., in *Harper/Collins Study Bible, op. cit.*, pp. 1379-1381.

[21] Finkelstein, I. and N. A. Silberman. 2001. *The Bible Unearthed, op. cit.*, p. 263.

[22] Roberts, J. J. M., "Isaiah: Introduction," in *Harper/ Collins Study Bible, op. cit.*, pp. 1011-1013.

[23] Campbell, E. F., in Coogan, M., ed., *op. cit.*, p. 315.

[24] McCarter, P. Kyle, Jr. 1996. *Ancient Inscriptions*, Washington, D.C.: Biblical Archaeological Society, pp. 103-104.

[25] Horn, Siegfried A., and McCarter, P. Kyle, Jr., in "The Divided Monarchy," in Shanks, Hershel, ed., *Ancient Israel, op. cit.*, pp. 161-162.

[26] Albright, W. F. 1969. *Archaeology and the Religion of Israel*, N.Y.: Anchor Books, p. 155.

[27] Campbell, E. F., in Coogan, M., ed., *op. cit.*, pp. 309-313.

[28] McCarter, P. Kyle, Jr., "The Divided Monarchy," in H. Shanks ed., *Ancient Israel, op. cit.*, pp. 156-158.

[29] McCarter, P.Kyle Jr., Illustration in Coogan, M., ed., *op. cit.*, p. 158.

[30] Finkelstein, I., and N. A. Silberman, The *Bible Unearthed, op. cit.*, p. 242.

[31] Friedman, R. E., *Who Wrote the Bible?*, San Francisco: Summit/Harper, pp. 81-82.

[32] Finkelstein, I., and N. A. Silberman, *op. cit.*, pp. 214-217.

[33] Ibid., pp. 219-220.

[34] Ibid., pp. 220-222.

[35] Campbell, Edward F., Jr., in Coogan, M., ed., *op. cit.*, p. 316.

[36] Thucydides. 1954. *The Peloponnesian War* (c.420-410 BCE), tr. Rex Warner, Hammondsworth, England: Penguin.

[37] Wilson, Robert R., *Harper/Collins Study Bible, op. cit.*, Notes, p. 591.

[38] Sayce, Archibald Henry, "Babylonia-Assyria," in *Encyc. Brit.*, 11th ed., Vol. 3, *op. cit.*, p. 105.

[39] Finkelstein, I., and N. A. Silberman, *op. cit.*, pp. 264-269; 348.

[40] Perdue, L. G., "Jeremiah", *Harper/Collins Study Bible, op. cit.*, pp. 1110-1113.

[41] Perdue, L. G., *op. cit.*, Notes, p. 1118.

[42] Finkelstein, I., and Silberman, N. A., *op. cit.* p. 293.

[43] Cogan, Mordechai, "Into Exile," in Coogan, ed., *op. cit.*, pp. 350-353; Albright, W. F., "The Biblical Period," in Finkelstein, Louis, ed. 1955. *The Jews*, Vol. 1, N.Y.: Harper and Bros., pp. 46-48.

[44] Albright, W. F., "The Biblical Period," in Finkelstein, Louis, ed., *The Jews, op. cit.*; Johnson, Paul. 1987. *A History of the Jews*, N.Y.: Harper and Bros., pp. 78-79.

[45] Johnson, Paul, *A History of the Jews, op. cit.*, pp. 78-79.

[46] Perdue, L. G., *Harper/Collins Study Bible, op. cit.*, Notes, pp. 1127, 1147.

8

Strangers in the Lands

In Egypt

Jeremiah and the refugees from Judah, after the assassination of Gedaliah in 582 BCE, found in Egypt already existing colonies of syncretist Yahwists. Jeremiah refers to the Israelites that then dwelt not merely in his own town of refuge Tahpanhes (Daphne) in the eastern Delta, from where he excoriated his fellow Judeans {Jeremiah 44:1-14}, but those that dwelt in the land of Egypt at Migdal, Memphis, and Pathros. As before in the Jerusalem homeland Jeremiah cries out against the profanation of idolatry of the people of Judah who now live in Egypt—their vows to the "Queen of heaven, libations, cakes marked with her image, both wives and husbands." He curses them: "...all the people of Judah who are in the land of Egypt shall perish by the sword and by famine until not one is left." {Jeremiah 44:27}.[1]

These colonies of Israelites and Judeans had been forming since the days of Assyria's attack on the Northern Kingdom, c.732 BCE.[2] For one hundred fifty years, until 582 BCE, the two Israelite political entities had been under siege mostly from the north. Those who felt the need migrated into that ancient well-watered motherland of the Nile and the Delta. Soldiers from Judah who had fought alongside the Assyrians when they invaded Egypt nearly a century earlier probably settled there.[3]

In addition, Hebrew troops, called Yeb, recruited probably from the time of Assyrian invasions, 671-667 BCE, of Judah, under King Manasseh and then by the Assyrian

vassal, Pharaoh Psammetichus I, 664-610 BCE, were then assigned to the southern island of Elephantine at the 1st Cataract of the Nile, opposite modern Aswan. Documents
from Elephantine, c.495-399 BCE, were discovered in the nineteenth century, CE. They
describe their appeals to both Samaria and Jerusalem during the Persian occupation
(they were then good Persian mercenaries) for assistance in rebuilding their temple
which had been destroyed by Egyptian priestly zealots in 410 BCE. Their appeal was to
the Persian governor of Judah, Bagohi, also to the governor of Samaria. They asked not
merely for financial help in rebuilding the temple but also requested information about
the procedures for observing the Feast of Unleavened Bread (Passover) and other cultic
matters. Some scholars believe that the Jews of Elephantine may have been of northern
Israelite origin, given their mention of northern shrines: "Anath-YHW, Eshem-Bethel,
Anat-Bethel." Bezalel Porten of Hebrew University believes that most scholars are
wrong in seeing the references to other gods besides YHW as indicating a northern syncretist Yahwism. His view is that these people went into Egypt during the heretical reign
of Judah's king, Manasseh, c.650 BCE, and that these refugees included Yahwist priests
from Jerusalem.[4]

The Second Isaiah, in Babylonian exile, c.550 BCE, states that Zion's children shall
return from the north, the west, and the land of Syene (1st Cataract—Aswan-Elephantine,
on the Nile). {Isaiah 49:12-14}. Also from the exile, they shall return from Egypt, from
Migdol (northeast), to Syene (south). {Ezekiel 29:10}.[5] The fate of these exilic colonies
in Egypt cannot be ascertained. After the conquest of Egypt from the Persians by Alexander, c.330 BCE, and the founding of his city Alexandria, a large Jewish population
was attracted to Alexandria. Whether these were from the Ptolemaic-controlled prov-
inces in Judea or from indigenous Yahwist colonists in Egypt cannot be known with
surety. Certainly, no mention is made of any Egyptian Jews returning to Yehud with
Persian hegemony and tolerance after 539 BCE, then, later, in the days of Nehemiah and
Ezra after the building of the Second Temple in Jerusalem. The numbers and power of
these Jewish inhabitants of Alexandria led to the translation of the Torah, now tradition-
ally structured. Then other parts of the Hebrew Bible were introduced, the *Nevi'im* (the
Prophets), and the *Kethuvim* (the Writings), plus some of the Apocryphal writings. This
was the *Septuagint*. The story is that 72 scholars were brought from Jerusalem to Alexandria to translate the Torah into Greek for the now-assimilated but practicing Jewish
population of Alexandria, c.280 BCE. At that time Ptolemy II, *Philodelphus* (man of

brotherly love), was ruler in Alexandria. He was a Greek, infatuated by scholarship and tradition.

The Jews of Egypt in the pre-Hellenistic period probably were absorbed into that rich ethnic composite that constituted ancient Egypt, from black Nubians to redheaded Celts, and assorted Semites in between. Essarhaddon, king of the Assyrians after his victories over the Egyptians at Memphis, in 674 BCE had a victory stele erected at Sinjirli, north of the gulf of Antioch. It shows the gifted if defeated Egyptian Pharaoh Taharqa, himself a Nubian outsider, with the features of a Negro.[6]

Israel's Assyrian Fate

The ten tribes of the Northern Kingdom, deportees from Assyrian-conquered Israel, disappeared after each of the events, after 732 BCE, for the kingdom in general, and then in 722 BCE from the capital Samaria itself. Finkelstein and Silberman believe that 40,000-50,000 people all told, twenty percent of the population west of the Jordan, were sent into exile, with the arid Trans-Jordan territories of Gilead then having a population of 150,000 people![7] The Assyrian empire began to come apart, c.650 BCE, with the revolt of Ashurbanipal's twin brother, Shamash-shum-ukin, who was made regent of Babylonia by their father Esarhaddon. Chaldeans, Arameans, Elamites went against the Assyrian king, as did the Indo-European Cimmerians in Asia Minor. The Assyrian viceroy twin (ruling in Babylon) lost his head in 648 BCE, as the formerly pacified south became unraveled with Kedarite Arab tribes coming into Transjordan (Gilead and Dan).[8]

It is quite possible that the exiles from Israel could have then drifted back into what was then Samaria. They had been away from their homeland for about seventy-five years. This was not much more time than the Judahites had lived in Babylonia, from 597-586 BCE, to after the Persian liberation of Babylonia and Judah, in 539-538 BCE. Many could have gone back to Samaria from their refuge in Judah, especially after that province came under Chaldean/Babylonian assault. The population of the formerly wealthy Israel never seems to have undergone the demographic blight that Judah suffered after the destruction of the Temple. Albright estimated that in the latter, a population of 20-25,000 (formerly 75-120,000—Jerusalem 15,000) remained in Judah after 582 BCE.[9] Thus the "ten lost tribes" of Israel might have quietly returned to their native homes alongside the Assyrian imported newcomers. We can thus explain the 80 elders from Samaria, Shechem, and Shiloh that Jeremiah tells us about, who came to mourn the destroyed Temple when Gedaliah and Jeremiah were at Mizpah. {Jeremiah 41: 4-5}.

Israel (which became Samaria) as well as Judah retained their basic Levantine ethnic mix which had been long established from the most ancient historic period (see Chapters 2-4). The returnees from Babylon now had created their own special sense of ethnic Judahite identity, attempting to separate themselves by marriage from the Samarians. The earlier traditions of intermarriage were quite variable, Moses' marriage to a Midianite; Ruth, the Moabite, which tribe was a product of the incestuous offspring of Lot and his unnamed daughter, and thus ancestor to David. Solomon's son, Rehoboam had a mother who was an Ammonite princess, the Ammonites a product of the incestuous offspring of Lot and a second unnamed daughter. {1 Kings 14:21}.

Samson married an unnamed Philistine charmer from Timnah. {Judges 14}. And, of course, the Ishmaelites were derived from Abraham and Hagar, his Egyptian concubine. Jael, loyal to Yahweh and the Israelites was a Kenite (Cain). The Edomites descended from Esau, Isaac's legitimate and eldest son. Then recall the half-Egyptian blasphemer during the Exodus, condemned by Moses. {Leviticus 24:10}.

Contrasting with the Biblical tradition of ethnic descent, is the Babylonian/Chaldean description of their own incursion into the Levant toward Judah: "In the seventh year, the month of Kislev, the king of Akkad [Babylon] mustered his troops to the Hatti-land, [sic], and encamped against the City of Judah..." {Babylonian Chronicle}. The Hatti were the Indo-European Hittites.[10]

The Babylonian Exile

In the year 695-694 BCE Jeremiah sent a letter to those who had accepted exile in Babylonia with King Jehoiachin in 697 BCE. Two envoys from King Zedekiah, then in vassalage in Jerusalem, took the letter addressed to the elders, priests, and prophets now residing in Babylon. The letter urged them to accept a seventy-year exile, thus to persuade all the people formerly of Judah to "seek the welfare of the city" of their exile, to marry, take wives for their sons and husbands for their daughters, and to multiply until they could return home again. {Jeremiah 29:1-7}.

The prophet Ezekiel was also a part of the Babylonian exilic community. He ministered for nearly thirty years to Judeans who lived in Tel-abib, a town on the Chebar Canal that ran through the city of Nippur near the ancient Sumerian city of Ur (of the "Chaldees").[11] Clearly, exiles to Babylonia from the three catastrophic events, 597, 586, and 582, BCE, constituted the elite of Judah, possibly ninety to ninety-five percent of the educated middle classes, the peasantry and working classes remaining behind.[12]

The situation in Babylonia was clearly different from what faced the Israelite exiles in Assyria or later on upon the sufferance of the Egyptians. The Chaldeans originally came from the area around Ur, near the mouths of Tigris and Euphrates rivers, and perhaps further back in time from Arabia or the area of what is known today as Quwait. In their day, the Chaldeans added a new Semitic overlay to the original Sumerian population of the two rivers.

A variety of exilic populations already existed throughout the Assyrian/Babylonian empires. Despite the practical barbarity of Chaldean Nebuchadressar, he also was intensely concerned with strengthening an empire weakened by the bloody costs, in human and material resources. This was his heritage, the results of the continuous wars in the area. Especially of concern was the destruction of Babylon by the Assyrian Ashurbanipal, during the uprising of his brother Sama-sum-yukin, with the help of the Chaldean/Babylonians, c.650 BCE, barely fifty years before the first Judean exile. The Judeans were expected to assist in the rebuilding, and to reap the rewards of their contributions.

Babylon had a rich cultural tradition that stretched back to the days of Sumer, 2500 years in the past. It was a culture of learning in which the kings and priests were literate, knowledgeable, intellectual, in contrast to what supposedly characterized the Assyrian war machine. The Assyrian capital Nineveh, was formerly believed to be an armed camp.[13] Babylon retained the residual power inherent in its traditions of culture, similar to that held by Athens for the militaristic Roman conquerors, a power that intoxicated an intelligent Assyrian such as Sama-sum-yukin.

Ashurbanipal's twin brother became Assyrian viceroy of Babylon in 668 BCE, on the death of his father Esarhaddon (son of Sennacherib). Ashurbanipal, the twin chosen to be king, ultimately faced a revolt by his own blood. With Chaldean assistance (as noted in Chapter 7), Sama-sum-yukin took the road toward glory, lost, and was beheaded. The revolt had surprising elements. Sama-sum-yukin was fascinated with then historic Babylonian culture. He attempted to reinstate the Sumerian language as the official tongue of his Babylonian/Chaldean province.[14] Sumerian was not a Semitic tongue, but was regarded as we regard Latin, only a greater linguistic distance existed here than between Latin and modern English. Yet Sumerian was still taught in the various Babylonian academies in appreciation of the conjoint heritage of geography. This link was long cemented in the many Babylonian libraries with their vast collections of the ancient

Sumerian tablets. Here had developed a treasured repository of a common mythology, literature, and civilization's glue, its systems of law.

Ashurbanipal himself has been described as "luxurious and indolent, entrusting the command of his armies to others whose successes he appropriated." He was cruel and superstitious, but, too, a great patron of art and literature. The extensive library of Nineveh was to a considerable extent his creation, and "scribes were kept constantly employed in it copying the older tablets of Babylonia..."[15] These Assyrian brothers show us that the intelligence of the Assyrians was acute, their respect for art and learning high. But power and military hegemony were the inertial dynamics of this northern Semitic nation. In 610 BCE, Scythians (Medes-Cimmerians) took Haran from the Assyrians, with Babylonia/Chaldean help, and Assyria was at its last gasp. [16]

At a distance, the Judeans could still celebrate: "Nineveh is like a pool whose waters run away. 'Halt! Halt'—but no one turns back." {Nahum 2:8}. Don't rejoice yet, Jerusalem, Josiah, your king, would be killed by an Assyrian ally, Egypt, in 609 BCE, and Nebuchadrezzar soon would be on his way!

The King of Judah, Jehoiachin, was released from prison in Babylonia in 561 BCE by Amel-marduk (c.562-560 BCE), son of Nebuchadrezzar.[17] Both Jeremiah and the second Deuteronomist Historian agree that this new king set Jehoiachin above the other kings in Babylon, gave him an allowance and had him dine regularly at the Chaldean/Babylonian king's table. {2 Kings 25:27-30; Jeremiah 52:31-34}.

A mysterious interval of four years and Nabonidus, 556-539 BCE, became king of Chaldean Babylonia. Cogan says Nabonidus was not of Chaldean ancestry. He argues that Nabonidus' devotion to the Moon God Sin, (Sinai), from his native city of Haran, the city of Abraham, Isaac, and Jacob, argues for Aramean (Indo-European-Mitanni?) ancestry.[18] Perhaps one of the most unique characters to lead a nation, Nabonidus reminds us of the role of Akhenaten, c.1350 BCE, attempting to irrevocably alter the national religion (see Chapter 4) and Julian the Apostate, 363-365 CE, attempting to return Rome from Christ to Aristotle. Nabonidus, however, incurred the wrath of the well-established priestly establishment that served Babylon's great god Marduk.

Nabonidus had the images of the various Babylonian gods transferred from the ancestral local shrines to Babylon, ostensibly for safekeeping.[19] He attempted to do as Hezekiah and Josiah had attempted to do in Judah, to centralize worship. In this case, of course, the centralization was for the god Marduk, at Babylon. His efforts also were directed to the beautification of Babylon's temples. Centralization and the control it connoted did alienate the local priesthood without satisfying the upholders of Marduk in the capital. Isaiah 2 comments from first-hand on these well-advertised Babylonian events: "Bel [Baal-Lord-Marduk] bows down, Nebo ["Nob," son of Marduk] stoops, their idols are on beasts and cattle; these things you carry are loaded as burdens on weary animals. They stoop, they bow down together; they cannot save the burden, but themselves go into captivity. {Isaiah 2.40-55; 46:1-2}.

The military were repelled by Nabonidus' antiquarian tastes; his fascinations with the history of the land of the two rivers. He had authored a standard chronology of the emperors of Babylon—from Sumerian days on. He centered his own theogeny at Haran in his worship of Sin (Sinai), but also of Shamash (the sun god), and Ishtar (goddess of love and war). He also revived the ancient temple rites, c.3000 BCE, at Sumer's Ur, and appointed his eldest daughter to be the high priestess there.[20]

In the early years of his reign, Nabonidus fought in northern Syria and the west against various Indo-European, Cimmerian, and Mede incursions. Then, suddenly, he gave over the running of the state and the wars to his son Belshazzar (Bel [Baal]-shar-usur), suddenly retiring to Tema (Sinai?) in northwestern Arabia, for ten years of contemplation.[21] For a number of years, the New Year's festival for Marduk had to be postponed because the king was not there.

The Israelite prophet Habakkuk, late 7th to early 6th century, the time of the agony of Judah, is quoted: "God came from Teman, the Holy One from Mount Paran. His glory covered the heavens, and the earth was full of his praise. The brightness was like the sun; rays came forth from his hand where his power lay hidden." {Habakkuk 3:3-4}. Stager believes that the Exodus tradition of Moses and the Midianites might best be interpreted as seeing "the mountain of God" as connected with Edom, Seir, Paran, Teman, Cushan (Arabia), and Midian, Tema being a large town in northwest Arabia south of Qurayyah and Timna.[22] We might ask why did Nabonidus choose Tema for his contemplation? Was there any relationship in this to his origins in Haran, Ur-homeland of the Hebrews of the Bible?

Nabonidus finally returned to the wars. He fled to Babylon after defeats by the Medes at Sippara. The governor of Kurdistan, Gobryas, entered Babylon without a fight. The priests of Marduk had apparently opened the gates to the enemy. {Daniel 5}. He hid himself in one of the temples, to no avail. "Nabonidus was dragged out of his hiding place, and Kurdish guards were placed at the gates of the great temple of Bel [Baal-Merodach-Marduk] where the services continued without intermission."[23]

Isaiah 2 echoes the general hope of deliverance from the disintegrating empire of this problematic emperor:

"Listen to me, O house of Jacob, all the remnants of the house of Israel, who have been borne by me from your birth, carried from the womb; even to your old age I am he, even when you turn gray I will carry you. I have made, and I will bear; I will carry and I will save...Listen to me, you stubborn of heart, you who are far from deliverance: I bring near my deliverance, it is not far off, and my salvation will not tarry; I will put salvation in Zion, for Israel my glory." {Isaiah 2. 46:3-4, 12-13}.

Cyrus, the Persian, soon arrived. He began his propaganda campaign promising to liberate all the people of Mesopotamia from the seemingly unstable Nabonidus, appealing to the Marduk-worshipping Babylonians as well as the captive Israelites. Nominally a follower of Zoroaster, he pursued a policy of religious neutrality.[24] "Thus says the LORD to his anointed [*sic*], to Cyrus, whose right hand I have grasped to subdue the nations before him and strip kings of their robes, to open doors before him—and the gates shall not be closed..." {2 Isaiah 45:1.

The hope was now to be a reality: "By the rivers of Babylon—there we sat down and there we wept when we remembered Zion. On the willows there we hung our harps. For there our captors asked us for songs, and our tormentors asked for mirth, saying, 'Sing us one of the songs of Zion'. How could we sing the LORD's song in a foreign land? If I forget you, O Jerusalem, let my right hand wither! Let my tongue cling to the roof of my mouth, if I do not remember you, if I do not set Jerusalem above my highest joy." {Psalm 137:1-6}.

Only with the Scrolls

When they left Jerusalem in exilic waves, setting their backs on a destroyed city and their Temple in ashes, the Israelites carried with them neither images of remembrance, nor the silver and gold embellishments of sanctity. Nebuchadrezzar and his captains had no special animus against the Israelite YHWH. But they did see the political power inherent in the Temple and its worshipful political demands. These were the same values that Hezekiah and Josiah had understood. The religion of the Judeans, and the Temple in Jerusalem could be the glue to hold this people together during these threatening times, to firm up a patriotism, a centripetality that could preserve the domain. That is why the "good kings" warred against the high places, and the ancient syncretic, if now corrupting, Canaanite rites that so entranced the rural folk.

What the Israelites, the elders, the priests, the prophets, the skilled and educated of the land, took with them, were their scrolls, the documents that bound them to this devastated land. These scrolls were the bricks that would become a great edifice of both memory and determination. The Tabernacle, the Ark that housed the scrolls of the Ten Commandments of Moses, was easily transportable. By the rivers of Babylon, the faith, the history, the discipline could be renewed and made eternal.

The history that the "J" and "E" writers had set down hundreds of years before; the chronicles of the kings of Israel and Judah; the priestly code "P", all contain some very early material, which was known in Jerusalem before Ezra, c.450 BCE, (almost 100 years after Cyrus allowed the Israelites to return and rebuild Jerusalem). The scrolls from which Ezra preached to the *golah* (the elite faithful) were now reintroduced into Jerusalem priestly circles, probably long edited into the Pentateuch during the exile in Babylon.[25] R. E. Friedman believes that most of "P" was written in the time of Hezekiah, but also recognizes that some portions were subject to editing during the Babylonian captivity and beyond, to the beginning of the second Temple.[26]

The Deuteronomic history, Deuteronomy through 2 Kings, has two editions, the first "discovered" and written during the rule of Josiah in Jerusalem, c.639-609 BCE, the second, probably during the exilic period. But there is much controversy concerning its ultimate authorship, and how it clarifies the varying allegiances and sources of the priesthood that would arrive in Babylon, and begin the critical editing of the Pentateuch.

Norman Gottwald maintains that the Deuteronomic Law Code {Deut. 12-26:} was edited in the 7th century BCE.[27] Certain sections, however, were proto-Deuteronomic, from the north, and part of an ancient tradition that seems to have been derived from the pre-monarchical era, but edited together in the time of Hezekiah, 727-698 BCE, and influential in Hezekiah's Judean reforms.[28]

Richard Friedman concurs, believing that the Deuteronomic Law Code was probably written by Shiloh priests descended from Moses who came south after the 722 BCE destruction of Israel.[29] However, Friedman has argued that Jeremiah, or his scribe, Baruch, son of Neriyah, who went into exile in Egypt with Jeremiah (!) put together the entire Deuteronomic histories.[30] This is naturally puzzling, since the compilation of Deuteronomy 1 and 2 seems to have taken place in Babylonia and after. An example of Friedman's analysis is given in relation to the Law Code, {Deut. 20:10-20}. Here Moses gives terrifying instruction as to how to deal with enemies. A) Those distant peoples: kill the men and take the women and little ones into captivity along with the cattle etc.

Closer peoples who should be under the inheritance of the Lord thy God "thou shalt save alive nothing that breatheth—utterly destroy them—namely the Hittites, Amorites, Canaanites, Perizzites, Hivites, Jebusites."

Yahweh gives such a promise of suzerainty over these people to Abraham, as part of his covenant. {Genesis 15:18-21-J source} Still, Friedman, sees the above Deuteronomic section as authored by "other" than D1 or D2, not E or P![31]

HOWEVER! {Exodus 34:11—J-source} has the same statement, same tribal enemies, so, too, see above, {Gen. 15:18-21—J-source} but without the terrible description of slaughter. Did Jeremiah copy this ancient "J" text?

Edward Campbell interprets the facts somewhat differently. The scrolls found by Josiah comprised the Book of Deuteronomy, c.622 BCE. The intellectual, political and religious perspective within derives primarily from the Levite Priesthood outside of Jerusalem. Here, the north, Israel and Shechem (Friedman—Shiloh) become important, hearkening back to its dominant role in ancient Canaanite tradition, 17-16 century BCE. A large Canaanite temple had long existed in Shechem, establishing for the patriarchal (and tribal) tradition its primary position. So, too, for Moses and Joshua, at Mt. Ebal (Baal), above Shechem. Reminiscent of the covenant at Mt. Horeb in the wilderness, this later gathering reflects the need for a central Canaanite location to worship Yahweh. Here would be accentuated the ancient tribal tradition, in seeming opposition to kingship.

Thus, argues Campbell, in Deuteronomy we discern a Mushite, rather than an Aaronite orientation. Further, Shechem retained a family connection with the Kohathites [Kohen?] among the Levites. The Deuteronomic Historians and the later (5th-4th centuries BCE) writers of Chronicles both concentrated on the centrality of Jerusalem. But they did not want to erase the more ancient footprint of a Shechemite-Levitical tradition. There is thus hinted in the Deuteronomic books a proto-Deuteronomical perspective under the influence of Davidic Jerusalem.[32]

And, of course, of great importance, a treasure trove of writings of the various prophets existed, already part of the Israelite religious and moral experience, and in some cases brought north into Babylon by followers. Finally, we should note the existence of many writings of seers, prophets, priests that were lost, later rejected for one reason or another. Clearly, this was a rich and diverse heritage that had to be renewed, so that this chosen people could live closer to the God of the Covenant. In doing so they would be allowed once more to return to that land of milk and honey," that Zion on a hill that had been promised as their inheritance, if they were but worthy.

A Higher Faith

The exilic intellectual elite had to come to grips with the tension between an awareness that their faith in the moral and physical power of YHWH would in the end redeem their land, together with the awareness of their own moral culpability in the ruin of their kingdoms. Thus the tone was set for their work in exile. This was underscored by their impotence, deprived of the power inherent in political independence and the symbol of their own holy shrine in Zion, wherein resided their God. They needed once more, as in the Exodus, to rededicate themselves to an unconditional commitment to the laws of YHWH.

What did this faith stand for? What was its uniqueness in the family of nations that now surrounded them in Babylon? In what way could they claim the superiority of their own faith, so superior that it could surmount the defeats, the pain, the loss?

They had a history, a thousand-year-old tradition of strangeness, aliens, with only their God to direct them. This history would separate and identify them, from the time of their patriarch, Abraham, coming south from Ur and Haran, now close at hand to their ultimate homeland in Canaan. Their history defined them as a people, but as a "chosen people" only when they embraced the tight defensive moral and social mode of observance of the meanings of this historical togetherness.

One God, YHWH, compared to the polytheism that existed among all the peoples with whom they had lived. One God, who could not be pictured, or sculpted, or made into graven images for worship, an abstract idea, a concept of a God. Indeed, this God, YHWH, had appeared in person to Moses, to Elijah, but as time and learning continued, the anthropomorphism diminished. He became an over-arching principle, passing moral judgment on human behavior, an exemplar that could not be reified into the Sun or the Moon. There was not a more transcendent God of nature and man. Power, YHWH had, but only for the guidance of his people through time and destiny, placing them on the anvil of righteousness, thus to survive and prosper, or be cursed for their infidelity.

Jeroboam, in founding the state of Israel, did set up young bulls as golden pedestals of the invisible YHWH, emphasizing the northern Canaanite tradition of Elohim, in the temples at Beth-el and Dan. In Jerusalem Solomon built his Temple, which included an inner sanctum the Holy of Holies with two statues, the cherubs, four legged animals, head of a human, wings like a bird, carved out of olive wood and plated with gold. They, too, represented the throne platform of YHWH, and also, very much in the Canaanite cultic tradition. Under the wings of the cherubs was the Tabernacle and within it was the ark, and the tablets of the Ten Commandments, given to Moses by YHWH. {Psalm 61:5}.

We must remember the difficulty that ordinary humans have with higher principles that are not things. We create demi-gods out of ordinary political chieftains and invest them with our patriotism. Our other gods are heroes of sports and entertainments. Today, images of saints, Madonnas, saviors, infiltrate modern religious worship. It is difficult to worship an unseen power that represents high moral discipline and behavior.

The Temple is a concession to tangible reality, a home for YHWH, in the tabernacle, the ark, and the written covenant with YHWH. Ritual is necessary for humans. Holidays can mark symbolically historically important emotional events—the Passover for example, in which the sacrifice of a lamb for the feast, is required. Increasingly, as the Israelites approached their time of destiny in Israel and Judah, their prophets, if not their priests separated symbolic representation in cultic activities from the magical and mythological. The kuppuru rites for the Mesopotamian New Year festival, Akitu, became the Day of Atonement for the sins of the individual—similar to Hittite and Assyro-Babylonian purification ceremonies.[33] Here the abstinence from fleshly satisfaction was richly substituted with prayer and Temple consecration.

Sacrifice also underwent a long process of spiritual purification. Who can doubt, as we have documented in earlier chapters, that in the most ancient historical times these tribal peoples actually gave their young into the fires for the gods? The stories of Isaac and Cain were altered to represent later priestly/scholarly sentiments, the sensibilities of a newer, urban era. Indeed, the strictures of Jeremiah reflect the adjustment that the laws of YHWH had undergone under the constant prophetic ethical admonishment by Israelite intellectuals. Even the stories that emanated from the Mosaic tradition of the Exodus stir fearful memories of terrible life surrendering rites, the seeming necessities for the appeasement of the judgment of fiery YHWH.

Unlike the religions of their contemporaries, no female goddesses entered the Israelite pantheon. The message of the Patriarchs and Moses, as derived from YHWH, was that the female principle as practiced in contemporary religions involved sexual rites exemplifying the weakness of humans. Inevitably came disgust with temple prostitution, both male and female. In the ritual worship of sexuality, nations opened the door to powerful and throbbing rhythms, physical elements that led to violence and war, values that would inevitably lead to the dissolution of defensive community life, Ashtarte (Asherah), Athena. The sexual must be disciplined. In recognition of human nature, the Israelite male was given greater leeway, in numbers of wives, in sexual relationships with unmarried women, but always under the strict supervision of Biblical law. Why the control over the female? Because the female principle was so central to the life and dynamic of a community, it had to be strictly patrolled, channeled into procreation, the fostering of the family, and the survival of the community.

The practices of the great urban societies of the time led to the dissipation of personal discipline and rigor, the corruption of family life, inevitably, God's wrath. These corruptions also had their internal political character. Here the autocratic rulers could dissipate human energies, independence of thought, even subversion. It was ancient exemplification of what modern dictators often resorted to: at the first whiff of rebellion, open the cinemas to pornography.

Circumcision is another example of the gradual spiritualization of what at first was a tangible physical rite of religious demarcation. In the beginning it was a sign of the covenant between Abraham and God, then a bond between God and Israel. (Gen. 17:7*ff.*—P-source). Recall, in {Exod. 4:24-26—J-source}, the frightening circumcision of Moses' son by Zipporah, the rite of "the bloody bridegroom" in which she consecrates Moses with the child's foreskin, and perhaps saves him from YHWH's wrath. So, too, before the Israelites can enter Canaan, Joshua must renew the rite of circumcision, which was ignored by the new generation, the people "not having listened to the voice of the LORD." {Joshua 5:6}. In the days of Jeremiah the ritual takes on a new metaphorical meaning: "Circumcise your heart to the Lord and remove the foreskins of your heart." {Jeremiah 4:4}.

In Deuteronomy, it is transposed back in time, though the phraseology is Jeremiah's: "Circumcise therefore, the foreskin of your heart and be no more stiff-necked." {Deut. 10:16}. Likewise: "...the LORD, your God, will circumcise your heart...so that you will love the LORD your God with all your heart and with all your soul." {Deut. 30:6}. This leads, of course, into Paul's and Christianity's non-literal interpretation of the ritual, which facilitated their ability to proselytize to the non-Semitic Roman masses.

The compilers of the ancient scrolls, in attempting to bring them together into a document for the faithful in the ages to come, still were influenced by the historical character of the Israelite experience. They were hesitant about effacing that which seemed crude and un-modern, even in 6th century Levantine society. Thus they respected the past, perhaps even submitted to it, as part of their religious devotion.

The priestly tradition, whether in part during the reign of Judah's Hezekiah (R. E Friedman), else as with the majority of scholars during the Babylonian captivity and later, attempted to fill out the sacramental, ritualistic elements in the Mosaic law, to make it a dynamic, working element in official Temple worship and consecration. Several hundred years later, and under a quite different cultural ethos, the Hellenistic, many of these rules would appear to be superstitious and archaic, representing a world that had passed below the historical horizon. It is one thing to search for a law that will preserve sexual purity. However, the priestly, "P", regulation of adultery as it applies to a married woman under suspicion by her husband, engraved into the Pentateuch, reminds us that the evolution of the religion of Israel was still in process:

"The priest shall set the woman before the LORD, dishevel the woman's hair, and place in her hands the grain offering of remembrance, which is the grain offering of jealousy. In his own hand the priest shall have the water of bitterness that brings the curse. Then the priest shall make her take an oath saying, 'If no man has lain with you, if you have not turned aside to uncleanliness while under your husband's authority, be immune to this water of bitterness that brings the curse'….When he has made her drink the water, then, if she has defiled herself and has been unfaithful to her husband, the water that brings the curse shall enter into her and cause bitter pain, and her womb shall discharge, her uterus drop, and the woman shall become an execration among her people. But if the woman has not defiled herself and is clean, then she shall be immune and be able to conceive children…This is the law when a spirit of jealousy comes on a man…then he shall set the woman before the LORD….The man shall be free from iniquity, but the woman shall bear her iniquity." {Numbers 5: *passim*—P-source}.

Later, during the Roman conquest of then-revolting Judea, Samaria, Galilee, the Pharisee/Rabbi Yohanan ben Zakkai, with the cooperation of the Roman emperor, Vespasian, c.69 CE, had himself smuggled in a coffin out of Jerusalem to Yavneh (the old Philistine city of Timnah). This town was now to be the site of the new Rabbinic Academy. It was he, Yohanan ben Zakkai, who suspended the above rule of the suspected adulteress, also the rite of the broken-necked heifer," involving community blood-guilt or innocence in the killing of a stranger. {Deuteronomy 21}.[34]

End and Beginning of Eras

The edict of Cyrus, 539 BCE, allowing the Israelites to return to the now-Persian province of Yehud, brought a trickle of returnees to that devastated homeland. They were mostly the children and grandchildren of the Davidic royalty, Shenazzar, and the priest, Zerubbabel (builder of the 2nd Temple), in search of their former fortune, but now firmly under the tutelage of a powerful, if beneficent, occupying power. {Ezra 1:8; 5:14; Chronicles 3:18}. Before the middle of the fifth century, c.450 BCE, hereditary Yahwist governors were already in control of Samaria and Ammon (Trans-Jordan).[35]

The bulk of the Israelite population in Babylonia remained there. Many moved to the cities of Persia, where they were useful to the monarchy, still with a relatively uncouth population of peasants and warriors. Hebrew communities could soon be found in cities in Asia Minor, such as Sardis, now also under Persian control.[36] The faith of their fathers was now portable. The Holy Writings could be copied and taken to new places where new communities of this ancient faith could be established.

By the days of Ezra and Nehemiah, also c.450 BCE, Israelites were widely dispersed in Babylonia and Persia. The Israelites of Nippur became wealthy, 28 settlements being recorded in this area, with extensive involvement in banking, agriculture, trade, military settlements. Some of those who chose to return to Yehud and the growing settlement in Jerusalem had male and female slaves that they were permitted to bring with them. {Ezra: *passim*}.[37]

The diminished land of Persian Yehud that the first returnees encountered, c.538 BCE, was but a shadow of the former pride of nationhood. Perhaps 25,000 inhabitants lived in this small region centered around and including Jerusalem.[38] Edomites, later called Idumeans, had occupied southern areas of ancient Judah, with its capital, Hebron. Ammonites and Moabites had returned to the lands east of the Jordan, where the assassins of Gedaliah had fled. Phoenicians moved south along the coast and the fertile valleys, the ancient tribal home of Asher, Zebulon, and Issachar. The ever-resourceful former Philistine towns along the southern coast again moved east into the Sheppelah hill country.

Those the Assyrians and Chaldean/Babylonians had left behind to tend the land, and who had incurred the wrath of the prophets for their syncretic and corrupt Yahwism, the *am har etz*, were suspect by the returnees. Increasingly intermarried, and casual in their worship, in both rituals and cult, especially the northerners of Samaria seemed different:

"Thus, when the small band of returnees arrived from Babylonia, they found a country that they did not know or recognize. They did not know its people or its mixture of different ethnic groups; presumably language was the only trait that they had in common. Culturally and religiously, the two groups had become strangers."[39]

Endnotes, Chapter 8

[1] Cogan, M., in Coogan, Michael D., ed. 1998. *The Oxford History of the Biblical World*, N.Y: Oxford Univ. Press, pp. 358-361.

[2] Finkelstein, I., and Silberman, N. A. 2001. *The Bible Unearthed*, N.Y.: The Free Press, p. 199.

[3] Albright, W. F., in Finkelstein, Louis, ed. 1955. *The Jews, Their History, Culture, and Religion*, Vol. 1, N.Y: Harper and Bros., p. 49.

[4] Purvis, J., and Meyers, D. E. 1999, "Exile and Return," in Shanks, Hershel, ed., *Ancient Israel*, Washington, D.C.: Biblical Archaeological Society, p. 204.

[5] Purvis, J., and Meyers, D. E. 1999, "Exile and Return," in Shanks ed., *Ancient Israel, op. cit.*, pp. 213-216.

[6] Sayce, Archibald Henry. 1910. "Babylonia and Assyria," *Encyclopedia Britannica*, 11th ed., Vol. 3, N.Y.: Cambridge Univ. Press, p. 105.

[7] Finkelstein, I., and Silberman, N .S., *The Bible Unearthed, op. cit.*, pp. 208, 221.

[8] Horn, S., and McCarter, P. Kyle, Jr. 1999. "The Divided Monarchy," in Shanks, *op. cit.*, pp. 186-187.

[9] Albright, Wm. F., in Finkelstein, L.,ed., *The Jews, op. cit.*, Vol. 1, pp. 49-51; Finkelstein, I., and Silberman, N. A., *The Bible Unearthed, op. cit.*, pp. 245, 306.

[10] Finkelstein, I., and Silberman, N .S., *The Bible Unearthed, op. cit.*, p. 293.

[11] Cogan, M., in Coogan, M., *The Oxford History of the Biblical World, op. cit.*, pp. 358-361.

[12] Cogan, M., "Into Exile," in Coogan *op. cit.*, p. 355; Gottwald, Norman. K. 1985. *The Hebrew Bible, A Socio-Literary Introduction*, Philadelphia: Fortress Press, p. 423; Purvis, J. D., "Exile and Return," in Shanks, ed. *op. cit.*, p. 202.

[13] Sayce, A. H., "Babylonia and Assyria," *Encyc. Brit. op. cit.*, 11th ed., Vol. 3, p. 106.

[14] Ibid., p. 105.

[15] Sayce, A. H., "Assurbanipal," *Encyc. Brit.*, 11th ed., 1910, Vol. 2, p. 789.

[16] Horn, S., and McCarter, P. Kyle, Jr. 1999. "The Divided Monarchy," in Shanks, *op. cit.*, pp. 190-191.

[17] Purvis, J., "Exile and Return," in Shanks ed., *Ancient Israel, op. cit.*, p. 208.

[18] Cogan, M., "Into Exile," in Coogan *op. cit.*, pp. 361-364.

[19] Roberts, J. J. M. 1993. Notes, "Isaiah," in *The Harper/Collins Study Bible*, New Standard Edition, London: Harper/Collins Publishers, p. 1078.

[20] Cogan, M., "Into Exile," Illustration of stele at Haran, in Coogan, *op. cit.*, p. 362; Saggs, H. W. F. 2000. *Babylonians*, Berkeley: University of California Press, p. 170.

[21] Stager, L. E., "Forging An Identity," in Coogan, *op. cit.*, pp. 143-144.

[22] Ibid., pp. 143-144.

23 Sayce, A. H., "Babylonia and Assyria," *Encyc. Brit. op. cit.*, 11th ed., Vol. 3, p. 106; Ibid., pp. 106-107; also, Sayce, A. H. "Belshazzar," *Encyc. Brit., op. cit.*, 11th edition, Vol. 3, pp. 711-712. The ancient records indicate that Nabonidus' son, Belshazzar (O Bel=defend the King) stayed on to fight at Sippur. On arriving at Babylon, Cyrus, with his typical political acumen, appointed Nabonidus to be Governor (Satrap) of the now-Persian Province of Karamania. Cyrus sent Gobryas up the river to fight Belshazzar, who was defeated and killed. Cyrus promptly proclaimed six days of mourning throughout Chaldean Babylonia, for death of Belshazzar!

24 Noss, John B. 1949. *Man's Religions*, N.Y.: Macmillan, pp. 458-459.

25 Albright, W. F., in Finkelstein, L., ed., *The Jews, op. cit.*, Vol. 1, p. 49; Gottwald, N. K, *The Hebrew Bible, op. cit.*; *Harper/Collins Study Bible* Editors and Scholars, *passim*.

26 Friedman, R. E. 1989. *Who Wrote The Bible?*, 2nd ed., San Francisco: Harper, p. 225.

27 Gottwald, N. K., *The Hebrew Bible, op. cit.*, p. 208.

28 Ibid.,. pp. 316-317.

29 Friedman, R. E., *Who Wrote The Bible?, op. cit.*, in Ch. 6, pp 117*ff.*

30 Ibid., pp. 146-148.

31 Ibid., p. 255.

32 Campbell, Edward F., in Coogan, ed., pp. 285-286.

33 Weinfeld, Moshe. 1989. "Israelite Religion," in Seltzer, Robert M., ed. 1989. *Judaism, A People and Its History*, N.Y.: Macmillan, p. 50.

34 Levine, Lee, "The Age of Hellenism," in Shanks, ed. *Ancient Israel, op. cit.*, p. 263.

35 Albright, W. F., "The Biblical Period," in Finkelstein, L., *The Jews, op. cit.*, p. 47.

36 Ibid., pp. 52-53.

37 Cogan, M., "Into Exile," in Coogan, ed., p. 357; Purvis, J. D. and Meyers, E. M., "Exile and Return," in Shanks, ed., *op. cit.*, pp. 205-207.

38 Albright, W. F., in "The Biblical Period," in Finkelstein, L., ed., *The Jews, op. cit.*, p. 49, estimates that the population was about 20,000; Finkelstein, I. and Silberman, N. A., in *The Bible Unearthed, op. cit.*, p. 308, estimate the population at 30,000.

39 Ahlstrom, G. W. 1986. *Who Were the Israelites?* Winona Lake IN.: Eisenbrauns, p. 105.

Bibliography

Abrahams, Israel. 1910. "Circumcision," in *Encyclopedia Britannica*, 11th ed., Vol. VI, N.Y.: Cambridge Univ. Press.

Ahlstrom, G. W. 1986. *Who Were the Israelites?*, Winona Lake, IN.: Eisenbrauns.

Ahlstrom, G. W. 1993. "The History of Ancient Palestine from the Paleolithic Period to Alexander's Conquest," Sheffield, England: *Journal of the Society of Old Testament Studies Supplemental Series,* 146.

Aitkin, M. J., *et al.*, eds. 1993. *The Origin of Modern Humans and the Impact of Chronometric Dating*, Princeton, N.J.: Princeton Univ. Press.

Albright, W. F. 1955. "The Biblical Period," in Finkelstein, Louis, ed. 1955. *The Jews, Their History, Culture, and Religion,* 2 vols., N.Y: Harper and Bros.

Albright, W. F. 1969. *Archaeology and the Religion of Israel*, Garden City, N.Y.: Doubleday.

Anderson, G. W. 1966. *The History and Religion of Israel,* N.Y.: Oxford University Press.

Anderson, G. W. 1975. *Understanding the Old Testament*, Englewood Cliffs, N.J.: Prentice Hall.

Andrews, P., and Stringer, C. 1993. "The Primates' Progress," in Gould, S., ed. 1993. *Life,* N.Y.: W. W. Norton, p. 233.

Arnold, P M. 1990. "Gibeah: The Search for a Biblical City," Sheffield, England: *Journal of the Society of Old Testament Studies Supplemental Series*, 79.

Asley-Montagu, M. F., and Brace, C. L. 1977. *Human Evolution,* N.Y.: Macmillan.

Barnett, R. D. 1953. "Mopsos," *The Journal of Hellenic Studies,* 73:143.

Bar-Yosef, O.1993 "The Role of Western Asia in Modern Human Origins," in Aitkin, M. J., *et al.,* eds. 1993. *The Origin of Modern Humans and the Impact of Chronometric Dating*, Princeton, N.J.: Princeton Univ. Press.

Bar Yosef, O. 1994. "Introduction: Dating Eastern Mediterranean Sequences," in Bar Yosef and Kra, eds. 1994. *Late Quaternary Chronology and Paleoclimates of the Eastern Mediterranean,* Tuscon, Ariz.: Univ. of Arizona.

Bar-Yosef, O. 1995. "Earliest Food Producers-Pre Pottery Neolithic (8000-5500)," in-Levy, Thomas, ed. 1995. *The Archaeology of Society in the Holy Land*, London: Leicester Univ. Press.

Bietak, M. 1996. *Avaris, the Capital of the Hyksos: Recent Excavations*, London.

Bodine, W. N., ed. 1992. *Linguistics and Biblical Hebrew*, Winona Lake, IN: Eisenbrauns.

Boling, Robert G. 1993. "Introduction to Judges," *Harper/Collins Study Bible.* 1993. New Standard Edition, London: Harper/Collins Publishers.

Bolk, L. 1926. *Das Problem der Menschenwerdung*, Jena: G. Fischer.

Breasted, J. H. 1905. *History of Egypt*, N.Y.: Scribner.

Breasted, J. H. 1916. *Ancient Times*, Boston: Ginn.

Breasted, J. H. 1934 ed. *The Dawn of Conscience,* N.Y.: Scribner.

Brettler, M. L. 1999. *The Creation of History in Ancient Israel*, London: Routledge.

Bright, J. 1981 (1972). *A History of Israel*, 3rd ed., Philadelphia: Westminster Press.

Brues, A. 1977. *People and Races,* N.Y.: Macmillan.

Callaway, J. A., and Miller, J. M. 1999., "The Settlement in Canaan," in Shanks, Hershel, ed. 1999. *Ancient Israel*, Washington, D.C.: Biblical Archaeological Society.

Campbell, B. 1985. *Human Evolution,* 3rd ed., N.Y.: Aldine De Gruyter.

Campbell, Edward F. 1998. "A Land Divided," in Coogan, Michael D., ed. 1998. *The Oxford History of the Biblical World*, N.Y.: Oxford Univ. Press.

Clottes, Jean. 2001. "Chauvet Cave," in *National Geographic*, August, 104-121.

Clottes, Jean. 2001. *La Grotte Chauvet: L'Art des Origines,* Paris: Editions du Seuil.

Coats, G. W. 1988. *Moses*, Sheffield Engl: Sheffield Acad.

Cogan, Mordechai. 1998. "Into Exile," in Coogan, Michael D., ed. 1998. *The Oxford History of the Biblical World,* N.Y.: Oxford Univ. Press.

Coogan, Michael D. 1998. "In The Beginning: The Earliest History," in Coogan, M. D., ed. 1998. *The Oxford History of the Biblical World,* N.Y.: Oxford Univ. Press.

Cook, Stanley Arthur. 1911 . "Jews," in *Encyclopedia Britannica,* 11th ed., Vol. 15, N.Y.: Cambridge Univ. Press.

Cook, Stanley Arthur. 1911. "Aaron," in *Encyclopedia Britannica,* 11th ed., Vol. 1, N.Y.: Cambridge Univ. Press.

Cook, Stanley Arthur, 1911. "Moses," in *Encyclopedia Britannica,* 11th ed., Vol. 18, , N.Y.: Cambridge Univ. Press.

Cook, Stanley Arthur. 1911. "Philistines," in *Encyclopedia Britannica,* 11th ed., Vol. 21, N.Y.: Cambridge Univ. Press.

Cook, Stanley Arthur, 1911. "The Exodus," in *Encyclopedia Britannica,* 11th ed., Vol. 10, N.Y.: Cambridge Univ. Press.

Coon, C. S. 1962. *The Origin of Races,* N.Y.: Knopf.

Cornfeld, Gaalyah. 1976. *Archaeology of the Bible: Book by Book,* N.Y.: Harper and Row.

Cowley, Arthur E., 1911. "Hebrew Literature," in *Encyclopedia Britannica,* 11th ed., Vol. 13, N.Y.: Cambridge Univ. Press.

Daiches, D. 1975. *Moses: The Man and His Vision,* N.Y.: Praeger.

Darlington, C. D. 1969. *The Evolution of Man and Society,* London: George Allen and Unwin.

Davidson, I., and Noble, W. 1993. "Tools and Language in Human Evolution," in Gibson, K. R., and Ingold, T., eds. 1993. *Tools, Language, and Cognition in Human Evolution,* Cambridge, Eng.: Cambridge Univ. Press.

deBeer, G. 1958. *Embryos and Ancestors,* 3rd ed., Oxford: Oxford Univ. Press.

DeMoor, J. C. 1990. *The Rise of Yahwism,* Leuven: Leuven Univ. Press.

Dennel, R. 1997. "The World's Oldest Spears," *Nature,* Feb.

Diamond, Jared. 1997. *Guns, Germs, and Steel,* N.Y: W. W. Norton.

Dothan, T., and Dothan, M. 1992. *People of the Sea,* N.Y.: Macmillan.

Eisley, L. 1957. *The Immense Journey,* N.Y.: Random House.

Finkelstein, I., and Silberman, N. A. 2001. *The Bible Unearthed,* N.Y.: The Free Press.

Finkelstein, Louis, ed. 1955. *The Jews, Their History, Culture, and Religion,* 2 vols., N.Y: Harper and Bros.

Freud, S. 1939. *Moses and Monotheism*, N.Y.: Knopf.

Friedman, R. E. 1987/1997. *Who Wrote The Bible*? San Francisco: Summit/Harper.

Friedman, R. E. 1999. *The Hidden Book in the Bible*, San Francisco: Harper.

Gabunia, L, *et. al.* 2000. "Earliest Pleistocene Hominid Cranial Remains from Dmanisi, Republic of Georgia: Taxonomy, Geological Setting, and Age," *Science*, 288:12, May.

Gibeon, Raphael. 1971. "Les bedouins Shosu des documents egyptiens," Leiden, 1971, Nos. 6a, 16a.

Gibson, K. R., and Ingold, T., eds. 1993. *Tools, Language, and Cognition in Human Evolution*, Cambridge, Eng.: Cambridge Univ. Press.

Gitin, S., *et al.* 1998. *Mediterranean Peoples in Transition: 13th-10th Century B.C.E.*, Jerusalem.

Gordis, Robert. 1955. "The Bible As a Cultural Monument," in Finkelstein, Louis, ed. 1955. *The Jews, Their History, Culture, and Religion,* 2 vols., N.Y: Harper and Bros Vol. 1.

Gottwald, N. K. 1979. *The Tribes of Yahweh*, Maryknoll, N.Y.: Orbis.

Gottwald, N. K. 1985. *The Hebrew Bible, A Socio-Literary Introduction*, Philadelphia: Fortress Press.

Gould, S., ed. 1993. *Life,* N.Y.: W. W. Norton.

Grant, Michael A. 1984. *History of Ancient Israel,* N.Y.: Charles Scribner.

Greenstein, E. L. 1993. "Introduction to Exodus," in *Harper/Collins Study Bible*. 1993. New Standard Edition, London: Harper/Collins Publishers.

Guthrie, R. Dale. 1984. "Mosaics, Allelochemics and Nutrients," in Martin, P. S., and Klein, R. G., eds. 1984 *Quaternary Extinctions*: a *prehistoric revolution*, Tucson, Ariz.: Univ. of Arizona Press.

Hackett, Jo Ann, 1993. "Introduction to Numbers," in *Harper/Collins Study Bible.* 1993. New Standard Edition, London: Harper/Collins Publishers.

Hackett, Jo Ann 1998. "There Was No King in Israel," in Coogan, M. D., ed. 1998. *The Oxford History of the Biblical World,* N.Y: Oxford University Press.

Halpern, B. 1988. *The First Historians: The Hebrew Bible and History*, San Francisco: Harper and Row.

Harrold, Francis B. 1989. "Mousterian, Chatelperronian and Early Aurignacian in Western Europe: Continuity or Discontinuity, in Mellars, P. A., and Stringer, C. P., eds. 1989. *The Emergence of Modern Humans*, Edinburgh: Univ. of Edinburgh Press.

Hendel, R. S. 1995. "Finding Historical Memories in the Patriarchal Narratives," *Biblical Archaeological Review,* 21/4.

Herrmann, S. 1967. "Der Name Jhw in den Inschriften von Soleb," *Fourth World Congress of Jewish Studies,* Vol. 1, Jerusalem.

Horn, Siegfried A., and McCarter, P. Kyle, Jr. 1999. "The Divided Monarchy," in Shanks, Hershel, ed. 1999. *Ancient Israel,* Washington, D.C.: Biblical Archaeological Society.

Huxley, G. L. 1966. *The Early Ionians,* London: Faber.

Ilan, David, in Levy, Thomas, ed. 1995. *The Archaeology of Society in the Holy Land,* London: Leicester Univ. Press.

Isserlin, B .S. J. 1998. *The Israelites,* London: Thames and Hudson, Ltd.

Itzkoff, S. W. 2000. *The Inevitable Domination by Man, An Evolutionary Detective Story*, Ashfield MA.: Paideia Publishers.

Jepson, G. L., Simpson, G. G., and Mayr, E., eds. 1963. *Genetics, Paleontology and Evolution,* N.Y.: Atheneum.

Johnson, Paul. 1987. *A History of the Jews*, N.Y.: Harper and Bros.

King, M., and Slobodin, S. B. 1996, article in *Science* on which J. N. Wilford based his article, "American Arrowhead Found in Siberia," *The New York Times,* Aug. 2.

King, Philip J., 1993, "Micah," in *Harper/Collins Study Bible.* 1993. New Standard Edition, London: Harper/Collins Publishers.

Klein, R. G. 1989. *The Human Career,* Chicago: Univ. of Chicago Press.

Klein, Ralph W. 1993. "Introduction" to Chronicles, *Harper/Collins Study Bible.* 1993. New Standard Edition, London: Harper/Collins Publishers.

Kramer, S. N. 1963. *The Sumerians,* Chicago: Univ. of Chicago Press.

Leakey, R. 1981. *The Making of Mankind.* N.Y.: Dutton.

Leiden Papyrus 348: Sarna, Nahum/Shanks, Hershel. 1999. "Israel in Egypt," cited in Shanks, Hershel, ed. 1999. *Ancient Israel*, Washington, D.C.: Biblical Archaeological Society.

Lemaire, Andre. 1999. "The United Monarchy," in Shanks, Hershel, ed. 1999. *Ancient Israel,* Washington, D.C.: Biblical Archaeological Society.

Lemche, N. P. 1991. "The Development of the Israelite Religion in the Light of Recent Studies on the Early Religions of Israel," *Supplements to Vetus Testamentum.*

Levine, Lee. 1999. "The Age of Hellenism," in Shanks, Hershel, ed., *Ancient Israel,* Washington, D.C.: Biblical Archaeological Society.

Levy, Thomas, ed. 1995. *The Archaeology of Society in the Holy Land*, London: Leicester Univ. Press.

Marshack, A. 1972. *The Roots of Civilization,* London: Weidenfield and Nicolson.

Marshack, A. 1974. "The Meander as a System, etc.," in Ucko, P., ed., *Biennial Conference of the Australian Institute of Aboriginal Studies*, May-June, 16, Canberra Australia.

Martin, P. S., and Klein, R. G., eds. 1984. *Quaternary Extinctions*: a *prehistoric revolution*, Tucson, Ariz.: Univ. of Arizona Press.

Mays, James L. 1993. "Hosea," in *Harper/Collins Study Bible.* 1993. New Standard Edition, London: Harper/Collins Publishers.

Mazar, Amihai. 1990. *Archaeology of the Land of the Bible, 10000-526 BCE*, N.Y.: Doubleday.

McBride, Dean, Jr. 1993. "Deuteronomy," in *Harper/Collins Study Bible.* 1993. New Standard Edition, London: Publishers.

McCarter, P. Kyle, Jr. 1993. "1, 2, Samuel," in *Harper/Collins Study Bible.* 1993. New Standard Edition, London: Harper/Collins Publishers.

McCarter, P. Kyle, Jr. 1996. *Ancient Inscriptions*, Washington, D.C.: Biblical Archaeological Society.

McCarter, P. Kyle, Jr., and Hendel, R. S. 1999, "The Patriarchal Age," in Shanks, Hershel, ed. 1999. *Ancient Israel*, Washington, D.C.: Biblical Archaeological Society.

Mellars, P. A. 1996. *The Neanderthal Legacy,* Princeton: Princeton Univ. Press.

Mellars, P. A., and Stringer, C. P. eds. 1989. *The Emergence of Modern Humans*, Edinburgh: Univ. of Edinburgh Press.

Mellars, P. A., and Stringer, C. P., eds. 1989. *The Human Revolution—Behavioral and Biological Perspectives on the Origins of Modern Humans*, Princeton: Princeton Univ. Press.

Milgrom, Jacob. 1993. "Leviticus," in *Harper/Collins Study Bible.* 1993. New Standard Edition, London: Harper/Collins Publishers.

Neusner, J. 1978. *The Glory of God Is Intelligence*, Provo, UT: Brigham Young Univ.

Nohrenberg, J. 1995. *Like Unto Moses*, Bloomington, IN: Univ. of Indiana Press.

Noss, J. B. 1949. *Man's Religions,* N.Y.: Macmillan.

Noth, M. 1981. *The Deuteronomistic History*, Sheffield, Eng.: Univ. of Sheffield Press.

Owen, D. L., and Wilhelm, G. 1995. *Studies in the Civilization and Culture of Nuzi. and the Hurrians*, Vol. 7, Bethesda, MD: CDL Press.

Owen, D. L., and Wilhelm, G. 1996. *Studies in the Civilization and Culture of Nuzi. and the Hurrians*, Vol. 8, Bethesda, MD: CDL Press.

Papyrus Anastasi VI, quoted from J. B. Pritchard. 1969. *The Ancient Near East in Pictures Relating to the Old Testament*, 3d ed., Princeton, N.J.: Princeton Univ. Press.

Papyrus Brooklyn 35, 1446, cited in Shanks, Hershel, ed. 1999. *Ancient Israel*, Washington, D.C.: Biblical Archaeological Society.

Patai, R. 1977. *The Jewish Mind*, N.Y.: Scribner.

Perdue, Leo. G. 1993. "Jeremiah," in *Harper/Collins Study Bible*. 1993. New Standard Edition, London: Harper/Collins Publishers.

Pitard, Wayne. 1998. "Before Israel," in Coogan, Michael D., ed. 1998. *The Oxford History of the Biblical World*, N.Y.: Oxford Univ. Press.

Poole, R .S., and Griffith, F. L. 1910. "Egypt," in *Encyclopedia Britannica*, 11th ed., Vol. 9, N.Y.: Cambridge Univ. Press.

Postgate, J. N. 1992 Early Mesopotamia: Society and Economy at the Dawn of History, N.Y.: Routledge

Pritchard , J. B., ed. 1958. *The Ancient Near East*, 3 vols., tr. Matthews and Benjamin; J. A. Wilson; E. A. Speiser, Princeton, N.J.: Princeton Univ. Press.

Pritchard, J. B. 1969. *The Ancient Near East in Pictures Relating to the Old Testament*, 3rd. ed., Princeton, N.J.: Princeton Univ. Press

Pritchard, J. B., ed. 1975. *The Ancient Near East: An Anthology of Texts and Pictures*, 2 vols., Princeton, NJ: Princeton Univ. Press.

Purvis, J., and Meyers, D. E. 1999. "Exile and Return," in Shanks, Hershel, ed. 1999. *Ancient Israel*, Washington, D.C.: Biblical Archaeological Society.

Raphael, Chaim. 1985. *The Road from Babylon: The Story of Sephardic and Oriental Jews*, London: Weidenfeld and Nicolson.

Redford, D. B. 1992. *Egypt, Canaan, and Israel in Ancient Times*, Princeton, N.J.: Princeton Univ. Press.

Redmount, Carol. 1998. "Bitter Lives," in Coogan, Michael D., ed. 1998. *The Oxford History of the Biblical World*, N.Y.: Oxford Univ. Press.

Roberts, J. J. M. 1993. "Introduction to Isaiah," *Harper/Collins Study Bible*. 1993. New Standard Edition, London: Harper/Collins Publishers.

Roddy, Nicolae. 2001. "Archaeology's 'New Vision' or Myopia?" review critique of Finkelstein and Silberman, in *Journal of Religion* and *Society*, Vol. 3, , p. 9 of 9 pp.

Rosenberg, Joel W. 1993. "Genesis," in *Harper/Collins Study Bible*. 1993. New Standard Edition, London: Harper/Collins Publishers.

Saenz-Badillos, A. 1993. *A History of the Hebrew Language.* Cambridge: Univ. of Cambridge Press.

Saggs, H. W. F. 2000. *Babylonians*, Berkeley: University of California Press.

Sanders, N. K. 1978. *The Sea Peoples 1250-1150*, London: Thames and Hudson.

Sarna, Nahum and Shanks, Hershel. 1999. "Israel in Egypt," in Shanks, Hershel, ed. 1999. *Ancient Israel*, Washington, D.C.: Biblical Archaeological Society.

Sayce, Archibald Henry. 1910. "Assurbanipal," in *Encyclopedia Britannica*, 11th ed., Vol. 2, N.Y.: Cambridge Univ. Press.

Sayce, Archibald Henry, "Babylonia-Assyria," in *Encyclopedia Britannica*, 11th ed., Vol. 3, N.Y.: Cambridge Univ. Press.

Schwarcz, H. P. 1994. "Chronology of Modern Humans in the Levant," in Bar Yosef, O., and Kra, R. S., eds. 1994. *Late Quaternary Chronology and Paleoclimates of the Eastern Mediterranean*, Tuscon, Ariz.: Univ. of Arizona.

Seltzer, Robert M., ed. 1989. *Judaism, A People and Its History*, N.Y.: Macmillan.

Shanks, Hershel, ed. 1999. *Ancient Israel*, Washington, D.C.: Biblical Archaeological Society.

Silver, M. 1995. *Economic Structures of Antiquity*, Westport, CT: Greenwood.

Simeons, A. T. S. 1962. *Man's Presumptuous Brain*, N.Y.: Dutton.

Simpson, G. G. 1944. *Tempo and Mode in Evolution*, N.Y.: Columbia Univ. Press.

Simpson, G. G. 1953. *The Major Features of Evolution*, N.Y.: Columbia Univ. Press.

Smelik, K. A. D., ed. 1991. *Writings from Ancient Israel: A Handbook of Documents*, Edinburgh: Univ. of Edinburg Press.

Smith, Patricia. 1995. "People of the Holy Land From Prehistory to the Recent Past," Levy, Thomas, ed. 1995. *The Archaeology of Society in the Holy Land*, London: Leicester Univ. Press.

Smith, W. Robertson, 1892. "Old Testament in the Jewish Church," cited in Smith, W. R., and Cook, S. A., "Decalogue," in *Encyclopedia Britannica*, 11th ed., 1911, Vol. 7, N.Y.: Cambridge Univ. Press.

Smith, W. Robertson, and Cook, Stanley Arthur. 1910. "Decalogue," *Encyclopedia Britannica*, 11th ed., Vol. 7, N.Y.: Cambridge Univ. Press.

Stager, L. E., 1998, "Forging an Identity: The Emergence of Ancient Israel," in Coogan, Michael D., ed. 1998. *The Oxford History of the Biblical World,* N.Y.: Oxford Univ. Press.

Stenning, John Frederick, "Exodus," in *Encyclopedia Britannica,* 11th ed., Vol. 10, N.Y.: Cambridge Univ. Press.

Tattersall, I. 1995. *The Last Neanderthal,* N.Y.: Macmillan/U.S.A.

Thomas, Hugh. 1979. *A History of the World,* N.Y.: Harper and Row.

Thompson, T. L. 1992. *Early History of the Israelite People from Written and Archaeological Sources,* Leiden: Brill.

Thompson, T. L. 1999. *The Mythic Past.* N.Y.: Basic Books.

Thucydides. (1954) c.420-410 BCE. *The Peloponnesian War,* tr. Rex Warner, Hammondsworth, England: Penguin.

Trinkaus, E., and Shipman, P. 1993. *The Neanderthals,* N.Y.: Knopf.

Tucker, Gene M., 1993, "Amos," in *Harper/Collins Study Bible.* 1993. New Standard Edition, London: Harper/Collins Publishers.

Ucko, P., ed., *Biennial Conference of the Australian Institute of Aboriginal Studies,* May-June, 16, Canberra Australia.

von Koenigswald, G. H. R. 1962. *The Evolution of Man,* Ann Arbor, MI: Univ. of Michigan Press.

Weber, Max. 1952. (1917-1918). *Ancient Judaism,* N.Y.: Free Press.

Weigall, A. 1923. *The Life and Times of Akhenaton,* N.Y.: Putnam.

Weinfeld, Moshe. 1983. "Social and Cultic Institutions in the Priestly Source against Their Ancient Near Eastern Background," in Proc. of the Eighth World Congress of Jewish Studies, Jerusalem, 1983.

Weinfeld, Moshe. 1989. "Israelite Religion," in Seltzer, Robert M., ed. 1989. *Judaism, A People and Its History,* N.Y.: Macmillan.

Wellhausen, J. 1957 (1885). *Prolegomena to the History of Ancient Israel.* N.Y.: Meridian.

White, R. 1989. "Production Complexity and Standardization in Early Aurignacian Bead and Pendant Manufacture: Evolutionary Implications," in Mellars, P. A., and Stringer, C., eds. 1989. *The Human Revolution—Behavioral and Biological Perspectives on the Origins of Modern Humans,* Princeton: Princeton Univ. Press.

Whitehouse, O. C. 1911. "Hebrew Religion," in *Encyclopedia Britannica,* 11th ed., Vol. 13, N.Y.: Cambridge Univ. Press.

Wilford, J. N. 1996. "American Arrowhead Found in Siberia," *The New York Times* Aug. 2; from article in *Science*, 8/2/96, by King, M., and Slobodin, S. B.

Wilford, J. N. 1997. "Ancient German Spears Tell of Mighty Hunters of Stone Age," *The New York Times,* 3/4/97.

Wills, C. 1998. *Children of Prometheus,* Reading, Mass.: Perseus Books.

Wilson, Robert. 1993. "1, 2 Kings," in *Harper/Collins Study Bible.* 1993. New Standard Edition, London: Harper/Collins Publishers.

Wolpoff, M .H., and Caspari, R. 1997. *Race and Human Evolution*, N.Y.: Simon and Schuster.

Wooley, L. 1958. *Art of the World.* London: Methuen.

Wormington, B. H. 1960. *Carthage,* London: Hale.

Wright, S. 1963. "Adaptation and Selection," in Jepson, G. L., Simpson, G. G., and Mayr, E., eds. 1963. *Genetics, Paleontology and Evolution,* N.Y.: Atheneum.

Young, J. D., ed. 1981. *Ugarit in Retrospect*, Winona Lake, IN: Eisenbrauns.

Index

Acknowledgments

Illustrations/Maps: I, VIII, X—Hammond Inc.; Illustrations/Maps: II, III, IV, VII—
    Oxford University Press; Illustrations/Maps: V—Bible Archaeological Society;
    Illustrations/Maps: VI—Union of Hebrew Congregations; Illustrations/Maps: IX–
    British Museum.
Frontispiece: The Jerusalem Museum.

Seymour W. Itzkoff was trained in philosophy at Columbia University. Now an Emeritus Professor, he taught for many years at Smith College. He is the author of nineteen scholarly books, including several studies of the neo-Kantian philosopher, Ernst Cassirer, and a book on the art of 'cellist Emanuel Feuermann. Most recently, his *Inevitable Domination by Man, An Evolutionary Detective Story*, has received critical scientific acclaim.